THE

# RISE AND PROGRESS

OF

# THE ENGLISH CONSTITUTION.

BY

E. S. CREASY, M.A.,

BARRISTER-AT-LAW;
PROFESSOR OF HISTORY IN UNIVERSITY COLLEGE, LONDON;
LATE FELLOW OF KING'S COLLEGE, CAMBRIDGE.

FOURTH EDITION.

REVISED, AND WITH ADDITIONS.

NEW YORK:
D APPLETON AND COMPANY
443 & 445 BROADWAY.
1865.

DEDICATED TO

# HENRY PEARSON, ESQ., M.A.,

OF THE MIDDLE TEMPLE, BARRISTER-AT-LAW,

BY HIS FRIEND,

THE AUTHOR.

# PREFACE.

In 1848 I prepared and published a small pamphlet, called "The Text Book of the Constitution," in which were arranged the texts of Magna Carta, the Petition of Right, and the Bill of Rights, with historical comments, and with remarks on the People's Charter and other political topics of that year. Independently of its politics, that pamphlet has been found useful as an historical compilation; but the extent to which its latter pages were occupied with political discussions, made me unwilling either to employ it myself or to see it employed by others in education. I do not wish to disavow any of the opinions which I expressed in it, but a teacher of History has no right to avail himself of the position in which he stands towards his pupils, for the purpose of training up broods of young Tories, Whigs, or Radicals, according to his own party predilections. I therefore intended to prepare an edition of that little treatise, which should deal only with the Past, and in which the spirit of party pamphlet should be entirely got rid of. But the work has grown under the pen; and I have been led to make additions, omissions, and re-arrangements, which have rendered it a distinct book, and one to which the name it now bears is much more applicable than the title of its predecessor would have been.

Except in the earlier part of the volume, I have entirely avoided ecclesiastical topics. I have found it impossible to deal with them, without mingling in some of the hottest controversies of the present day.

My obligations to Guizot, Palgrave, Kemble, Latham, Worsaae, Bowyer, Warren, Macculloch, Forsyth, Pashley, and, above all, to Hallam, are self-apparent in these pages. Wherever I have found truths well stated by others, I have preferred useful compilation to worthless novelty.

E. S. CREASY.

*University College, London,*
*October* 18, 1853.

# PREFACE

## TO THIRD EDITION.

---

I HAVE tried to show a fit sense of the public favour which this little book has received, by correcting it carefully, and by making such useful additions as I could blend in it without running into party politics, and without turning it into that proverbial evil, *Μέγα βιβλίον*. The account of the present distribution of political power in England will be found to be now much fuller than it was in the preceding editions; and I have joined with it some comments on our old English principle of Local Self-government in Local matters; a subject to which I had not previously given due prominence.

E. S. CREASY.

2, *Mitre Court Chambers, Temple,*
*December 12th*, 1855.

# CONTENTS.

CHAPTER VI.



CHAPTER VII.



CHAPTER VIII.



CHAPTER IX.



CHAPTER X.



CHAPTER XI.



CHAPTER XII.



CHAPTER XIII.

## CHAPTER XIV.



## CHAPTER XV.



## CHAPTER XVI.



## CHAPTER XVII.

# THE RISE AND PROGRESS

OF THE

# ENGLISH CONSTITUTION.

---

## CHAPTER I.

Meaning of the term "English Constitution."—Is there an English Constitution?—Primary Principles of the Constitution.—Magna Carta, the Petition of Right, and the Bill of Rights form its Code.—General Ignorance of these Statutes.—Scope of the present Work.—Constitutional Law of Progress.—How to learn the Constitution.—Classification of Constitutional Functions.—Importance of studying Leading Scenes in History.—History of the Elements of our Nation, why material.—Exclusion of Party Politics.

WHATEVER may be thought of the execution of this work, I have little fear of being censured, so far as regards the design. An attempt to arrange in a simple form, and to place before the public, in a few easily accessible pages, the great principles of our Constitution,—to prove their antiquity, to illustrate their development, and to point out their enduring value, will surely, in times like the present, not be discouraged as blamable; and, in the strange dearth of useful treatises on this important topic, it will hardly be slighted as superfluous.

It is, in the first place, necessary to have a clear understanding of what we mean when we talk about "the English Constitution." Few terms in our language have been more laxly employed : and so uncertain is the knowledge, so very vague are the ideas which many have of the constitution of their country, that when the opponent of a particular measure or a particular system of policy cries out that it is unconstitutional, the complaint generally means little more than that the matter so denounced is something which the speaker dislikes.

Still, the term, "the English Constitution," is susceptible of full and accurate explanation : though it may not be easy to set it lucidly forth, without first investigating the archæology of our history, rather more deeply than may suit hasty talkers and superficial thinkers, but with no larger expenditure of time and labour, than every member of a great and free State ought gladly to bestow, in order that he may rightly comprehend and appreciate the polity and the laws *in* which, and *by* which he lives, and acts, and has his civic being.

Some furious Jacobins, at the close of the last century, used to clamour that there was no such thing as the English Constitution, because it could not be produced in full written form, like that of the United States, or like those with which Sièyes stocked the pigeon-holes of his bureau, to suit the varying phases of the first years of the French Revolution. The same cavil is occasionally repeated in our own times. In order to meet it, there is no occasion to resort to the strange dogma of Burke, that our ancestors, at the Revolution of 1688, bound, and had a right to bind, both themselves and their posterity to perpetual adherence to the exact order of things then established : nor need we rely solely on the eulogies, which foreign as well as native writers, a hundred years ago, used to heap upon the British constitution. Those panegyrics, whether exaggerated or not, were to a great extent supported by reasonings and comparisons, which are now wholly inapplicable. But, without basing his political creed on them, an impartial and earnest investigator may still satisfy himself that England has a constitution, and that there is ample cause why she should cherish it. And by this it is meant, that he will recognise and admire, in the history, the laws, and the institutions of England, certain great leading principles, which have existed from the earliest period of our nationality down to the present time ; expanding and adapting themselves to the progress of society and civilization ; advancing and varying in development, but still essentially the same in substance and in spirit.

These great primeval and enduring principles are the principles of the English Constitution. And we are not obliged to learn them from imperfect evidences or precarious speculation ; for they are imperishably recorded in the Great Charter, and in the Charters and Statutes connected with and confirmatory of Magna Carta. In Magna Carta itself, that is to say, in a solemn instrument deliberately agreed on by the king, the prelates, the great barons, the gentry, the burghers, the yeomanry, and all the freemen of the realm, at an epoch which we have a right to consider the commencement of our nationality, and in the statute entitled *Confirmatio Cartarum*, which is to be read as a supplement to Magna Carta, we can trace these great principles, some in the germ, some more fully revealed. And thus, at the very dawn of the history of the *present* English nation, we behold the foundations of our great political institutions imperishably laid.

These great primeval and enduring principles of our Constitution are as follows :—

The government of the country by an hereditary sovereign, ruling with limited powers, and bound to summon and consult a parliament of the whole realm, comprising hereditary peers and elective representatives of the commons.

That without the sanction of parliament no tax of any kind can be imposed; and no law can be made, repealed, or altered.

That no man be arbitrarily fined or imprisoned, that no man's property or liberties be impaired, and that no man be in any way punished, except after a lawful trial.

Trial by jury.

That justice shall not be sold or delayed.

These great constitutional principles can all be proved, either by express terms, or by fair implication, from Magna Carta, and its above-mentioned supplement.

Their vigorous development was aided and attested in many subsequent statutes, especially in the Petition of Right and the Bill of Rights; in each of which the English nation, at a solemn crisis, solemnly declared its rights, and solemnly acknowledged its obligations:—two enactments which deserve to be cited, not as ordinary laws, but as constitutional compacts, and to be classed as such with the Great Charter, of which they are the confirmers and the exponents.

Lord Chatham called these three "The Bible of the English Constitution," to which appeal is to be made on every grave political question. The great statesman's advice is still sound. It deserves to be considered by subjects as well as by princes; by popular leaders without the walls of parliament, as well as by ministers within them.

And, indeed, it is not only to those who are prominently engaged in political struggles, but to all who would qualify themselves for doing their duty to their country,—to all who are conscious of what Arnold has called "the highest earthly desire of the ripened mind, the desire of taking an active share in the great work of government,"—that these texts of our Constitution ought to be the objects of peculiar study; in order that, first, we may learn from them what our Constitution really is, and whether it deserves to be earnestly upheld by us as a national blessing, or ought to be looked on as an effete incumbrance, whose euthanasia we should strive to accelerate; and, secondly, that when we have convinced ourselves of its merit, we may be able to test proposed measures by their conformity with or their hostility to its principles.

It is painfully strange to observe how few even of well educated Englishmen possess, or have so much as ever read these three Great Statutes. Magna Carta, in particular, is on everybody's lips but in nobody's hands; and, though perpetually talked of, is generally talked of in utter ignorance of its contents, beyond a vague impression that it prohibits arbitrary taxation and arbitrary imprisonment, and that it is in favour of Trial by Jury. The original charter of King John is not even printed in the common editions of the statutes. With respect to the two other great laws which Lord Chatham ranks with Magna Carta, namely, the Petition of Right, and the Bill of Rights, it may safely be asserted that hundreds have never read a line of them, who would be justly indignant if we were to doubt their familiarity with the Attic legislation of Cleisthenes, or with the Roman reform bills of Terentillus and Licinius Stolo.

The texts of Magna Carta, the Petition of Right, and the Bill of Rights will here be laid before the reader; and I have endeavoured to make the perusal of them more interesting and more useful, by not only giving explanations of the legal and archæological terms which they contain, but by also adding historical introductions and comments. Unless this is done, the spirit of the Constitution cannot be perceived; and, if the letter of the Constitution deserves admiration, still more does its spirit. It is only thus that some of its essential characteristics can be discerned; and, by studying it thus, the more we convince ourselves of its reality and its antiquity, the more confident shall we become of its future durability. For, the same earnest and long-continued studies, which teach the historical inquirer to believe in and to venerate the great principles of the English Constitution, also display to him the workings of its normal law of progress, its plastic power of self-amelioration and expansion, through which we may hope to see all growing exigencies of modern times supplied, not only without danger, but with aid and corroboration to the fundamental institutions of ages past.

The student of the English Constitution ought not only to be familiar with the chief portions of Magna Carta, the Petition of Right, and the Bill of Rights; but he ought also to have a clear knowledge and an appreciative feeling of the circumstances under which each of the three primary laws came into existence; of the immediate purposes for which each was framed; and of the enduring general benefit to the nation which each was also designed to secure. He ought to trace and examine the development of the great principles which these statutes embody; and his especial attention should be directed to such other statutes as confirm, extend, or explain the leading enactments. He ought also to watch how far the constitutional rights, which these laws sanction and provide, have been extended to all members of the community. This is to be carefully noted, not only in respect of the protections from positive wrong, which the Constitution affords, but also in respect of the other benefits which it offers. We must observe what classes and what numbers of the population have from time to time taken part in the active functions of the government of the State. And it is always to be remembered that the active functions of political government include not merely such rights as the right of sitting in parliament, the right of voting for members of parliament, and the like, but they include such rights as the right of eligibility to any magistracy or executive office, and the right of electing others thereto; they include, also, the right of taking any part in criminal or civil trials, as, for example, the right of acting as jurymen. I follow here the greatest of all writers on the subject of human political institutions. Aristotle classifies the constitutional functions of a member of a State under these three heads: 1st, the Deliberative; 2ndly, the Administrative; 3rdly, the Judicial.*

We shall, necessarily, in thus studying the history of our nation and its institutions, be led to observe, in connection with the great primary principles that have been enumerated, many supplemental constitutional rules that have been successively introduced, and gradually established, during the six centuries of our national existence. The amount of authority, to which each of these rules is entitled, may perhaps vary, according to the weight of the reasons which may be found for the origin and maintenance of each, according to the extent to which each seems to carry out the true spirit of the primary principles, and also

* Ἔστι δὴ τρία μόρια τῶν πολιτειῶν πασῶν, περι ὧν δεῖ θεωρεῖν τὸν σπουδαῖον νομοθέτην ἑκάστῃ τὸ συμφέρον. ὧν ἐχόντων καλῶς, ἀνάγκη τὴν πολιτείαν ἔχειν καλῶς, καὶ τὰς πολιτείας ἀλλήλων διαφέρειν, ἐν τῷ διαφέρειν ἕκαστον τούτων. Ἔστι δὲ τῶν τριῶν τούτων ἓν μέν τι τὸ βουλευόμενον περὶ τῶν κοινῶν. Δεύτερον δὲ τὸ περὶ τὰς ἀρχάς· τοῦτο δὲ ἔστιν ἃς δεῖ καὶ τίνων εἶναι κυρίας· καὶ ποίαν τινὰ δεῖ γίγνεσθαι τὴν αἵρεσιν αὐτων. Τρίτον δέ τι τὸ δίκαζον.—*Aristot. Polit.*, lib. iv. c. 14.

according to the length of time by which the existence of each has been hallowed. But they ought all to be carefully noted; and they all deserve the respectful attention even of those who would modify their influence, or except particular cases from their operation. The study of their causes is indispensable for a right judgment of their effects.

I have endeavoured to compile and arrange in these pages information respecting the origin, the character, and the progress of our Constitution, with regard to all the points of view, the importance of which I have been indicating. I am far from venturing, on this account, to call this little volume a complete history of the English Constitution, but it may aid the student as an introduction to other more learned and elaborate treatises; and, perhaps, even the well-informed politician may sometimes find it useful as a manual for immediate reference. I believe, indeed, that with regard to Constitutional history, as well as with regard to general history, much has been done to secure a present knowledge and a permanent recollection, when the intellect has once thoroughly comprehended and the imagination has once vividly reproduced a small but well-chosen number of leading scenes in the long and complicated drama. Such scenes abide clearly in the memory when the general mass of the story becomes dim; and, when they so abide in the memory, they are valuable, not only by reason of the intrinsic importance of their own immediate topics, but because they serve us as landmarks for an improved survey of the whole subject. They are also most beneficial in enabling us to realize the utility of the incidental information as to particular passages of history, which our other studies, and even our desultory reading for mere amusement's sake, continually throw in our way. He who has the knowledge of certain great leading historical events firmly implanted in his mind, has in his mind a set of bases, between and round which he naturally fixes and groups all the historical facts that he reads or hears of. His memory is thus continually refreshed. Each piece of new information awakens in him intelligible and connected ideas ; and he addresses himself to the acquisition of fresh facts, or to the consideration of rival theories, with far higher powers and advantages, than can be possessed by the man, who may, indeed, have read much more, but who has read without selection and system ; and whose mind, as to history, must (to borrow a phrase of Dryden) be only full of "a confused mass of thoughts, tumbling over one another in the dark."

Attention is, therefore, here drawn to the acquisition of the Great Charter, the passing of the Petition of Right, and that of the Bill of Rights, as leading scenes in our Constitutional history. The first of these has been treated at far greater length than either of the other two ; both because there is not the same opportunity of referring my readers to other writers on the subject, and because, as it occurs at the very opening of our national history, a right comprehension of it forms the very foundation of our Constitutional knowledge. This is premised, lest it should be thought that the investigations of the Constitutional history of each element of our nation, which are introduced before discussing the Great Charter itself, have been foisted in here merely for the sake of inopportunely parading ethnological theories, or of swelling the size of this volume. The tenets there brought forward are essential for the fixing of the corner stone of my position respecting the English Constitution. I maintain that the principles of our Constitution have been in existence ever since we, this English nation, have been in existence. This is to be proved not merely by quoting the Great Charter, but by making good the assertion that the epoch when the Great Charter was granted is the epoch when our nationality commenced. For this purpose it is absolutely necessary to analyze our nation, to trace the separate current of each of its primary sources, and to watch the processes of their intermingling. Perhaps I may venture to hope that one effect of studying our history in this manner, may be to give it an additional interest, from its evident connection with our classical studies. The main stream of our nation is Germanic; and he, who devotes himself to the histories of Greece and Rome, will find Greek history blending in Roman, and Roman blending in Germanic. The institutions of our Germanic ancestors commanded the anxious interest of the master-minds of ancient Rome. Those same institutions are the first subjects to which the inquirer into our laws and our political organization must bend his thoughts. They have, indeed, been greatly modified by the other elements with which they have been mingled here, but they have exercised more influence than any others. The Germania of Tacitus is equally a hand-book for the student of modern and for the student of ancient history. It thus demonstrates the unity of all history.

I hope that my work, in its present form, may be useful to young readers, in aiding to educate them for the future discharge of political duties; but I have earnestly sought to keep these pages free from party politics. I know, from my experience as a lecturer for thirteen years, how difficult it is to discuss English history without the line of instruction being affected by the instructor's own political bias. But I hope that the same experience has enabled me to surmount that difficulty. I have throughout this work kept its main object steadily in view, and have rigidly rejected every topic and every sentence that seemed calculated to serve other purposes. I advocate here neither Conservatism nor Liberalism, in the sense in which those slogans of modern party-warfare are commonly understood; but I strive to point out those great principles of the Constitution, which both Conservatives and Liberals ought to know, and must acknowledge, however they may differ as to the relative importance which they would fain see each principle acquire.

## CHAPTER II.

Our Constitution coeval with our Nationality.—Thirteenth century the Date when each commences.—The Four Elements of our Nation.—The Saxon, *i. e.* the Germanic, the chief Element.—Parts of the Continent whence our Germanic Ancestors came.—Their Institutions, Political, Social, and Domestic.—Date of the Saxon Immigrations into this Island.—What Population did they find here?—The British Element of our Nation, Romanized Celtic.—Primary Character and Institutions of the British Celts.—Effect of Roman Conquests.—How far did the Saxons exterminate or blend with the Britons?—Evidence of Language.

It has been stated in the last chapter that Magna Carta is coeval with the commencement of our nationality; in other words, that we have had our present Constitution, as represented in Magna Carta, throughout the whole time of our true national history, except some brief periods of revolutionary interruption. The proof of this depends on the date at which we fix the commencement of the history of the English nation, as a complete nation. This date is the 13th century.*

* I am glad to be able to cite the high authority of Mr. Macaulay in support of the position that the history of the English nation commences in the 13th century. Mr. Macaulay, in the 17th page of the first volume of his History, after speaking of the Great Charter as the first pledge of the reconciliation of the Norman and Saxon races, says—"Here commences the history of the English nation. The history of the preceding events is the history of wrongs inflicted and sustained by various tribes, which, indeed, dwelt on English ground, but which regarded each other with aversion, such as has scarcely ever existed between communities separated by natural barriers." Two eloquent pages are devoted to the illustration of this fact. I may be permitted in justice to myself to remark, that I had frequently in my lectures maintained the position that the history of the English nation does not commence before the 13th century; and it will be found also in my "Text-book of the Constitution," which was published before the appearance of Mr. Macaulay's History.

The accuracy as well as the importance of this date will be more readily discerned, if we remember the difference that there is between the history of *the English* and the history of *England* ;—between the history of our nation, and the history of the island on which we now dwell.

Our English nation is the combined product of several populations. The Saxon element is the most important, and may be treated as the chief one ; but, besides this, there is the British (that is to say, Romanized Celtic), there is the Danish, and there is the Norman element. Each of these four elements of our nation has largely modified the rest ; and each has exercised an important influence in determining our national character and our national institutions. It is not until we reach the period when these elements were thoroughly fused and blended together, that the history of the English can properly be said to begin. This period is the 13th century after the birth of our Saviour. It was then, and not until then, that our nationality was complete. By nationality is meant the joint result of unity as to race, language, and institutions. In the 13th century these unities were created. Let us prove this separately. First, with respect to race. Though the coming over of the Normans in the 11th century made up the last great element of our population, a long time passed away before it coalesced with the others. For at least a century and a half after the conquest,

See also, in connection with this subject, the first of Arnold's Lectures on Modern History. I do not ágree with that great and good man in thinking that the Britons, who lived here before the coming over of the Saxons, are in no respect connected with us as our ancestors, and that, "nationally speaking, the history of Cæsar's invasion has no more to do with us than the natural history of the animals which then inhabited our forests." But it was from his pages that I was first led to appreciate the paramount importance of the Germanic source of our nation, and also to realize the full meaning of the terms "national" and "nationality."

there were two distinct peoples, the Anglo-Norman and the Aglo-Saxon, dwelling in this island. They were locally intermingled with each other, but they were not fellow-countrymen. They kept aloof from each other in social life, the one in haughty scorn, the other in sullen abhorrence. But when we study the period of the reigns of John, and his son and grandson, we find Saxon and Norman blended together under the common name, and with the common rights, of Englishmen. From that time forth, no part of the population of England looks on another part as foreigners; all feel that they are one people, and that they jointly compose one of the States of Christendom. Secondly, with respect to language. In the 13th century, our English language, such substantially as it still is, became the mother tongue of every Englishman, whether of Norman or of Saxon origin.* So, finally, with respect to our institutions; it was during this century that the Great Charter was obtained, and the statutes connected with and confirmatory of it were passed, in which we can trace the great primary principles of our Constitution. It was in this century that Parliaments, comprising an Upper House of Temporal and Spiritual Peers, and Lower House of Representatives of Counties and Boroughs, were first summoned. It was in this century that our legal system assumed its distinctive features, and was steadily enforced throughout the realm.

It is clear, therefore, that it is at this period, that our true nationality commences; for our history, from

* The earliest extant specimen of the English language, as contradistinguished from the Saxon and Semi-Saxon, is the proclamation of Henry III. to the people of Huntingdonshire, A.D. 1258. See Latham on the "English Language," p. 77. The reader need hardly be reminded that, for the first century and-a-half after the Conquest, the Normans in England spoke French.

this time forth, is the history of a national life, then complete and still in being. All before that period is a mere history of elements, and of the processes of their fusion. But it is a preliminary history that must be studied in order to comprehend aright the history that follows. In order to understand the Great Charter, we must catch the spirit of the age in which it was granted. To do this, we must form to ourselves a vivid and a true idea of the people that obtained it; and we must, for that purpose, trace the early career, we must mark the characteristics, and watch the permanent influence of each of the four elementary races by which the English people has been formed. Of these four elements the Anglo-Saxon is unquestionably the principal one. Our language alone decisively proves this; for it is still substantially the same language which our ancestors spoke in Germany before they left the banks of the Eyder and the Elbe for the coasts of Britain.* We may, therefore, advantageously first see who and what the Anglo-Saxons were in their original homes; and then examine who and what the inhabitants of this island were whom the Anglo-Saxons found here. The subsequent immigration of the Danes, and the final influx of the Normans, will next be separately considered: and, then (after watching also the processes and the results of the partial fusion of these races, both that which took place with respect to the first three before the arrival of the Normans, and that which afterwards took place with respect to the Norman conquerors themselves, and those whom they subdued), we may proceed to the consideration of the first part of our immediate subject, to ascertain the condition of the various classes of the community at

* There are extant two Anglo-Saxon poems, "Beowulf" and the "Lay of the Traveller," which are proved by internal evidence to have been composed before our Saxon ancestors came to Britain.

the time when the great national movement took place, by which King John was compelled to sign Magna Carta (A.D. 1215).

The chief element of our nation is Germanic, and we have good cause to be proud of our ancestry. Freedom has been its hereditary characteristic from the earliest times at which we can trace the existence of the German race. The Germans, alone, of all the European nations of antiquity that Rome assailed, successfully withstood her ambition and her arms. They never endured either a foreign conqueror, or a domestic tyrant. Similarly proud and unblemished by servitude are the pedigrees of two more of the elements of our nation. The Danes and the Normans, who came among us, were and ever had been freemen. It was only the British portion of our elements that had endured foreign conquest and arbitrary rule; and even this source of our nation had become so largely tinged by the fusion of the Roman conquerors with the conquered Celts, that we can regard it, if not with pride, at least without humiliation.

The Germans who settled in this island during the fifth and sixth centuries are usually spoken of as Saxons, Angles, and Jutes. The collective name of Anglo-Saxons has been given to them by historians, for the sake of distinguishing them from the Saxons of modern Germany; and it is a name which it is convenient to employ.

There has been, and there continues to be much learned controversy as to the exact localities on the Continent, whence the Germanic conquerors of Britain came, and as to their precise degrees of affinity one with the other.* Without entering into these

* I think that Kemble and Latham have proved that no Jutes from the country now called Jutland took part in the Anglo-Saxon Conquest of this island. See Kemble's "Saxons in England," and Latham's

deep (though very valuable and interesting) discussions, we may be safe in adopting the general statement that the Anglo-Saxons were Germans of the sea-coast between the Eyder and Yssel, of the islands that lie off that coast, and of the water systems of the lower Eyder, the lower Elbe, and the Weser. It is important to observe that these are all parts of Germany, which were less affected by contact with the Romans, and with which the Romans were less acquainted, than was the case with the parts of Germany that lie near the Rhine and the Danube, the two boundary rivers of the Roman continental empire in Europe. And yet it is almost exclusively from Roman writers that we gain our information about the institutions and usages of our Saxon ancestors in their primeval fatherland. Caution must be used in admitting and applying to them the details which we read in Cæsar and Tacitus respecting the manners and institutions of the Germans. But we may gain thence some general knowledge which may be safely relied on, especially when taken in connection with what we know of the Anglo-Saxons, at a later period. Our German ancestors were freemen, having kings with limited authority, who were selected from certain families. *Reges ex nobilitate, duces ex virtute sumunt. Nec regibus infinita nec libera potestas.* (Tac. Mor. Germ., vii.) Besides these kings, they had chieftains whom they freely chose among themselves for each warlike enterprise or emergency. All important state affairs were discussed at general assemblies of the people; matters of minor consequence being dealt with by the chief magistrates alone. *De minoribus rebus principes consultant, de majoribus omnes: ita tamen ut ea quoque quorum penes plebem*

"English Language," third edition. See also, for the original homes of the Anglo-Saxons, Latham's "Ethnology of the British Islands," and his edition of the "Germania" of Tacitus.

*arbitrium est, apud principes pertractantur.* (Tac. Mor. Germ., xi.) Any person might be impeached and tried for his life at the chief popular assembly. *Licet apud concilium accusare quoque, et discrimen capitis intendere.* (Ib., xii.) The head men, or magistrates, who were to preside in the local courts, were also elected at popular assemblies; and the organization of the men of each district into Hundreds, for the purposes of local self-government and for being joint securities for the good behaviour of each other, appears also to have existed among them. *Eliguntur in iisdem consiliis et principes qui jura per pagos vicosque reddant. Centeni singulis ex plebe comites consilium simul et auctoritas adsunt.** They had no cities or walled towns, but they had villages, where each man dwelt in his own homestead.†

It is very important to mark this; and to observe that the ancient Germans were equally distinguished from the Classic Greeks and Romans, who were essentially dwellers in cities, and from the wandering tribes of Central Asia, who have ever been dwellers in tents, without settled home or habitation. The love of individual liberty, the spirit of personal independence, which characterized the German warrior, as contrasted with the classic citizen, to whom the state was all and the individual nothing, were perfectly compatible with a respect for order, and a capacity for becoming the member of a permanent and civilized community, such as never existed in the Scythian of antiquity or the Tartar of modern times.

Slavery existed among the ancient Germans, but

* I do not mean that Tacitus had precisely the idea of the German "Centeni" which I have stated; but such was, most likely, the institution of which he was partly informed. See Latham's note at p. 60 of his "Germania," and the chapter in Kemble's "Anglo-Saxons" on "The Tithing and the Hundred."

† Tac. Mor. Germ., xvi.

it was generally of a very mitigated kind. They had few domestic slaves, like those of the classical nations, or the negroes in America; and the term "serf" would more accurately describe the German "Servus"* whom Tacitus speaks of. The serf had his own home and his land, part of the produce of which he was bound to render to his master; that was the extent of his servitude; but he was destitute of all political rights.

Military valour was the common virtue of the nations of the North. The Germans possessed this, but they had also peculiar merits. The domestic virtues flourished nowhere more than in a German home.† Polygamy was almost entirely unknown among them; and infanticide was looked on with the utmost horror. The great ethnologist, Pritchard, in his survey of the different races of mankind, truly observes that "In two remarkable traits the Germans differed from the Sarmatic as well as from the Sclavic nations, and, indeed, from all those other races to whom the Greeks and Romans gave the designation of barbarians. I allude to their personal freedom and regard to the rights of men; secondly, to the respect paid by them to the female sex, and the chastity for which the latter were celebrated among the people of the North. These were the foundations of that probity of character, self-respect, and purity of manners, which may be traced among the Germans and Goths even during Pagan times, and which, when their sentiments were enlightened by Christianity, brought out those splendid traits of character which distinguish the age of chivalry and romance."‡

Much indeed of the spirit of chivalry, and even

* Tac. Mor. Germ., xxv.

† Ibid., xviii., xix.

‡ Pritchard's "Researches into the Natural History of Mankind," vol. iii. p. 423.

the germs of some of its peculiar institutions, may be found in the customs of our Germanic ancestors as they are described by Tacitus. The young warrior was solemnly invested with the dignity of arms by some chief of eminence; and the most aspiring and adventurous youths were wont to attach themselves as retainers to some renowned leader, whose person they protected in war, and whose state they upheld in peace. (*In pace decus, in bello præsidium.*) These were the "Gesithas" of the Anglo-Saxons; they fed at the chief's table, they looked to him for gifts of war-horses or weapons, as rewards for deeds of distinguished valour. Their relation to him was that of Fealty; and we may see here a species of Feudalism, with the all-important exception that the relation between retainer and chief had no necessary connection with the tenure of any land.*

Such were our Anglo-Saxon forefathers, who, in the fifth century of the Christian era, came across the German ocean and changed the Roman province of Britain into England, *i. e.* the land of the English; the new collective name of the whole island being taken from the Anglian portion of the conquerors, though the names of some of its new subdivisions, such as Sussex, Essex, Wessex, &c., have immediate reference to the Saxons. Whether the current story of the landing of Hengist and Horsa in Kent, of Vortigern and Rowena, &c., &c., is to be dismissed to the now populous region of myths, or whether it is to be regarded as substantially true,† is not a subject to be discussed here; but the main facts may be taken as certain, that a great Germanic immigration into Britain took place during the fifth century,‡ and that

* See the excellent chapter in Kemble, on "The Noble by Service."

† See Kemble's "Saxons in England," and some sensible observations on the other side of the question in Craik's "History of the English Language."

‡ I disbelieve the new theory of a large settlement of Saxons here in

it was effected not by one great movement, but by a number of unconnected expeditions of successive squadrons under independent chiefs.

We now come to the consideration of the second element of our nation. We have to examine what the population was which the Anglo-Saxons found here, and to ascertain to what extent they displaced or blended with it.

The Saxons found Celts* here, but they were not unmitigated Celts. They were Romanized Celts. In order fully to understand that term, we must investigate the normal state of the British Celts, and consider also how and to what extent they were influenced by Roman conquest before the arrival of the Saxons.

The description which Cæsar gives of the inhabitants of Britain is the earliest that we possess. Some valuable information is also to be obtained from Strabo and Diodorus Siculus.† The south-west part of the island had been known by the civilized nations of the ancient world at a much more remote period. The Scilly Islands and Cornish coasts were frequented in very early times by the Phœnician and Cartha-

the fourth century. The fact of there having been then a "*Comes littoris Saxonici*" on the east coast of Britain, proves no more than the fact of the subsequent existence of English lords of the Welsh and Scottish marches. No one supposes the districts which these officers ruled to have been inhabited by the Welsh or the Scotch. Such a name merely shows that the district was peculiarly exposed to the ravages of the nation by which it is designated.

* The evidence of language, as shown by the names of our rivers and mountains and the other great natural objects of the island, being Celtic, is conclusive of the fact of a Celtic population having been spread over Britain. The extreme north was probably occupied by a Norse race at a very early time; but that does not affect *English* history. With respect to the Belgic inhabitants of Britain, I agree with those who hold that they were Celts, and that the difference of their language from that of the other Celts was merely a difference of dialect. See Latham's "Ethnology of British Islands," p. 61.

† See Latham's "Ethnology of Britain," chap. 1 and 2. See also the chapter on Towns, in Kemble's "Anglo-Saxons."

ginian traders, who obtained from our mines the tin which they imported to their own countries and to the other states round the Mediterranean, and which must have been required for the purpose of making the bronze, which we know to have been so largely used for purposes of utility, warfare, and ornament. From the Phœnician merchants and miners the native Britons acquired the art of working metals, and of forming the bronze weapons and other implements which are found in some of the ancient tombs in this island. But the Phœnicians here, like the Portuguese in the East Indies, seem merely to have established factories, and not to have influenced materially the condition or the usages of the great mass of the native inhabitants. At a period nearer to the time of Cæsar's landing, merchant-vessels from Gaul carried on some intercourse with our south-eastern shores. Hence, as Cæsar relates, the tribes of the maritime districts were less barbarous than those of the interior, and agriculture was more practised in the south than was the case further north. The population of the island is said by him to have been large,* a statement which Diodorus confirms, but which is not to be taken according to our modern ideas of density of population. The buildings of the ancient Britons were numerous; but they had no fortified towns, and used, for the purposes of defence, spots among their woods which were naturally difficult of access, and which they strengthened by a ditch and stockade. They were subdivided into numerous independent tribes, with many kings and petty rulers, and their wars with each other were not so frequent as was generally the case among the nations of antiquity.† We have no means of knowing their political institutions, beyond the fact of their having kings and other

* "Hominum est infinita multitudo." Bell. Gall. v. 12.
† Diod. Sicul., v. 21.

rulers. If their polity resembled (as is probable) that of their kindred Celts in Gaul, they had a noblesse, and the mass of the people was destitute of all rights and franchises.* Their religion was Druidism; and Britain is said to have been the parent-seat of that creed. The Druids were not only priests, but they were, also, almost the sole civil magistrates and administrators of the law.† Perhaps the point in which the British Celts contrast most unfavourably with the ancient Germans, is in respect to the sanctity and purity of the marriage tie. We have seen how this was respected among our Germanic ancestors; but the Celts, whom Cæsar found here, had a custom, which, I believe, is only paralleled among the savages of some of the South Sea Islands. They formed socialist communities of ten or twelve in number, who had their wives in common.‡

Against these Celts, possessing, together with many of the vices of the savage state, its usual merit of irregular valour, Cæsar led the Roman legions about half a century before the Christian era. But his invasion, though attended with victory, and successfully renewed in the following spring, was rather a transient inroad than an attempt at permanent conquest. After the withdrawal of his troops, Britain was left to her rough independence for nearly a century; when the Romans again attacked her, and, after a forty years' war, brought almost all that part of the island which lies south of the Friths of Forth and Clyde completely under the dominion of the emperors of Rome.

Seneca's observation, that "Wheresoever the Roman conquers, he inhabits," was made while Britain

* Cæsar, Bell. Gall., vi. 13. "Plebes pæne servorum habetur loco, quæ per se nihil audet et nullo adhibetur consilio."

† De Bell. Gall., vi. 13, 14.

‡ Ibid., v. 14.

was being subdued, and it is true of this as of the other conquests which were effected by that remarkable people.

Unlike most nations of antiquity, the Romans neither sought to exterminate nor to make a slave population of those whom they invaded. By planting colonies, and by taking the towns into the pale of the Roman citizenship as "municipia," a nation of Romans was gradually formed in each conquered province. Britain (which, with the exception of Dacia, was the last acquired, and which was one of the earliest lost of the Roman provinces) was not Romanized so completely as was generally the case; But Roman civilization flourished here for three centuries, and some of its fruits still survive. Thirty-three townships were established under the Romans in this island, each possessing powers of self-government and taxation, and the inhabitants of each electing their own decurions or senators, from among whom the magistrates were appointed. We may be partly indebted to this, the Roman influence on the British element of our population, for the system of municipal freedom and local self-rule, to which so much of our glory and our power has justly been attributed.*

It is to be borne in mind, that it was not exclusively an Italian stream that blended with the Celtic source of our nation, while Rome ruled the land. From the reciprocal intercourse between the various portions of the Roman empire, the British population must have been sensibly tinged with the blood of the various races that acknowledged the Imperators of Rome. And a similar result must have been effected

* See, with respect to the order of Decurions in the Roman Municipia, Guizot's "Lectures on European Civilization;" Savigny's "History of the Roman Law" (vol. i. translated by Calcraft); Kemble's "Anglo-Saxons," vol. ii. chap. 7; and Guizot's "History of Representative Government," lecture 22.

by the presence of the Roman legions, especially in consequence of the policy which the emperors adopted, of pensioning off the veteran legionaries with grants of land in the countries where they had been stationed. Now, we must remember that the Roman legions under the empire were raised and supplied by recruits drawn from all parts of the Roman dominions, and that during the later times of Roman history, they were levied promiscuously from the different provincials and from the barbarians of the frontiers. So that, under the Roman eagles, men of every race and clime must have been assembled, with no common tie save that of discipline, and that of a partially-acquired knowledge of the Latin tongue. And even in the best times of the empire every legion was accompanied by a corps of barbaric auxiliaries, whose scene of operation was carefully appointed at a distance from the country which supplied them.*

These are important points, when we are considering the British element of our nation; but it is certain that, however varied the population of the south of the island thus became under Roman rule, a community of Roman civilization was generally diffused, and the language, the literature, and, above all, the laws of Rome, became naturalized in Britain.†

* See Latham's "Ethnology of the British Islands," p. 98.

† Mr. Macaulay, in the opening of his History, underrates the extent to which Britain was Romanized. There is an excellent article on the subject in the "Edinburgh Review," No. cxci. Sir F. Palgrave's words, in his History of the English Commonwealth, on this point, deserve citation. "The country was replete with the monuments of Roman magnificence. Malmesbury appeals to those stately ruins as testimonies of the favour which Britain had enjoyed; the towers, the temples, the theatres, and the baths, which yet remained undestroyed, excited the wonder and admiration of the chronicler and the traveller; and even in the 14th century, the edifices raised by the Romans were so numerous and costly, as almost to excel any others on this side the Alps. Nor were these structures among the least influential means of establishing the Roman power. Architecture, as cultivated by the ancients, was not merely presented to the eye; the art spake also to the mind. The walls

As the power of imperial Rome decayed, her British province began to suffer more and more from the inroads of the savage tribes from the north of the island, and from the attacks of the sea-rovers from the Saxon shores. Rome gradually withdrew her troops; and, at last, about five centuries after the first landing of Cæsar, she reluctantly abandoned her reluctant province to nominal independence, but to real anarchy and devastation. The arrival of the Saxons checked the progress of the Caledonian marauders. These were driven back to their northern fastnesses, but the German new comers soon claimed supremacy over the British inhabitants. A long chaotic period of savage warfare ensued; and nearly two hundred years of slaughter and suffering passed away before our Saxon ancestors established their Octarchy in the island; and, even then, a considerable portion of the western district remained in the possession of the British, or, as the Saxons termed them, the Welsh.

How far in the parts of the island, which the Saxons subdued, they exterminated the British, or to what extent the two populations were blended together, deserves next our earnest inquiry; and it is a matter on which the correctness of our classification of the elements of our nation must depend.

The Germanic origin of our language, and the peculiarly savage nature of the warfare by which the Anglo-Saxons conquered this island, have led some writers to assert that the provincials of Britain were

covered with the decrees of the legislature, engraved on bronze, or sculptured on marble; the triumphal arches, crowned by the statues of the princes who governed the province from the distant Quirinal; the tesselated floor, pictured with the mythology of the State, whose sovereign was its Pontiff—all contributed to act upon the feelings of the people, and to impress them with respect and submission. The conquered shared in the fame, and were exalted by the splendour of the victors."—See also his "History of Normandy and England," chap. 1.

almost entirely exterminated, and that the land was repeopled by the rapid influx and continued increase of German colonies. This hypothesis would exclude the Celtic element from our nation. Arnold goes so far as to say that "The Britons and Romans had lived in our country, but they are not our fathers; we are connected with them as men indeed, but, nationally speaking, the history of Cæsar's invasion has no more to do with us, than the natural history of the animals which then inhabited our forests. We,—this great English nation, whose race and language are now overrunning the earth from one end to the other,—we were born when the white horse of the Saxons had established his dominion from the Tweed to the Tamar."

On the other hand, Sir F. Palgrave and other authorities consider that a very large portion of the population of England, during the Anglo-Saxon period, was of British descent. I believe that this is a subject on which the recent labours of comparative philologists have supplied the historian with new and valuable light. I incline so far to the opinion of Arnold, as to regard the Germanic as the main stream of our race, but I cannot wholly exclude the Celtic; nor can I dismiss Caractacus as an alien in blood, though we can proudly claim a still closer relationship with Arminius. In opposition to the Palgravian hypothesis, the reader may be usefully reminded that the Saxon invasion of Britain differed from the usual course of the barbarian conquests on the Continent over the severed fragments of the Roman Empire. *There* the military superiority of the assailants was generally self-evident and uncontested. Moreover, the Germanic invaders of Gaul, of Spain, and Italy, were generally warriors from tribes that had been influenced to some extent by intercourse with the Romans, both in peace and in war. Their chiefs were not wholly unfamiliar with Roman discipline and Roman art, and were ready to appreciate Roman civilization. Many, also, of the Germanic conquerors on the Continent had been converted to Christianity before their inroads had been commenced, nearly all were converted before their settlements were concluded. But the Saxons had never been confined by peaceful approximation to the Roman frontier. No missionary had set his foot among their forests or on their coasts. They were pagan pirates. They invaded Britain by detachments, and under different independent chiefs. They never landed in such imposing force as to awe the invaded into bloodless submission, but merely in sufficient numbers to fight their way—to conquer indeed—but only to conquer inch by inch. Their savage paganism inflamed them with peculiar frenzy against all that the Christianized Britons held most sacred; each side upbraided the other with perfidy and fraud; no possible bond of fair union existed between them; and, probably, in no conquest were the victors more ruthless to the vanquished than in the desperate and chequered struggle by which the Saxons won their slow way over this island.

Led by this historical circumstantial evidence, and by the great fact of our language being essentially Germanic, I believe that the Saxons almost entirely exterminated or expelled *the men* of British race whom they found in the parts of this country which they conquered. But the same evidence (both the historical and the philological), when carefully scrutinized, leads also to the belief that it was only the male part of the British population which was thus swept away, and that, by reason of the unions of the British females with the Saxon warriors, the British element was largely preserved in our nation. I remind my readers that the British, whom the Saxons found here, were mainly Celts.

Besides those Celtic words in the English language which can be proved to be of late introduction, and those which are common to both the Celtic and Germanic tongues, there are certain words which have been retained from the original Celtic of the island. These genuine Celtic words of our language (besides proper names) are rather more than thirty in number. The late Mr. Garnett formed a list of them; and in his opinion the nature of these words showed that the part of the British population which the Saxons did not slay, was reduced into a state of complete bondage, inasmuch as all these words have relation to some inferior employment. Now, if the reader will carefully examine the list, he will see that not only do these Celtic words all apply to inferior employments, but that by far the larger number of them apply to articles of feminine use or to domestic feminine occupations. They are as follows:—*Basket, barrow, button, bran, clout, crock, crook, gusset, kiln, cock* (*in cock-boat*), *dainty, darn, tenter* (*in tenter-hook*), *fleam, flaw, funnel, gyve, griddel* (*gridiron*), *gruel, welt, wicket, gown, wire, mesh, mattock, mop, rail, rasher, rug, solder, size* (*glue*), *tackle.*

This remarkable list of words is precisely what we should expect to find, on the supposition that the conquering Saxons put their male prisoners to the edge of the sword, except a few whom they kept as slaves, but that they took wives to themselves from among the captive daughters of the land. The Saxon master of each household would make his wife and his dependents learn and adopt his language; but in matters of housewifery and menial drudgery, their proud lord would scorn to interfere, and they would be permitted to employ their old own familiar terms. All the circumstances of the Saxon conquest favour this hypothesis. The Saxons came by sea, and in small squadrons at a time. They came also to fight their way, and were little likely to cumber their keels with women from their own shores. A few Rowenas may have accompanied the invading warriors, but in general they must have found the mothers of their children among the population of the country which they conquered.

This hypothesis also accounts for the difference which undoubtedly exists between ourselves and the modern Germans, both in physical and in mental characteristics. The Englishman preserves the independence of mind, the probity, the steadiness, the domestic virtues, and the love of order which marked his German forefathers ; while, from the Celtic element of our nation, we derive a greater degree of energy and enterprise, of versatility, and practical readiness, than are to be found in the modern populations of purely Teutonic origin.

## CHAPTER III.

Conversion of the Anglo-Saxons.—Its civilizing Effects.—They occupy the Roman Towns.—England attacked by the Danes.—The third, *i. e.* the Danish, Element of our Nation.—Danish Institutions and Customs.—Ferocity of their Attack on England.—Extent of their chief Settlements here.—Evidence of Danish Names of Places and Persons.—Alfred rescues Saxon England from them.—The Danish blends with the Saxon Element.—Fusion of the first three Elements of our Nation.

The conversion of the Anglo-Saxons to Christianity (which was principally effected during the seventh century) did much to mitigate the wild fierceness of the conquerors, and also to modify their political and social institutions. The ecclesiastics from continental Christendom, who were the first missionaries to Saxon England, and who continued to migrate hither in no inconsiderable numbers, came from lands where the old Roman civilization had survived in a much greater degree than was the case in Britain. They were familiar with municipal self-government practised in populous and important cities; they were familiar, also, with the idea of imperial power, as it once had been wielded by Roman emperors in the West, and still lingered in the ostentatious though feeble grasp of the emperors of Constantinople. The Church, moreover (within the pale of which St. Augustine and his coadjutors brought the English nation), had her councils, her synods, and the full organization of a highly complex, but energetic and popular ecclesiastical polity. She recruited her ranks from men of every race, and every class of society. She taught the unity of all mankind ; and practically broke down the barriers of caste and pedigree, by offering* to all her temporal advantages as well as her spiritual blessings. She sheltered the remnants of literature and science ; and ever strove to make the power of the Intellect predominate over brute force and mere animal courage. All these civilizing influences must have largely affected the converted Anglo-Saxons, and have given increased efficacy to the subdued but not exterminated element of our race, the Romanized British element, with which the Saxons had partially coalesced. Moreover, the very wars which the Saxons waged against the Britons and each other, must have made the Germanic conquerors appreciate the military advantages of occupying the walled towns and cities which the Romans had left in our island.† They who thus became dwellers in cities would naturally adopt the system of civic self-government, which Rome had once introduced, and which was so congenial to the free spirit of the new settlers. The remnant of the British population in the cities may have taught much of this, but it is probable that the clergy of the Roman See taught more. Thus many germs of order appeared in Saxon England when Christianized; but, before they could be fully developed, a new indraft of rough barbaric blood was poured into the population. Scandinavia sent hither her swarms of warriors, fresh from her rugged coast, unsoftened by any recollection of Imperial or any contact of Papal Rome, to struggle

* See, as to the influence of the Church of Rome as an instrument of modern European civilization, the admirable observations of the Protestant Guizot, "Histoire de la Civilization, en Europe," Leçons 5 et 6.

† I cannot adopt the opinion of Mr. Kemble (chapter on "The Towns," book ii., of the "Saxons in England"), that the Saxons generally suffered the Roman cities to perish, and that their own towns had a totally independent origin. The fact that the Saxons were almost always at war not only with the Britons, but with each other, is conclusive against supposing that they could have neglected the military advantages which the Roman fortifications offered.

long and fiercely for the mastery of the island, and to make the third great element of the English nation. The consideration of this element soon occupies the historical student, who has been tracing the progress of the Saxons in this island ; for the Danes commenced their ravages and partial conquests of England before the Anglo-Saxon Octarchy could be fused into the English kingdom ; before, indeed, any of the Saxon States had acquired a permanent predominance over the rest.*

In the year 787, thirteen years before the accession of Egbert to the throne of Wessex, some men of a strange race landed from three vessels at an eastern port in England. They slew on the beach the Saxon magistrate who came down to question them, plundered the neighbouring habitations, and hastily re-embarked with their spoil. Such was the first recorded appearance of the Danes in England ; but they darken the pages of the Anglo-Saxon Chronicles from that time forth to the year 1066, when our last Harold destroyed the last host of Scandinavian invaders at Stamford Bridge, only a few days before his own defeat and death at Hastings.

These northern sea-rovers, from whose ravages scarcely any European coast during the ninth and tenth centuries escaped, who everywhere appear as conquerors, and up to whom so many noble and royal pedigrees are traced, had much original affinity of race, language, and institutions, with the Anglo-Saxons whom they assailed so savagely in their settlements in this island.

The Scandinavian and the Germanic tongues are classed together by comparative philologists under the common title of the Gothic stock. Odin, Thor,

* Kemble has completely proved that the supposed Saxon Bretwaldas (or rulers of all Britain) are fabulous. See also Hallam's "Middle Ages," vol. ii. p. 349, 10th edition.

Freia, and the other principal deities of the Scandinavian Valhalla, had been also the gods of the Anglo-Saxons, while the Anglo-Saxons were in their primitive state of heathendom.* Both Anglo-Saxons and Scandinavians believed that the princely families out of which they chose their kings were descended from Odin. The Scandinavians seem in their political institutions to have been more turbulently free than even their Germanic kinsmen. The three Scandinavian countries, that ultimately became the monarchies of Denmark, Sweden, and Norway, were originally subdivided into numerous petty kingdoms. In each of these, whenever the king died, his successor was elected out of the descendants of the sacred stock by the choice of the assembled freemen of the State. Part of the population was in a state of slavery or thraldom (trœldom), the inevitable result of the perpetual wars and piracies in which the Scandinavians indulged. These unhappy beings were of course destitute of all political rights; but every freeman capable of bearing arms might attend at the "Ting," as the popular assemblies, both for legislative and judicial purposes, were called, and every freeman had an equal voice. Each Scandinavian State was subdivided into hærads or hundreds, which formed communities for local self-government, identical, probably, in nature with the hundreds of the primitive Germans, which have been already spoken of. They followed chiefs of their own choice in warlike expeditions; though the king was regarded as the natural leader of the national force on great occasions. But unless the assembled freemen in the Ting willed it, the king could neither make peace nor war, nor impose a tax, nor levy an army. He was little more than a military

* See Kemble's chapter on Saxon Heathendom, and Grimm's "Deutsche Mythologie."

chieftain, and was sure of being speedily deposed, if he did not exhibit sufficient spirit and energy in warlike enterprises to satisfy his subjects. War, especially war by sea, was the occupation in which a Danish freeman sought to live, and in which he prayed to die. Some gleams, however, of more civilized and civilizing feeling may be traced amid the martial gloom of the Scandinavian character. Women were regarded always with honour, and often with chivalrous devotion. The respect, also, of these warriors for their laws, as administered by freemen towards freemen, was general and profound. They delighted in poetry and minstrelsy. They held the arts of the miner and the worker of metals in estimation. Nor were their maritime skill and enterprise displayed only for purposes of destruction. They looked on commerce with respect; laws were established and strictly observed for the protection of merchant vessels; and an extensive traffic was carried on by Scandinavian adventurers with the far East, through Russia and along the great rivers of central Asia.* But the fierce excitement of battle was generally the prevailing attraction for which a Danish fleet was launched. Every free Scandinavian was a seaman; and the art of ship-building was brought early by them to considerable perfection; though they generally used in their predatory expeditions small vessels of little draught, so as to enable them to ascend the rivers of the countries which they attacked. It was chiefly by squadrons from the Danish part of Scandinavia that England was assailed, though the Norwegians co-operated: † and our chroniclers speak of

* For the Danish institutions and customs see Worsaae's book on "The Danes and Northmen in England, Scotland, and Ireland;" Crighton's "Scandinavia," vol. i. chap. iv.; and an article by Sir Francis Palgrave on our ancient Law-Courts, in the 75th Number of the "Edinburgh Review."

† According to Worsaae, Scandinavians from Denmark chiefly attacked

them generally as Danes. In France, and other countries of the Continent, they were known by their own favourite designation of Northmen.

The original affinity that had existed between the Danes and the Anglo-Saxons by no means mitigated the ferocity of the Scandinavian invaders towards the Germanic occupants of the island; it rather was a cause of exasperation. A change had taken place in the Anglo-Saxons since their settlement here, which had broken off every tie between them and their Scandinavian kinsmen.

The Anglo-Saxon had been converted to Christianity, while the man of the North still gloried in the title of Son of Odin; and hated, as a renegade, him who, once proud of the same descent from the Asas, had left his warrior faith for the new creed of the mass and the monk. Led by their Vikings, younger sons of royal houses, whose only heritage was the sea and such lands beyond its waves as their own swords could win them, these "Slayers from the North," as the old legends termed them, reappeared in England again and again, settling ere long on the shores which at first they merely ravaged, breaking down Saxon bravery by their ferocious and fanatic valour, overwhelming the three minor kingdoms of Mercia, East Anglia, and Northumbria, and nearly crushing that of Wessex, which had become the chief Saxon State of the south and centre of the island.

The genius and heroic patriotism of Alfred rescued Saxon England from utter destruction. A son and grandson worthy of him succeeded him on the throne of Wessex. The Danish population, which had spread

England; Scandinavians from Norway chiefly attacked Scotland. Of the three Scandinavian countries, Sweden sent the fewest assailants of this island. "Not that the Swedes were less piratical, but that they robbed elsewhere; in Russia, for instance, and in Finland."—*Latham's English Language*, p. 99.

over the northeast of England, was brought to acknowledge the authority, partly by victories in the field, partly by the influence of superior civilization, and still more by conversion to Christianity. Anglo-Saxon and Anglo-Dane became more and more assimilated; the Anglo-Saxon tongue, institutions, and habits generally acquiring the ascendancy. But there can be no doubt of the influence of the Danish having been strong and permanent. The evidence of language, both in difference of dialect and in the names of places and persons, still points out the parts of England where the Danish occupancy was strongest. In every shire where we find the compound names of places ending in *by*, (as in *Derby*, *Grimsby*, *Ormsby*, &c.,) we trace the Dane. The German (or Saxon) ending would be *ton.** The termination *son* to proper names of persons (as in *Adamson*, *Nelson*, i. e. *Nielson*, &c.) marks a Danish pedigree. Other proofs of a similar kind are collected by the modern Dane, who shows a pride, which we may well share, in these marks of affinity between the combatants of Copenhagen.†

The troubles which shook Saxon England after the reign of Edgar (875) caused fresh attacks from Denmark. But Denmark was now consolidated into one kingdom, and had been brought within the civilizing pale of Christendom. The wars with Sveyn and Canute waged here during the end of the 10th and commencement of the 11th centuries were of a very different character to the savage devastations with which the old Northmen had swept the land. They were steady wars of conquest; and for a time were successful. Canute (or Knut, as the name is more properly written and pronounced) was undis-

* See Worsaae's "Danes in England," sect. viii.; and Latham's "Ethnology of British Islands," chap. 13.

† See Worsaae, p. 177, and pp. 186, 187.

puted sovereign of England from 1017 to 1035. He united also the crowns of the three Scandinavian kingdoms, and was one of the greatest princes that ever ruled in this island, whether we regard the extent of his power or his personal character. But his dynasty was not destined to take root here, and after the death of his son Hardicanute (1052), the Anglo-Saxon element showed its predominance over the Anglo-Danish; and the nation restored a prince of the old royal stock of Cerdic to the throne. From the accession of Edward the Confessor to the battle of Hastings, England may be again correctly termed an Anglo-Saxon kingdom.

We have thus brought together three of the four elements of our race; and watched their fusion. We have seen the general prevalence of the Anglo-Saxon over the British and the Danish: and henceforth we shall speak of the product of the combined three as Anglo-Saxon, in contradistinction to the fourth, the Norman element, that is yet to come. But before we turn our attention to Normandy, it is well to pause, and examine (so far as is practicable) the general nature of the Anglo-Saxon institutions before the Norman Conquest.

## CHAPTER IV.

Anglo-Saxon Institutions.—Classes of the Population.—Thralls, Ceorls, Thanes.—Townships.—Hundreds.—Tythings.—Frank pledge.—Lords.—The Were.—The Socmen.—The Towns.—The Witenagemote.—The King.—The Bishops.—The Clergy.—The Poor.—Deterioration of the Saxon Polity before the Conquest.

NOTWITHSTANDING the effects of the Norman Conquest, and the consequent introduction of the fourth element of our present nation, the foundations of so many of the most important of our institutions are Saxon, that a right understanding of the Anglo-Saxon system of government, and the condition of the various classes of the community under it, is indispensable in order to discern and appreciate the changes and modifications introduced by the Normans, and also those which "the great innovator, Time," has subsequently effected. And even at the present day we must look back to the Anglo-Saxon period, if we would properly comprehend the principles of many of the most important and the most practical parts of our laws and usages.

There is no branch of constitutional knowledge in which so much has been done during the last fifty years as in Anglo-Saxon history. It used to be studied merely with a view to modern politics, and it was misunderstood and distorted accordingly. It is now investigated with the desire of learning the truth, and the lessons which we derive from it are therefore trustworthy and sound. Extreme party-writers can no longer pretend to find, or fancy that they find, their favourite tenets in the Anglo-Saxon system; but we may all find much, the spirit of which is worthy of admiration and perpetuation, though the forms through which it acted are obsolete and incapable of revival.

It should be premised that the word "system," as applied to the Anglo-Saxon times, must be taken in a very modified sense, or it is calculated to mislead by giving an idea of uniformity, such as never existed. The Anglo-Saxon institutions were not arbitrarily created by any one lawgiver, or during any one age. They grew by degrees; and they grew also in a country which was an almost perpetual scene of war and tumult, and which was inhabited by races of different origin; so that the local development of these institutions varied, besides their temporary fluctuations. It is unsafe to attempt to give more than a general idea of their leading features, which must be variously worked out in detail, according to the particular reign, and the particular part of England, to which it is meant to be applied.

One class of the community in Anglo-Saxon times (though probably no very large portion) was in a state of absolute slavery. They were known in Saxon by the names of Theow, Esne, and Thrall. They probably originally consisted of conquered Britons; but as criminals, who could not pay the fine imposed by law, were reducible to this state, many unfortunate beings of German ancestry must in process of time have been comprised in this degraded and suffering class. The freemen of the land were classified by a broad division into the Ceorls who formed the bulk of the population, and into the Thanes who formed the nobility and the gentry. Sometimes the classification is made into Ceorls and Eorls; the title of Eorl having reference to birth, whereas the title of Thane had reference to the possession of landed property. It was this, the ownership of landed property, that mainly determined the *status* and political rights of a Saxon freeman, and therefore the classification into Ceorls and Thanes is the most convenient to follow.* There is an additional reason for doing so, because the Danes used the title Eorl (Jarl, Earl) to designate authority and command; and when the Danish influence extended in Saxon England, the title of Earl was employed, not to mark a man of good birth, but the ruler of a shire or other district.

Many other names of bodies of people among the Saxons, and among subdivisions of classes, might be cited and explained, but to do so would require a disproportionate amount of this treatise; and, for the broad general view of Anglo-Saxon institutions, which alone is aimed at here, the classification of freemen into Ceorls and Thanes is sufficient.

Both the democratic and the aristocratic principles entered largely into the Anglo Saxon polity; the latter finally obtaining the ascendancy, chiefly by reason of the strictness of the regulations, which it was found necessary to introduce, in order to maintain some degree of public peace, and to give some security for property and person, amid the tumult and confusion which prevailed so often and so generally in England during the troubled ages of the Anglo-Saxon rule. To adopt the technical language of a modern writer on political philosophy,† Security being the primary object of government, it was found necessary to trench largely on both Liberty and Equality, in order to preserve it.

* See on this subject, and on the position of an Earl, who had not the property requisite to make him a Thane, an excellent note in the new edition of Mr. Hallam's "Middle Ages," vol. ii. p. 256. See also Kemble's "Saxons in England," vol. i. p. 131.

† Bentham.

One great fact, however, never must be forgotten while we examine the Anglo-Saxon institutions, and mark the privileges which the thanes (*i. e.* the landed proprietors) possessed over the mass of the free commonalty, the ceorls. The superior body was not composed of an hereditary caste or noblesse. It was an aristocracy, but it was open to receive recruits from the ranks below it. Any ceorl, who could acquire a defined amount of landed property, could become a thane.

It is convenient to examine the Anglo-Saxon social body, by commencing with its component parts. This method is recommended by Palgrave, and (subject to some slight additions and qualifications) we may safely follow him in taking the Anglo-Saxon townships as the integral molecules, out of which the Anglo-Saxon State was formed. He says,* "Ascending in the analysis of the Anglo-Saxon State, the first and primary element appears to be the community, which in England, during the Saxon period, was denominated the Town, or Township. In times comparatively modern, this term became less frequently used, and it has been often superseded by the word 'Manor.' The latter is of Norman origin, and merely denotes a residence, and is frequently applied in ancient records to any dwelling or mansion, without any reference to situation, territory, or appendant jurisdiction. An explanation of the Saxon term may be required. Denoting in its primary sense the inclosure which surrounded the mere homestead or dwelling of the lord, it seems to have been gradually extended to the whole of the land which constituted the domain." There was a lord of every township, usually one of the more opulent thanes, though some townships belonged to the sovereign as their superior. We will,

* "Rise and Progress of the English Commonwealth," p. 65.

however, limit our attention to the ordinary and normal case, where a resident thane was lord of the township. He dwelt there on his own demesne lands. Round him there were grouped a number of ceorls, some occupying allotments of land, some tilling the lands of others.* Each township had its Gerefa, or Reeve, an elective chief officer; and also in each township four good and lawful men were elected, who, with the reeve, represented the township in the judicial courts of the hundred and the shire. All these appear to have been freely elected by the commonalty of each township from among their own body. The inhabitants of each township regulated their own police. They were bound to keep watch and ward; and if any crime was committed in their district, they were to raise the hue and cry, and to pursue and apprehend the offender.

Such were the townships; having, generally, each its own local court, with varying amounts of jurisdiction; and being subordinate to the hundred court, which was again subordinate to the shire moot or county court.

This leads us to consider the English hundreds, which subsist to this day, though the townships have become almost obsolete, having been superseded partly by the Norman manors, and partly in consequence of the ecclesiastical division into parishes having been adopted for the purposes of petty local self-government.

Whether our hundreds had originally any reference to *number* or not, it is certain that they ultimately became mere territorial divisions. And, both in order to facilitate the organization of the inhabitants for military purposes, and to afford better security against

* I am only endeavouring here to give a general sketch of a township, and therefore avoid entering into questions about Socmen, or Landboc, or Lon, or Infangthief, or Outfangthief, &c. Copious information on these points may be found in Palgrave and Kemble.

crime, the hundreds were subdivided into tythings. In one respect, the system of tything was more comprehensive than the system of townships, as there may have been land not included in any township, and which would yet be within a hundred, and consequently would, when hundreds were subdivided, be brought within a tything.

Every hundred had its court, which was attended by the thanes whose demesnes were within its boundaries, and by the four men and the reeve of each township. The hundred court was held monthly, and was subordinate to the court of the shire. The shire or county courts were held at least once a year. They were presided over by the bishop, and the eorlderman or earl. Each shire had also its reeve, who, in the absence of the eorlderman, was the president of its court, in conjunction with the bishop. All the thanes in the county, the four men, and the reeve of each township, and the twelve men chosen to represent each hundred, attended the county court, but it is justly doubted whether any but the thanes had a voice in it. Though an appeal from it seems to have lain to the Witenagemote, the supreme court of the kingdom, and though the Witan in some cases sometimes exercised an original jurisdiction, the shire moots were in practice the most important tribunals in the country, and both they and the minor ones, which we have referred to, were certainly of a very free and popular character.

So far the Anglo-Saxon system seems democratic enough; but even before we proceed to the consideration of the Witenagemote, there are two features to be attended to which are of a very different character.

Every member of the Anglo-Saxon commonalty was bound to place himself in dependence upon some man of rank and wealth, as his lord. The "lordless" man was liable to be slain as an outlaw by any one who met him. Besides this, by the system of frank pledge, every man was bound to be enrolled in some tything; the members of each tything being mutually responsible for each other's good conduct,—to this extent at least, that if any one of them committed a crime, the rest were bound either to render him to justice to take his trial, or to make good the fine to which, in his absence, he might be sentenced. The effect of these regulations was almost to limit every man to the place and neighbourhood of his nativity; for it was difficult and almost impossible to get enrolled in a tything or to find a lord in a place where a man was not known. At the same time, it is to be borne in mind that this species of compulsory settlement inflicted far less hardship in Anglo-Saxon times, when there was little traffic or communication between one district and another, and little inducement for a poor man to try to change his home, than has been in modern times caused by our laws of settlement and removal.

The recollection of this will keep us from exaggerating the importance of one point in the position of the ceorls, which has caused some writers to speak of it as a state of servitude. Many of the Saxon ceorls were legally annexed to the lands of their lords, and could not quit the estate on which they had to render their services. But the ceorl was in other respects personally free. He was law-worthy, to use the old expressive phraseology. Among the Anglo-Saxons (as among all the other northern nations) a composition, or *were-gild*, was fixed by the law for the slaying of any member of the State, according to the class to which he belonged. The were-gild for the death of a ceorl was 200 shillings, and was payable to his family, and not to the lord of the estate on which he lived. But the fine for killing a slave was paid to the slave's owner. The ceorl had the right of bearing arms. He was a legal witness. As already pointed out, he had political rights with regard to the magistracies of his township, his tything, and his hundred, both as an elector and as himself eligible to office. He could acquire and hold property in absolute ownership; and he needed no act of emancipation to pass into the class of thanes, if he acquired the requisite property qualification of five hides of land. Many of the ceorls were land owners to a smaller extent. Hallam considers the Socmen, who are frequently spoken of in Domesday Book, to have been ceorls of this description. He says, "They are the root of a noble plant, the free socage tenants, or English yeomanry, whose independence has stamped with peculiar features both our constitution and our national character." *

By far the larger part of the population in the Anglo-Saxon times was agricultural, but the towns were of considerable importance. The free spirit of local self-government which marks the Anglo-Saxon polity as displayed in its rural and village communities, was no less strongly developed in their cities and towns. The burg (as the town was usually called, meaning, literally, a fortified place) was organized like a hundred, having subdivisions analogous to those of the hundred, according to its size and population. The *Burhwara*, or men of the borough, elected from among themselves their local officers for keeping the peace, and other purposes of municipal government. They thus also freely chose their own borough-reeve, or port-reeve, as their head of the civic community was termed. This officer presided at their local courts (the burhwaremot, or hustings), and in time of war led the armed burgesses into the field. Sometimes the king, or a bishop, or a neighbouring lord, claimed and exercised seignorial rights within the borough; nor can any description of the Saxon municipal system

* "Middle Ages," vol. ii. p. 274.

be drawn that could be uniformly accurate. But, in general, we may safely assert that the Saxon boroughs were thriving and were free; that they were strongholds, where the germs of England's commercial prosperity, and of the capacity of the Anglo-Saxon race for local self-government, were matured, amid the turbulence of a rude age, and the attempted encroachments of royal and aristocratic power.*

I shall have occasion hereafter to revert to the subject of the Anglo-Saxon judicial system, particularly with reference to trial by jury; at present I will proceed to a brief account of the supreme assembly, the Witenagemote, which many political writers of the last century used to describe as a genuine English parliament annually elected by universal suffrage.

Palgrave, Hallam, and Kemble, however they may differ among themselves on points of detail, have effectually dispelled these monstrous and often mischievous delusions. The Witan was essentially an aristocratic body. It was summoned and presided over by the king. It was attended by the bishops, by the earls or eoldermen; the thanes generally had a right to attend; and probably those who resided in the neighbourhood of the place where a Witan was held did attend in considerable numbers. For the purpose of appealing against the decisions of inferior tribunals, and of procuring justice against powerful individuals, whom the minor courts could not reach, the magistrates of boroughs, and the four men or reeves of townships, and other similar officers, must have occasionally been present. This is what Sir Francis Palgrave terms "Remedial Representation." But there certainly were no representatives of the

* For further information as to the Anglo-Saxon boroughs, their guilds, &c., see the Appendix on Municipal Institutions, at the end of Lappenberg's "England under the Anglo-Saxon Kings." See, also, the chapter in Kemble on "The Towns," vol. ii. p. 262.

ceorls at the Witan with any power to take part in or vote in its proceedings.

The Witan made laws and voted taxes; but this last was a rare necessity. The king was bound to take their advice as to making war or peace, and on all important measures of government. The Witan had the power of electing the king from among the members of the blood royal. They on some occasions exercised the power of deposing him for misconduct: and they formed the supreme court of justice both in civil and criminal causes.

The nature and extent of the authority which the Anglo-Saxon kings possessed are partly shown by the description of the powers of the Witan. But, in addition to many minor rights, the royal prerogatives of appointing many of the principal officers of government, of commanding and disposing of the military force of the kingdom, were of considerable importance; and the personal character of the sovereign influenced materially the prosperity or adversity of the country, during the troubled centuries that passed between the accession of Egbert and the fall of the last Harold.

It has been stated that the bishops were members of the Witan. The influence of the clergy in the Anglo-Saxon times was very great; the humblest priest ranking with the landed gentry as a mass thane. The ecclesiastical distribution of the country into parishes (*i. e. preost scyres,* each being the district of a single priest) is Anglo-Saxon; a division since generally adopted for purposes of local self-government. It is to Saxon laws that modern disputants respecting tithes and church-rates refer for the original legal obligation on the English laity to provide those ecclesiastical revenues. Besides their right to these, the church was largely endowed with glebe for her parochial churches, and broad lands for her cathedrals and monasteries. The existence of one of these great ecclesiastical foundations in or near a city favoured the progress of municipal civilization; and many of our towns grew up round our ancient cathedrals. The high officers of the church, her bishops and archbishops, were recognised as the highest officers of the State also. Kemble has well remarked on the effect of this alliance between Church and State in the Saxon times, that, "guilty of extravagances the clergy were here, no doubt, as elsewhere; but on the whole their position was not unfavourable to the harmonious working of the State; and the history of the Anglo-Saxons is perhaps as little deformed as any by the ambition, and power, and selfish class-interests of the clergy. On the other hand, it cannot be denied that in England, as in other countries, the laity are under the greatest obligations to them, partly for rescuing some branches of learning from total neglect, and partly for the counterpoise which their authority presented to the rude and forcible government of a military aristocracy. Ridiculous as it would be to affirm that their influence was never exerted for mischievous purposes, or that this institution was always free from the imperfections and evils which belong to all human institutions, it would be still more unworthy of the dignity of history to affect to undervalue the services which they rendered to society. If in the pursuit of private and corporate advantages they occasionally seemed likely to prefer the separate to the general good, they did no more than all bodies of men have done,—no more than is necessary to ensure the active co-operation of all bodies of men in any one line of conduct. But, whatever their class-interests may from time to time have led them to do, let it be remembered that they existed as a permanent mediating authority between the rich and the poor, the strong and the weak, and that, to their eternal honour, they fully comprehended and performed the duties of this most noble position. To none but themselves would it have been permitted to stay the strong hand of power, to mitigate the just severity of the law, to hold out a glimmering of hope to the serf, to find a place in this world and a provision for the destitute, whose existence the State did not even recognise."

This last observation of Kemble's refers to the wretched position of those outcasts of the Saxon civil community who could find no place in one of the mutual associations, the tithings, and find no lord who would permit them to become his retainers. These friendless, helpless beings could not have been very numerous (we are not speaking of the wilful outlaws who lived by brigandage, but of the involuntary outlaws), but some of them must have existed. Such a being had no existence in the eye of the law, the civil State regarded him not, but abandoned him to arbitrary violence or starvation. But (to adopt again the eloquent words of Kemble) Christianity "taught that there was something even above the State, which the State itself was bound to recognise." The church impressed the heavenly law by which the poor and needy, whom the earthly law condemned to misery, were to be relieved; and the clergy presented their organization as an efficient machinery for the distribution of alms. There were other sources of relief for the poor. The tithes and other ecclesiastical revenues contributed their portion, and thus at every cathedral and every parish church there was a fund for the helpless pauper, and officers ready for its administration.

I leave unnoticed many points in the Anglo-Saxon system, of interest in themselves, but not indispensable for the general purpose of this treatise. But, in approaching the period of the Norman Conquest, it may be usefully observed, with Guizot, that in the last period of the Anglo-Saxon system the power of the great nobles was becoming more and more predominant, so as to menace both the independence of the crown and the freedom of the commonalty. The earls, or eorldermen, the rulers of large provinces, like Earl Siward, Earl Leofric, Earl Godwin and his sons, and others, were forming a separate order in the State, through the aggressive influence of which the political rights and liberties of the others would probably have decayed and perished. The catastrophe of the Norman Conquest prevented this ; a catastrophe terrible in itself; but, in all human probability, the averter of greater evils even to the Saxons themselves than those which it inflicted.

## CHAPTER V.

The Norman Element.—Different from the Danish.—Rolf the Ganger's Conquest of Neustria.—State of Civilization in France.—Characteristics of the Normans.—Their brilliant Qualities.—Their Oppression of the Peasantry.

LAST, but not least in importance, of the four elements of our nation, came the Norman. In some respects it may seem to be identical with the Danish: as Scandinavia was the parent country of both Norman and Dane. But there is this essential distinction. The Danes came to England direct from their Scandinavian homes. The Norman nation had dwelt in France for more than a century and a half between the time of its leaving Scandinavia and the time of its conquering England. During that interval the Normans had acquired the arts, the language, and the civilization of the Romanized Gauls and the Romanized Franks. They had done more than acquire the characteristics of others: they had created and developed a new national character of their own, differing both from that of their rude Danish and Norse kinsmen on the shores of the Baltic and the North Sea, and from that of the Romanesque provincials, whom they found on the banks of the Seine and the southern coast of the Channel.

Osker, Regner Lodbrok, Eric the Red, Biorn Ironside, Sidroc, and many more kings and jarls of the Norse or Dansker-men, had sailed up the Seine and spread the terror of their plunderings and slaughters through France, before a young Norwegian chief, named Rolf, and surnamed "Ganger" from his length of limb, left Norway with a fleet of warriors, and in 876 A. D., after some passing forays in England and Belgium, entered the estuary of the Seine, and made the familiar voyage of his countrymen up to Rouen. To say that he was enterprising, energetic, and fearless, is only to say that he was a Norse Viking. But tall striding Rolf was much more. He was a founder of empire. His brains were as good as his sinews. He was a man of thought as well as a man of action, and was worthy to be the lineal ancestor of England's sovereigns. He "formed the plan of substituting permanent colonization for periodical plunder. His host, his men, his 'baronage,' ultimately took possession of the city of Rouen, and the neighbouring country, measuring and dividing the land according to the Danish custom, by the rope."* But their settlement there was not effected at once. A long series of wars with the Frankish kings followed, varied by truces which were always bought of the Northmen with French gold. At last, in the year 912, King Charles Le Chauve formally ceded to Rolf the province which the jarl already firmly held, and which, from its new lord and his warriors, has thenceforth borne the name of Normandy.

Even in the crushed and miserable state of France under her last Carlovingian kings, Rolf, and his fellow-adventurers from Scandinavia, could perceive and appreciate the yet living fragments of a civilization superior to their own. This, in truth, the instinctive faculty of discerning and adopting the creations of the genius of others, peculiarly characterized the Normans, not only at the period of their first settlement in France, but throughout the ages of the rule of

* Palgrave's "Normandy and England," p. 518.

their dukes in Normandy. Rolf and his warriors embraced the creed, the language, the laws, and the arts, which France, in those troubled and evil times, during which the Carlovingian dynasty ended and that of the Capets commenced, still inherited from Imperial Rome and Imperial Charlemagne. Duke Rollo (such were the title and name which Jarl Rolf assumed) was succeeded in his duchy by a race of princes resembling him in mental capacity, as well as in martial bravery. The descendants also of the original Norman barons, taken as a body, were conspicuous for the same merits that had marked their sires. The century and a half which passed between Duke Rollo's settlement in Normandy and Duke William the Bastard's invasion of this island was an important period in mediæval history. France, throughout this time, was little more than a federation of feudal princes; and, during this period, the power, and pride, and predominance of the nobility, as a distinct order from the mass of the nation, grew rapidly, and assumed a peculiar social organization.

Amid the general disorder of France the noblesse fortified their castles where they dwelt; each baron in his stronghold, with his family and his band of favourite retainers round him. The management of horses and arms began to be regarded as the sole occupation worthy those of "gentle" blood. During this century and a half, chivalry, with all its romantic usages and institutions, grew into existence; and the germs of modern literature, of the poetry of the *Trouveur* and the *Troubadour,* appeared. Religious zeal, also, as manifested in distant pilgrimages, and in the lavishing of wealth and architectural skill upon abbeys, cathedrals, and shrines, was carried to a height previously unknown. In all these things, and in a generous respect for intellectual excellence by whomsoever and however manifested, the Normans were pre-eminent. Their national originality of character was at the same time shown in the free, but orderly and intelligent spirit which made them establish and preserve in their province a regularity of government, system, and law, which contrasted strongly with the anarchy of the rest of France. The Norman had a steady fixity of purpose, he had a discernment of the necessity of social union and mutual self-sacrifice of free-will among the individual members of a State for the sake of the common weal. Such qualities are the indispensable materials for national greatness; they were peculiar in those days to the Normans, especially as distinguished from the versatile and impatient noblesse of the rest of continental Christendom.

We have no trustworthy details of the institutions and laws of the Normans before the conquest of England. We only know generally that there was a council of the Norman barons, which the Norman duke was bound to convene and consult on all important matters of state; and that William the Conqueror's counts and chevaliers had not degenerated from the independent frankness of their Scandinavian sires.

Such were the brighter qualities of the Normans, who gave kings to our throne, ancestors to our aristocracy, clergy to our church, judges to our tribunals, rule and discipline to our monasteries, instructors to our architects, and teachers to our schools. We must proceed in our enumeration of the Norman gifts, and add, "who, beside the misery which their conquest caused to the generation then in being, gave, for many ages, tyrants to our peasantry, and brutal oppressors to our burghers and artizans." For there is a dark side of the Norman character, which the historian of English liberty must not omit; and even the aristocrats of ancient republican Rome were surpassed by the Norman nobility in pride, in state craft, in merciless cruelty, and in coarse contempt for the industry, the rights, and feelings of all whom they considered the lower classes of mankind.

Hitherto in speaking of the Normans in Normandy, we have been considering their usages and their characteristics, so far only as they themselves were concerned. It remains to view and judge them relatively to others.

The warriors of Rolf, and their descendants, were not the whole population of Normandy; they formed only a small minority of the human beings who lived in that province. The peasantry, whom the Norse conquerors found there, were not extirpated or evicted, but became part of the property of the new lords of the soil. They were taken with the land, like the other animals that were found on it. The mere fact of the foreign conquerors making slaves of the conquered natives, would present in itself nothing remarkable. Such was the established practice of ancient and mediæval times, nor can we say that modern ages have been pure from it. But the domination of the Normans over their *villeins* (as the Neustrian peasants were termed) was marked by its peculiar oppressiveness; and especially by the tyranny of the forest-laws which the Normans established. Sir Francis Palgrave says of this, that though the Normans did not destroy the old inhabitants of Neustria, "the conquerors gave the widest construction to the law of property; air, water, and earth were all to be theirs —fowl, fish, and beasts of chase, where the arrow could fly, the dog could draw, or the net could fall— sportsmen and huntsmen, the Danish lords appropriate to themselves all woodland and water, copse and grove, river, marsh, and mere. Their usurpation of the rights previously enjoyed in common occasioned in the days of Rollo's great grandson a fearful rebellion; and the spirit of the forest-laws, the pregnant source of misery to old England, has perhaps acquired additional bitterness in our present age; we retain the evil, whilst our pariahs have lost the compensation which mitigated mediæval tyranny."

It is worth while to read in the old Norman chronicler, William of Jumiege, his narrative of the insurrection which Palgrave refers to; not only for the information which it gives respecting its immediate subject, but, still more, for the insight which it affords into the prevailing sentiments among the Normans with respect to the labouring classes. Count Ranulph's cruelty to the insurgent peasants might be attributed to provocation or to individual ferocity of character. But De Jumiege wrote coolly and deliberately; and the tone in which he speaks of the sufferings and the duties of the peasantry, may be taken as accurately representing the general opinion of the Norman lords. After eulogizing the virtues of the then reigning duke Richard, De Jumiege says, "While he abounded in such goodness, it happened that in his youth a certain seminary of pestiferous dissensions arose within his dukedom of Normandy. For the peasants, one and all, throughout the various counties of Normandy, holding many assemblies, resolved to live at their own free-will; so that they should enjoy their own rights as to forest and to fishery, without the barrier of the law previously ordained. And for the purpose of establishing these schemes, two delegates were elected by each assembly of the mad rabble, who were to meet in a central convention for the purpose of confirming these resolutions. And when the duke knew it, he forthwith appointed Count Ranulph with a multitude of soldiers to repress the fierceness of the peasants, and disperse their rustic convention. And he, not delaying to do the duke's bidding, captured forthwith all the delegates, with some other peasants; and having cut off their hands and feet, he sent them back in that helpless state to their comrades; to check them from such practices, and to be warning to them not to expose themselves to something still worse. And when the peasants received this lesson, they forthwith abandoned their assemblies and their debates, and returned to their proper places at their ploughs." *

* William of Jumiege, book v. chap. 2.

## CHAPTER VI.

The Norman Conquest.—Extent of the Changes which it caused.—Numerical Amount of the Norman and Anglo-Saxon Populations.—Amount of Loss of Life caused by the Conquest.—Probable Number of the Normans and other New-comers from Continental Europe.—Did the Population increase in the Century and a half preceding the signing of Magna Carta?—The Miseries of Stephen's Reign.—Period of Tranquillity under Henry II.—Probable Amount of Population in 1215.

THE morning of the 29th day of September, 1066, saw a host of the Norman chivalry land upon the coast of the South Saxons (Sussex), and the setting sun of the following 14th day of October saw them the conquerors and lords of England.* The last of the Saxon kings, with his brethren, and most of the bravest thanes of the south and centre of the island lay dead on the field of Senlac. The two great northern earls, Edwin and Morcar, were timid and irresolute. There was no vigorous native chief to renew the war. The fortification of the strong places throughout England had been neglected: and as there was no post whither the shattered remains of Harold's army could retreat, and where they could halt in safety until reinforcements arrived, and until further measures of defence could be organized, a single defeat placed the whole country in the power of the invader.

Duke William had, indeed, some slight pretexts of right to the English crown, besides the cogent title

* See the Battle of Hastings, chap. 8 of "The Fifteen Decisive Battles of the World."

of the sword. His relationship to Edward the Confessor, and the alleged bequest of the sovereignty of England to him by that king, gave a colourable excuse, both to his own conduct in undertaking his great enterprise, and to the conduct of the Saxons who submitted to him, instead of prolonging a hopeless war after the battle of Hastings.

He was crowned King of England by the Saxon archbishop with the ancient Saxon forms, and after taking the coronation oath of the Saxon kings, on Christmas Day, 1066. At first his rule was comparatively mild. By confiscating the large estates of King Harold and Harold's family, and principal adherents, William obtained the means of appeasing (if he could not satisfy) the rapacity of his followers, while he left for a time the greater number of the English landowners in the enjoyment of their property. But, under any disguise, conquest is to a brave people a bitter draught. The sense of foreign domination, and the insolence of William's Norman barons and prelates, weighed heavily on the spirits of Saxon thane and Saxon ceorl. Then came fierce local risings, with delusive partial success over the foreigners; soon crushed by the disciplined troops and the high military genius of the Conqueror. Then followed more sweeping confiscations, and darker cruelties: the results not so much of hasty anger, as of a stern, remorseless policy. William resolved that his English subjects should fear him, if they hated him; and no feeling of mercy ever made him pause in any measure that seemed adapted to increase and consolidate his power.

There are some yet standard works on our history and our laws, in which the Norman Conquest of England is spoken of in terms which would lead the reader to imagine that it amounted to little more than the substitution of one royal family for another on the throne of this country, and to the garbling and changing of some of our laws through the "cunning of the Norman lawyers." But it is certain that the social and political changes which that Conquest introduced into England, excelled in importance the effect of any similar event which had occurred in mediæval Christendom, and that they have not been equalled by the results of any subsequent conquest which one Christian nation has effected over another. In consequence of the triumph of the Normans here, new tribunals and tenures predominated over the old ones, new divisions of race and class were introduced, whole districts were devastated to gratify the vengeance or the caprice of the new tyrants, the greater part of the lands of the English were confiscated and divided among aliens, "the very name of Englishman was turned into a reproach, the English language rejected as servile and barbarous, and all the high places in Church and State for upwards of a century filled exclusively by men of foreign race." The words of Thierry * on this subject are no less true than eloquent. He tells his reader that "if he would form a just idea of England conquered by William of Normandy, he must figure to himself, not a mere change of political rule, nor the triumph of one candidate over another candidate, of the man of one party over the man of another party, but the intrusion of one people into the bosom of another people, the violent placing of one society over another society, which it came to destroy, and the scattered fragments of which it retained only as personal property, or (to use the words of an old act) as 'the clothing of the soil.' He must not picture to himself—on the one hand, William, a king and a despot—on the other, subjects of

* Thierry's "Norman Conquest." See, too, Hallam's "Middle Ages," vol. ii. p. 304.

William's, high and low, rich and poor, all inhabiting England, and consequently all English: he must imagine two nations, of one of which William is a member and the chief—two nations which (if the term must be used) were both *subject* to William; but as applied to which the word has quite different senses, meaning in the one case *subordinate*, in the other *subjugated.* He must consider that there are two countries—two soils—included in the same geographical circumference; that of the Normans rich and free,—that of the Saxons poor and serving, vexed by *rent* and *taillage*;—the former full of spacious mansions, and walled and moated castles,—the latter scattered over with huts of straw and ruined hovels; —that peopled with the happy and the idle—with men of the army and of the court—with knights and nobles,—this, with men of pain and labour—with farmers and artizans;—on the one, luxury and insolence, —on the other, misery and envy—not the envy of the poor at the sight of opulence which they cannot reach, but the envy of the despoiled when in presence of the despoiler."

We have now traced the four great elements of our nation from their respective origins, until they were all brought together in this country. The period which elapsed between the introduction of the last of these in point of date (that is to say, the Norman), and the national rising against King John in the early part of the 13th century, is a period of fusion; very interesting, as to many of its events, and as to the personal characters of many who figured during it. In particular, the Conqueror himself, the brave Saxon chieftain Hereward, the Archbishops Lancfranc and Anselm, King Henry the Second, Archbishop A'Beckett, and William Longbeard, the Saxon burgess, who strove in vain to defend the oppressed commonalty of the capital against their Norman tyrants, all deserve the careful attention of the student of English history, and of the student of human nature. But to avoid prolixity, I pass over the details of this period ; and proceed to examine the number and condition of the various classes of the population of England in the reign of John, the epoch of the true dawn of our complete nationality. In making that examination, we shall be led to consider several of the most important events which had then happened in the interval since the Conquest.

One primary point, before we notice the subdivisions of the population, is to ascertain, as well as we are able, the numerical amount of the whole. And this is closely connected with a topic, which ought not to be omitted when we speculate on the comparative importance of each of the four elements of our race ; I mean the proportion which the Normans and other new-comers from Continental Europe bore to the Anglo-Saxons and Anglo-Danes, among whom they settled as conquerors.

The population of England at the time of the Norman conquest is variously estimated at from a million and a half to two millions. It is necessary to bear this in mind, when we read of the losses sustained by defeats in the field, and other calamities of this period ; because we are too apt to think of the England of bygone centuries as of the England of our own times in point of population. Unless we correct this anachronism in our ideas, we shall not attach sufficient importance to the destruction of two or three hundred thousand human beings in that age, as being a catastrophe, not only shocking in itself with regard to the immediate sufferers, but calculated seriously to thin the land of its old inhabitants.

I propose to determine as far as possible, 1st, the extent to which the Saxon population was diminished by its afflictions under the Normans ; and, 2ndly, the probable number of the Normans and other Continental Europeans who settled here. We shall find that these calculations will supply us with our primary data for estimating the number of the population at the epoch of the Great Charter.

The Saxon army which perished with Harold, at Hastings, is said not to have been a very large one. But the slaughters of the Saxons, which followed, in consequence of their subsequent insurrections against the Conqueror, were numerous and severe: nor can we estimate the total number that perished by the edge of the sword, during William's invasion and reign, at less than a hundred thousand. The number of exiles also was considerable; as very many of the Saxons sought refuge in Scotland; and many fled beyond seas from the tyranny of their Norman lords. But the massacres perpetrated in cold bood by William's command destroyed more than fell fighting, or fled into exile; and the famines and pestilences caused by his merciless devastations of wide tracts of populous and fertile territory were more destructive still. One of his most atrocious acts of this kind was his laying waste the country between the Humber and the Tyne, partly out of anger for a rising of some of the inhabitants against him, and partly as a measure of precaution, because he expected an invasion from Denmark, and thought that the Danes would most likely land in the North of England, where the population was most nearly akin to them. The Norman monkish chronicler, Ordericus Vitalis, who is generally William's unscrupulous panegyrist, thus speaks of his devastation of Northumbria: "He extended his posts over a space of one hundred miles. He smote most of the inhabitants with the edge of the avenging sword: he destroyed the hiding-places of others: he laid waste their lands: he burned their houses, with all that was therein. Nowhere else did

William act with such cruelty: and in this instance he shamefully gave way to evil passion; while he scorned to rule his own wrath, and cut off the guilty and innocent with equal severity. For, excited by anger, he bade the crops, and the herds, and the household stuff, and every description of food, to be gathered in heaps, and to be set light to and utterly destroyed altogether: and so that all sustenance for man or beast should be at once wasted throughout all the region beyond the Humber. Whence there raged grievous want far and wide throughout England; such a misery of famine involved the helpless people that there perished of Christian human beings, of either sex, and every age, upwards of a hundred thousand." *

A large part of Hampshire was similarly made a wilderness by his orders, so as to supply him with a "New Forest," wherein he might pursue his favourite sport of the chase. Many other acts of his might be mentioned, all tending to waste the people who were his victims from off the face of the land: and an infinitely larger number of cruel and destructive acts were perpetrated by him and his Norman followers, no special record of which has survived, but to which the lamentations of the old Saxon chroniclers bear emphatic though confused testimony. For instance: one of these old writers† tells us that he forbears narrating, in detail, the conduct of the Normans to the mass of the population, "because it was hard to express in words, and because it would appear incredible by reason of its excessive barbarity." Many more such phrases of the Saxon monks who saw and mourned over the miseries of their countrymen might be cited. And there is also the explicit proof which

* Ordericus Vitalis, lib. iv.

† Hist. Eliens.

the figures in Domesday Book* supply of the decay of the populations of the great cities and towns, and it was during the first 20 years of the Norman rule in this country. Altogether, I believe that the old population of the island was diminished by, at least, a third, during the invasion and the reign of William the Conqueror.

It remains to be considered how far this gap was filled up by the Normans and their companions.

William's army at Hastings is said to have numbered 60,000 fighting men. Of these, a fourth fell in the fight; but we must add largely for the non-combatants who accompanied the troops. We have an account also of another even larger host, which he summoned over here from the Continent, in the 19th year of his reign, when he expected an invasion from Scandinavia ; and a constant stream of new population from the Continent was poured into England during the times of all her first Anglo-Norman monarchs.

Few of these adventurers returned to their homes. So that it is probable that, during the reigns of the Conqueror and his sons, from two hundred thousand to three hundred thousand Normans and other immigrants from the Continent became inhabitants of this country.

The accession of population to England from the Continent continued during the reigns of Stephen and Henry II., especially the latter ; when the Plantagenet heritage in the south of France contributed to the influx. The introduction also of a large colony of Flemings, who were principally settled in the neighbourhood of Wales, is not to be omitted. I do not, however, think that the aggregate population of the various races in England was larger at the death

* See Hallam's "Middle Ages," chap. 8, p. 2.

of Richard I. than at the epoch of the Conquest. The misery which the country suffered during the reign of Stephen must fearfully have reduced the number of human beings in the land. No description of that misery can be more emphatic than that which the old chroniclers give. They tell us that "The nobles and bishops built castles, and filled them with devilish and evil men, and oppressed the people, cruelly torturing them for their money. They made many thousands die of hunger. They imposed taxes upon towns, and when they had exhausted them of everything, set them on fire. You might travel a day, and not find one man living in a town, or in the country one cultivated field. The poor died of hunger; and they who were once men of substance now begged their bread from door to door. Never did the country suffer greater evils. The very Pagans did not more evil than those men did. If two or three men were seen riding up to a town, all its inhabitants left it, taking them for plunderers. To till the ground was as vain as to till the sand on the sea-shore. And this lasted, growing worse and worse, throughout Stephen's reign. Men said openly that Christ and his saints were asleep."

During the long and prosperous reign of Henry II., the country recovered from "that shipwreck of the commonwealth," as one of Henry's Acts of State emphatically calls the condition of the land in the time of Stephen. But looking generally to the character of the other reigns, I do not think there is any reason to suppose that the total population of the realm, in the time of John, exceeded the largest census which is assigned to Anglo-Saxon England, namely, about two millions.

## CHAPTER VII.

General View of the Feudal System.—Meaning of the terms "Feudal" and "Allodial."—General Sketch of the Progress of a Germanic Settlement in a Roman Province.—Causes of Feudalism.—Progress of "Sub-infeudation."—Aristocratic Character of Feudalism.—Its Oppressiveness to the Commonalty.—Its brighter Features.

In order to understand the classes into which the two millions of human beings, who dwelt here at the time of the grant of the Great Charter, were divided, and the system of government which then existed, a right comprehension of the principles of the Feudal System is indispensable. Even the state of the enslaved peasantry of England at the commencement of the 13th century cannot be thoroughly discerned, unless we view the peasants in relation to their feudal lords. And, when we proceed to the great events of the century, it would be utterly impossible to give any intelligible account of the greatest of all, the acquisition of Magna Carta, without continually pausing to explain feudal terms and usages, if we should not have taken a preliminary survey of that strange body of social and political institutions, so long and so generally prevalent over Europe, to which historians and jurists have given the title of Feudal.

The inquiry is, indeed, far from being one of mere antiquarian interest. The forms of our Constitution cannot be understood without it; and the student of our law, especially of the law of real property, must still resort to the feudal system for the principles, and even for the practice, of his art.*

I am not, however, going to discuss here, either the etymology, or the date of the birth, or the exact pedigree of Feuds. Suffice it, for the present occasion, to say generally, that the feudal system was gradually matured during the six or seven centuries of confusion which followed the irruption of the Germanic nations into the Western Roman empire: and that, at the epoch which we treat as the dawn of complete English history (about A. D. 1215), the feudal system was established, though with different modifications, in every European country that had been a Roman province and had been overrun by German conquerors. The feudal system was also then established in Germany itself.

There are many things which are the more easily understood by first obtaining an understanding of their opposites. This is the case with the word "Feudal." The term used in contradistinction to it, by European jurists, is "Allodial." Allodial land was land in which a man had the full and entire property; which he held (as the saying is) out and out. But feudal land (and the land itself so held was called a Feud, or Fief) was land which a man held of some other man, from whom or whose ancestors the holder (or his ancestor) had received permission to possess and enjoy the fruits of the land; but the property and ultimate dominion of it remained in the giver, or, as he was technically called, the lord. The idea of the sovereign owner of land allowing individuals to have the possession of portions of it, and even to transmit such possessory interest to their heirs, on condition of rendering certain services, usually military, may be found in the institutions of almost every

* See "Haynes on Conveyancing," vol. i. p. 6. Fifth edition. See, also, Stephens' "Blackstone," vol. i.

ancient European nation, and in those of many Asiatic States at the present time. But it was only in mediæval Europe that this simple idea and natural custom were elaborated into a complete system of government and of social organization, to which everything else was made subordinate, and by reference to which every public office and every private right were determined.

In order the more clearly to picture to ourselves the chief causes of the establishment of Feudalism, we may sketch in our minds the progress, and watch the position, of some one of those numerous bands of Teutonic conquerors that had won their way into a Roman province at the fall of the ancient Western empire. The sketch I am about to give, is applicable to Romanized Europe generally, not specially to England. My object at present is to give the leading ideas of feudalism. When we come to apply them to the state of things in this island, some important modifications must be introduced: but still the general theory must be first learned. Here, again, in order to illustrate and explain feudalism, I shall first illustrate its negation, allodialism.

When, by degrees, the bands of Germanic warriors, who had broken in upon Gaul and the other Roman provinces, began to lose their spirit of fierce restlessness, and to wish for some permanent settlement in the territories which they had conquered from the provincials, and had long fought for with each other, the ownership of land acquired a value in their eyes, not merely of a higher degree, but of a wholly different nature, to that which it had in the eyes of their ancestors, who dwelt amid their primitive forests and wildernesses; and also to that which it had had in their own, so long as they were a mere troop of adventurers, roving in quest of plunder, or seeking fresh enterprises for the sheer sake of the excitement.

Let us imagine an army of Germanic conquerors in this mood for becoming inhabitants of the land which they had conquered, and let us mark what would be the natural results. Some part of the territory might probably be left in the hands of the conquered population; but the conquerors would share the rest. The points to attend to, are to see, first, how they would share it; and secondly, what other system of parcelling out domains would soon ensue. It is to be remembered that each barbaric king was not the sovereign of an army of subjects in the sense in which we employ the term "sovereign" and "subject;" but of free and independent warriors, each of whom would claim his share of the spoil as a right, as something to hold at his own free will, not as a boon revocable at a despot's caprice. The portion of land, which the German soldier thus took, he took as his property; and his estate in it was termed, by the Franks, Allodial. As the conquerors dwelt among a numerically superior population, their safety must have required them to keep up their military organization; and the subordination, which is the essence of all military discipline, must have greatly facilitated the change of tenure which, as we shall next see, generally occurred.*

I have described the distribution of land that took place among the free warriors who composed a Germanic army, and the terms on which that land was usually assigned; but all the confiscated territories was not thus portioned out. Large demesnes were reserved for the king, called fiscal lands. Out of the royal demesnes the sovereigns granted lands to their most favoured or distinguished personal followers, under the title of fiefs or benefices. Whether any definite services were at first affixed to a beneficiary grant

* See Note 8, to Robertson's "View of the State of Europe."

is uncertain ; but in the nature of things, some return would be expected from the favoured follower ; an expectation which would soon ripen into a demand : and military service against foreign or domestic foes would, in such a state of society, be the return most desirable to the grantor, and most easily and willingly accorded by the receiver. But the ownership of the fief did not pass out of the grantor. The favoured individual (the Feudatory, in the technical phrase) received, not a right of property, but a mere license of possession and enjoyment, an usufructuary right, which some authors suppose to have been at first precarious and arbitrarily revocable ; though the feudatory's interest soon became more certain and permanent, enduring for his life, unless forfeited by some act of misconduct towards the giver, or, as we will term him, assuming the feudal phraseology, the lord. And gradually fiefs became hereditary ; though, throughout the development of the system, the ultimate property was and is held to be in the lord, as evidenced both by legal forms and symbols, and by the liabilities of the fief to revert to the hand that gave it—liabilities which long afforded sharp and practical symptoms of its original character.

As the privileges of the feudatory thus became certain, so were his duties systematized, and the consequences of his breach of them defined. Military service, fidelity in counsel, respect for the person and honour of his lord, attendance at his lord's tribunal, pecuniary contribution in certain cases, formed the essence of these duties, varying, however, in detail, at different times and in different countries.

Corresponding duties of protection from the lord to the feudatory existed ; and the general character of the relation between the lord and vassal may be defined in Mr. Hallam's words as a mutual contract of support and fidelity.

I have been describing a case of feudalism in its simplest form, where the feudatory, to whom the sovereign lord of the land granted it, continued to hold the land himself. But the process of "Sub-infeudation" was common, and then a far more complex state of things arose. The feudatory, who received large grants of land from his sovereign, frequently had dependents of his own, to whom he carved out portions of his fief, to be held of himself on terms similar to those by which he held it of his lord. His sub-grantees thus became vassals under him, and he was a feudal lord to them. They again might subdivide their sub-fiefs, and grant them to others. And the process might be indefinitely renewed as often as each subdivided piece of feudal land was capable of still further subdivision. So that many links in the feudal chain might intervene between the original grantor, or lord paramount, and the actual occupant of the soil, who was termed the Tenant Paravail. Thus, there arose a seignioral hierarchy, specious in appearance, and which Blackstone has eulogized, but in reality productive of very great confusion. For, as it was in respect of the land that the feudal relation arose, and not in respect of any personal *status* of the individual, the same two men might be and often were lords and vassals of each other in respect of different lands, and an endless conflict of obligations and rights were created.

Still, some protection was gained from the system; and as times grew more and more troubled after the dissolution of the empire of Charlemagne, the oppressed and isolated allodialist was glad to seek even temporary shelter, by becoming one of the liegemen of some powerful baron in his neighbourhood. Frequently, also, the feudal barons possessed themselves with the strong hand of the little properties of their feebler neighbours. "During the 10th and 11th centuries," says Mr. Hallam, "it appears that allodial lands in France had chiefly become feudal; that is, they had been surrendered by their proprietors, and received back again upon the feudal conditions; or more frequently, perhaps, the owner had been compelled to acknowledge himself the man or vassal of a suzerain, and thus to confess an original grant which had never existed. Changes of the same nature, though not, perhaps, so extensive or so distinctly to be traced, took place in Italy and Germany. Yet it would be inaccurate to assert that the prevalence of the feudal system has been unlimited; in a great part of France allodial tenures always subsisted, and many estates in the empire were of the same description."

The influence of the feudal system was not limited to the lay part of the population, or to the rural districts of the state. "The prelates and abbots were completely 'feudal nobles;' they swore fealty for their lands to the king or other superior; received the homage of their vassals, enjoyed the same immunities, exercised the same jurisdiction, maintained the same authority as the lay lords among whom they dwelt." * Very frequently the bishops and abbots gave fiefs to knights on condition of defending the cathedral or the abbey; and of supplying and leading the contingent of troops, which the lord paramount demanded. The towns and cities also had their feudal lords. Sometimes the rights of war and conquest gave to the sovereign or some powerful noble the feudal seigniory over a civic community: sometimes the burghers voluntarily placed their city under the feudal seigniory of some celebrated chieftain, or neighbouring baron, for the sake of military protection. The extent of the jurisdiction of the feudal lord over a borough varied according to the terms of the original compact, where it had been voluntarily

* Hall. i. 194.

created; and according to the terms which the burgesses were able to purchase, where the lords' right over them was the sweeping right of conquest. The modes by which the boroughs obtained their charters of liberties, their municipal organizations, and their own leagues with one another for self-protection, form one of the most interesting portions of mediæval history, but can only be glanced at here.

The spirit of the feudal system was essentially aristocratic. It required, indeed, the existence of a single lord paramount, whether termed Emperor, or King, who was theoretically the supreme fountain of honour and justice, and the motive centre of authority both in peace and war. But, in practice, the feudal aristocracy was an aggressive power, that ever sought to aggrandize itself at the expense of monarchy. The process of sub-infeudation was the great cause of this. Each baron, who girt himself with martial vassals sworn to serve him, and who made the revenues of provinces and cities his own, became the founder of an "*imperium in imperio.*" He did not, indeed, often throw off the semblance of allegiance to his sovereign, but he claimed and exercised the right of resisting his sovereign by open force, if the sovereign carried his feudal prerogatives too far, and of making formal war on him as on a stranger, if his sovereign did him wrong on any matter unconnected with their feudal relationship. He claimed and freely exercised the right of similarly making war on any of his fellow-subjects, on the neighbouring barons or others who offended him. This right of private warfare was the greatest affliction to feudal Europe. Another point on which the feudal lords strove to assert their independenee of the crown, was the right of administering justice in their own territories. Each feudal lord had his baronial court, at which his military tenants attended, and where the judicial combat was the favourite mode of determining controversies between the litigants, whether of a civil or a criminal nature.

While the feudal aristocracy was thus encroaching upon the natural powers of the monarchy, it was no less aggressive upon the commonalty of the land. The feudal barons and their retainers gradually formed an aristocracy of birth as well as of tenure. It has been pointed out, in describing our Norman ancestors before the Conquest, how each baronial castle became a military school, wherein the exercises indispensable for the training and duties of the armed cavalry of those ages were taught to the barons' sons, and to the youths of similar birth who were nurtured with them. It is to be observed, that every holder of a fief by military tenure, however small his strip of land, was a noble, as distinguished from the tiller of the soil, the burgess, and the artisan, and even from him who held land by a less martial title. The superiority of the feudal warrior who was thus trained up, and who fought on horseback, protected by his coat-of-mail armour, over the common people who fought on foot and without armour of defence, was effective in war, and tended more and more to encourage the pride of superiority of class. Men who belonged to this equestrian rank (as the class of feudal aristocracy in its early stage may be correctly called) retained the same feelings of elevation, even though they had parted with their land. Their children did the same. The institutions of chivalry, and the adoption of distinctive armorial bearings by members of particular families, aided powerfully in creating this mixed feudal aristocracy, based partly on tenure of land, and partly on birth. The nobility, and the knights and members of knightly families, made up a warrior caste, who termed themselves gentle by birth; and who looked down on the great mass of the lay community as beings of almost inferior nature. According to the favorite theory of the admirers of the feudal system, men were divided under it into three classes—warriors, teachers, and producers. The feudal nobles and knights with their vassals and military followers were the first class; the clergy were the teacher class; and the rest of the people were the third, the productive class.[*] Unhappily, the general tendency of feudalism was to depress the producers. The peasantry and the little allodialists were ground down with servitude, and forced to till the soil as abject dependants of the barons; while the stores of the merchant and the earnings of the artizan were too often treated as the legitimate objects of knightly rapacity and violence. If we investigate feudalism in its social aspects, we shall find ample cause for the inextinguishable hatred with which, as Guizot truly states, it has ever been regarded by the common people.[†] But this ought not to make us blind to its brighter features. There was much in feudalism, especially as developed in the institutions of chivalry, that was pure and graceful and generous. It ever acknowledged the high social position of woman, it zealously protected her honour. It favoured the growth of domestic attachments, and the influence of family associations. It fostered literature and science. It kept up a feeling of independence, and a spirit of adventurous energy. Above all, it paid homage to the virtues of Courage and Truth in man, and of Affection and Constancy in woman.

* Weber, "Universal History," 109.
† "Civilization en Europe."

## CHAPTER VIII.

Distinction between Feudalism as developed in England, and Feudalism as generally developed on the Continent.—How far did it exist among the Saxons before the Conquest; how far among the Normans?—Character of William the Conqueror.—Feudalism which he introduced.—His checks upon the Baronial Power.—Great Authority of the First Anglo-Norman Kings.

In applying to English history the description of the principles of feudalism which was given in the last chapter, we must remember several important points of distinction between this island and the Continent, respecting the adoption and the development of the feudal system. The Roman province of Britain underwent two, if not three, successive conquests by nations of Germanic race. First there was the Saxon conquest, the peculiarities of which, as contradistinguished from the Germanic conquests of Roman provinces on the Continent, have been adverted to in a previous chapter. There was afterwards the great conquest of Saxon England by the Normans, who came from semi-Germanized and semi-civilized France, and who brought with them a system of feudalism already moulded in its essential parts. Perhaps the extensive immigration of victorious Danes, which occurred in the interval between the Saxon and Norman conquests, ought to be reckoned as a conquest itself. In no continental province of the old Roman empire did similar events occur. But the distinction between feudalism in England, and feudalism in France, Germany, Italy, or Spain, is even more due to the sagacious mind and resolute will of one great man, of William the Conqueror himself.

Before we examine this, there are two topics which have been already adverted to, but which must be again glanced at. These are, first, the question how far feudalism existed among the Saxons in England before the Conquest; and secondly, how far did it exist among the Normans in Normandy before the Conquest?

On the first of these questions volumes have been written, and many more will probably appear. I am not going to discuss the conflicting theories that have been put forward; and will only observe, that, so far as the *forms* of feudalism are concerned, there are few, if any, of which we cannot trace occasional precedents or analogues among the Anglo-Saxons; but that no general elaborate system of feudal form and ceremonies existed in Saxon England, like that which we find here afterwards. So far as regards the *spirit* of feudalism, there was certainly little here before the Conquest. The Saxon ceorl and his thane were in a far different position relatively to each other, from that in which the Anglo-Norman villein stood relatively to his lord. On the whole, I would affirm that there were many institutions among the Anglo-Saxons of a partially feudal nature, which much facilitated the subsequent introduction of feudalism; but that the feudal system, as a system, cannot be said to have existed here before the overthrow of Saxon independence at Hastings.

With regard to the other topic—how far feudalism prevailed among the Normans themselves in Normandy before they conquered this country, Sir Francis Palgrave, in his recent history of Normandy, disputes the commonly-received opinion of Sismondi and others, that Duke Rollo and his Northmen, when they became permanent denizens of Normandy, introduced a complete system of feudality.* Palgrave's contradiction of Sismondi appears to be verbally right, and substantially wrong. There seems to be no evidence, direct or inferential, of either Duke Rollo, or any other Norman duke, having suddenly composed and introduced among his subjects an elaborate system of feudalism, with all the laws and incidents of tenure designed and provided for. But a perusal of Dudon de St. Quentin, of William of Jumiege, and Wace, abundantly proves that feudalism, in all its essential principles, either had been established, or had grown up in Normandy, before William the Bastard became duke ; and one great point, namely, that the Norman peasantry were tyrannized over as villeins, in the fullest intensity of feudalism, is shown by the narrative of the insurrection of those unhappy men against Duke Richard the Second, which I have quoted in a preceding chapter. The clear evidence also, which we possess, of how William dealt with landholders in England, is cogent proof that he was familiar with the feudal tenure in his own duchy. I believe, on the whole, that it is substantially correct to say, that William introduced the feudal system into this country, though some portions of it were not fully developed till after his time, and though Henry the Second and his Justiciars, when they re-organized the kingdom, after the "shipwreck" which it underwent in Stephen's time, probably made several innovations.

Hallam correctly describes William the Conqueror as a cold and far-sighted statesman, of great talents, with little passion or insolence, but utterly indifferent to human suffering. These qualities were all eminently displayed in the way in which he organized feudalism in this country, adopting it so far as it tended to confirm his conquest and consolidate his power, but modifying it from the form in which it

* P. 673.

existed on the Continent, so as to guard his throne from being overshadowed by a haughty and turbulent nobility, in the manner in which he himself and the other great peers of France overawed the French Crown. Nor ought we, in justice to William, to doubt but that the instinctive appreciation of Order, which is a characteristic of great men, must have strongly influenced him in the precautions which he took against the development here of the baronial insubordination, which filled the Continent with petty violences and local miseries. Guizot truly says that "there are men whom the spectacle of anarchy or of social stagnation strikes and distresses, who are intellectually shocked thereat as with a fact which should not be, and who become possessed with an uncontrollable desire to change it and to plant some rule, some uniformity, regularity, and permanency, in the world before them." And such a man, notwithstanding his selfishness, his pride, and his hardness of heart, was William, Duke of Normandy, and, by conquest, King of England.

He established as an universal rule throughout the country, that he himself was the supreme lord of all the land. Such continues to be the theory of our law to the present hour. "All the lands and tenements in England in the hands of subjects," says Coke, "are holden mediately or immediately of the king; for in the law of England we have not properly allodium."*

This feudal supremacy of the Crown was solemnly acknowledged at the great assembly which William convened at Salisbury, in 1086. Every man of the least note who held land in England attended there:† and they all took the oath of fealty to William as their liege lord; and each of the vast multitude performed the ceremony of homage to him.

* Coke "Littleton," cap. i. sect. 1. † "Saxon Chron." 290.

Each landowner, whatever his rank or wealth, knelt openly and humbly before William as he sat on his throne. Each placed his clasped hands within the king's hands, and pronounced the formal words, "I become your man, from this day forth, of life, of limb, and of earthly worship, and unto you will be true and faithful, and bear you faith for the land I hold of you, so help me God."

But while William thus made feudalism universal in England, he at the same time made an important alteration in its system, by which he strengthened the authority of the Crown, and provided against his great vassals acquiring the insubordinate powers which the feudal nobility on the Continent enjoyed. He did not, indeed, prohibit sub-infeudation. That was not done till two centuries later. But William at the Salisbury convention made all the sub-tenants of his *Tenants in capite* (i. e. of those who held land immediately from himself), take the oath of fealty to him, the king, as the lord paramount of all. Whereas on the Continent, the vassal who held lands took an oath of fealty to his own immediate lord;—to the sovereign, if he held directly from him, but to the mesne lord, if (as in the great majority of cases) some peer or baron, or perchance several of them, intervened between the Crown and the occupant of the soil.

Besides thus "breaking in upon the feudal compact in its most essential attributes, the exclusive dependence of a vassal upon his immediate lord,"* William took other effective measures to keep down the influence of the aristocracy, and exalt that of the Crown. While lavishly generous in his grants of land to those who had served him, he took care to reward each leading Norman noble by estates scattered over different parts of the kingdom, and not by compact little principalities, which might serve as

* Hallam, vol. ii. p. 312.

bases of rebellion, and form independent States. He maintained also in effective force the supreme authority of his own royal tribunal; and kept within as narrow limits as possible the territorial jurisdiction which each lord of a manor exercised in his court baron. He had the wisdom also to retain the Saxon popular tribunals of the county court and the court of the hundred, although he diminished the dignity of the county court by withdrawing ecclesiastical matters from its cognizance. For all purposes of temporal jurisdiction it was preserved. It may, indeed, be said to have acquired vigour, and to have become more democratic in character under the Anglo-Norman kings, than it had been before the Conquest. Under the Anglo-Saxon system only the thanes, that is, the gentry, could act and vote as members of the county court. Under the Anglo-Norman rule all persons who held any land by a free tenure had a right to attend the county court and to take part both as suitors and voters in its proceedings. While these democratic courts of the shire and the hundred flourished, and while also the power of the king's courts was gradually extended (as was done by the Conqueror's wisest successors), it was impossible for any feudal lord in England to raise his baronial court into the judicial importance which was arrogated by each count and seignior on the Continent.

Such licensed anarchy, as is implied by a recognized right of private warfare, was little likely to be permitted under the iron rule of William. Every man, small or great, was bound to keep the king's peace, and was amenable to the criminal law for the breach of it. Instances of violence and strife between rival nobles, that seem to amount to private warfare, may certainly be found in the Anglo-Norman times, but these, even when unpunished, were looked on as breaches of the law, and not as things done in the exercise of legal privileges.*

Thus, Norman feudalism in England secured more order and regularity, and embodied a stronger central governing power, than could be maintained in the feudal States of Continental Christendom. There were other causes for the predominant importance and authority of Anglo-Norman royalty. One of these was the immense wealth of the Crown, independently of any contributions from its subjects. William kept nearly 1500 manors, and almost all the cities and towns of any note, as his own share of the spoils of the Conquest. Another cause was the readiness with which the Saxon part of the population ever served the king against any of their Norman barons who rebelled. A third, and not the least important cause, was the remarkable intellectual capacity and energy which characterized not only the Conqueror himself, but all his successors on our throne, until John became king of England.†

We shall have occasion hereafter to observe the happy peculiarity of our Constitution, by which England secured the blessing of a Nobility, but escaped the curse of a numerous Noblesse, such as overspread the other feudal States of Europe. At present our attention has been limited to the distinctive points of English feudality, prior to the reign of John.

We may now direct our attention to the condition of the population of the land, at the time when this degenerate inheritor of the Conqueror's sceptre roused all classes of freemen into a joint struggle against the abused predominance of royal power.

* See Hallam, vol. ii. p. 345. The instances cited by Allen (on the Royal Prerogative, p. 120) seem to confirm Hallam's remarks.

† See Palgrave's "Normandy and England," pp. 704, 707.

## CHAPTER IX.

**State of the Mass of the English Nation at the Commencement of the Thirteenth Century.—The Peasantry.—Villeinage: its Incidents: its probable Origin and Extent; and the Modes of becoming emancipated from it.—State of the Lower Classes in Towns.—State of the Middle and Upper Classes.—The various Tenures of Land.—State of the Boroughs after the Conquest.—Their partial Recovery of their Liberties.**

Of the two millions of human beings who inhabited England in the reign of John, a very large number, probably nearly half, were in a state of slavery. Those who are disposed to listen to tales about "Merrie England," and "the good old times," should remember this fact. At the commencement of true English history, we start with the labourers in abject wretchedness. The narrative of the changes in their social and political positions thenceforward to modern times, is certainly a history of progressive amelioration, though lamentably slow and imperfect.

The technical name for the kind of slavery which prevailed in Anglo-Norman England is Villeinage. Some slaves were annexed to certain lands, and passed into the dominion of the heirs or purchasers of those lands whenever the ground, which was considered the more important property, changed owners. These were called "Villeins regardant." Others were bought and sold, and passed from master to master, without respect to any land. These were termed "Villeins in gross;" the ancient law applying to them the same uncouth but expressive phraseology, by which it spoke of rights of common and other inanimate legal entities.

It is probable that the number of villeins in gross was never very considerable: but there are good grounds for believing that, at the commencement of the thirteenth century, the greater part of the labouring agricultural population of England (including not only actual farm-labourers, but the followers of those handicrafts which are closely connected with husbandry, and were practised on the land) were villeins regardant, and were looked on merely as so much of the live-stock of the land to which they belonged.

The best description of the ancient state of villeinage is contained in Mr. Hargreaves' celebrated argument in the case of the Negro Somerset, in 1772; where he successfully maintained the noble position, that a slave who touched British ground became free. He proved this by showing that the law of England had never [that is to say, never since the formation of the Common Law] recognized any species of slavery, except the ancient one of villeinage, then long extinct; and that our law had effectually guarded against the introduction of any new sort of slavery into England. In doing this, Mr. Hargreaves was led to make the most full and accurate investigation of the nature of villeinage which has ever been effected; and the law-tract to which I refer, is consequently of the highest value to the student of early English history.

"Slavery," says Mr. Hargreaves, "always imports an obligation of perpetual service; an obligation which only the consent of the master can dissolve. It generally gives to the master an arbitrary power of administering every sort of correction, however inhuman, not immediately affecting the life or limb of the slave; and sometimes even these are left exposed to the arbitrary will of the master, or they are protected by fines, and other slight punishments, too inconsiderable to restrain the master's inhumanity. It creates an incapacity of acquiring, except for the master's benefit. It allows the master to alienate the person of the slave, in the same manner as other property. Lastly, it descends from parent to child, with all its severe appendages."

The condition of a villein involved most of these miserable incidents. The villein's service was uncertain and indeterminate, being entirely dependent in nature and amount on the caprice of his lord. In the emphatic terms of some of our old law-writers, "*The villein knew not in the evening what he was to do in the morning, but he was bound to do whatever he was commanded.*" He was liable to beating, imprisonment, and every other chastisement that his lord thought fit to inflict; except that the lord was criminally punishable if he actually killed or maimed his villeins, or if he violated the person of his *neif*, as a female villein was termed. The villein was incapable of acquiring property for himself; the rule being, that all which the villein got became the lord's. He usually passed to each successive owner of the land, as if he had been a chattel attached to it. But the lord, if he pleased, could sever him from the land, and separate him from his family and children, by selling him as a villein in gross by a separate deed. This wretched condition of slavery descended to the children of villein parents; and even if the father only was a villein, the children inherited the same sad lot from him. Indeed, at one time, the severity of the law was such, that if a villein who belonged to one lord married a neif who belonged to another lord, the children of such a marriage were equally divided between the two slave-owners.*

* See Hargreave's "Jurisconsult Exercitations," vol. i. p. 19.

Such was the wretched state in which we find the bulk of the English peasantry at the time when the full history of our nation commences. We cannot track the precise steps by which the law of villeinage had become so established; but we have every reason to suppose, that this took place in the interval between the Conquest and the reign of Henry II., when we find villeinage completely settled,* as appears by the book of Chief Justice Glanville. The Norman lords had then brought the peasantry of England into much the same state as that to which their ancestors had formerly reduced the peasantry of Normandy. "By a degradation of the Saxon Ceorls, and an improvement in the state of the Saxon Thralls, the classes were brought gradually near together, till at last the military oppression of the Normans, thrusting down all degrees of tenants and servants into a common slavery, or at least into strict dependence, one name was adapted for both of them as a generic term—that of *villeins regardant.*" This last remark is taken from Sir Henry Ellis's Introduction to Domesday Book; and it is from the valuable statistics which he has compiled of the number of "Villani" and "Servi" therein recorded, relatively to the numbers of other classes which are there mentioned, and by bearing in mind the probable character of the parts of the population not registered in Domesday Book, that the best data are to be obtained for calculating the number of villeins in the reign of John: having regard, also, to the probable deterioration in the lot of the lower orders, which had been going on in the interim, or at least until the time of Henry II.

It remains to mention the facilities which the law, as established in the thirteenth century, gave for the emancipation of villeins, and the difficulties which it placed in the way of any accession to their number.

* Glanville, lib. v. c. 6.

The lord might, at any time, enfranchise his villein; and there were also many acts of the lord, from which the law inferred an enfranchisement, though none could be proved to have actually taken place. If the lord treated the villein as a freeman, by vesting the ownership of lands in him, or by accepting from him the feudal solemnity of homage, or by entering into an obligation under seal with him, or by pleading with him in an ordinary action, the law held that the lord should never afterwards be permitted to contradict his own act by treating him as a villein. There were many other modes of constructive enfranchisement. One of the most important was, that if a villein remained unclaimed by his lord for a year and a day in any privileged town (that is to say, in any town possessed of franchises by prescription or charter), he was thereby freed from his villeinage. Moreover, in all disputes on the subject of villeinage the presumption of law was in favour of liberty. The burden of proof always lay upon the lord. And there were only two ways in which villeinage could be proved. One was, by showing that the alleged villein and his ancestors before him had been the property of the claimant and of those through whom he deduced title for time whereof the memory of man ran not to the contrary; the other was, by showing that the alleged villein had solemnly confessed his villeinage in a court of justice. The first of these modes of proof was always liable to be defeated by showing that the alleged villein, or some one of his ancestors, through whom villeinage was said to be traced, had been born out of wedlock. For, as the law held that an illegitimate child was *nullius filius*, it also held that an illegitimate child could not possibly inherit the condition of villeinage.

Thus, while, at the period when we first can assert the common-law of the complete English nation to commence, we find this species of slavery so widely established in the country, we also find the law providing means for its gradual, and ultimately certain, extinction. We know little of the Justiciars of Henry II., in whose time this branch of our law can first be traced distinctly. But if, as is probable, Chief Justice Glanville and Abbot Samson of St. Edmunds,* and others, their fellows on the judicial bench, while they found the power of the lords over their villeins too firmly established to be called in question without shaking the rights of property, devised and encouraged these numerous methods, by which villeinage could gradually be extinguished, they ought to be reckoned among the truest benefactors of their country that England has ever produced.

Our means of knowledge respecting the condition of the artizans and lower orders in our cities and towns at this period are very scanty.

No large portion of them, if any, can have been in a state of slavery. It has been seen that in Henry II.'s time the villein from the country, who resided, unclaimed by his lord, for a year and a day in a town with franchises, became thereby free; and it is difficult to suppose that any one born within the town would be in a worse condition. The absolute slaves, the theows and thralls of the Saxon times, cease to be mentioned soon after the Norman Conquest. The villeins in gross (who alone could be in an analogous position to that of those Saxon thralls who lived in the towns) were few in number throughout Anglo-Norman England; nor am I aware that any positive mention of them in the towns can be traced.† Gen-

* See the account of Abbot Samson in the "Chronicle of Jocelin de Brakelonde," partly translated in Carlyle's "Past and Present." Henry II. employed Abbot Samson as a judge.

† In the Inquisition made in the Borough of Ipswich in the second year of John's reign, mention is made of various privileges enjoyed by

erally speaking, we may consider that villeinage in John's time existed only among the rural population; but it is to be remembered that the relative proportion of the number of the dwellers in the country to the number of the dwellers in the towns was much greater then than it has become in modern times.

The free labouring population, therefore, in John's time, included the lower classes in the towns, and those portions of the peasantry who had either escaped being reduced to villeinage, or had been emancipated from it. This class was gradually increasing in number; but the whole amount of free labourers in England in the early part of the thirteenth century cannot have been considerable. This is proved by the absence of any complaint in the legislation, and of any in the law chronicles of those times, about vagrant beggars and paupers—subjects which we find so repeatedly noticed in the statutes and histories of the next and subsequent centuries.* The villeins on each estate were maintained by the lord of it, like his other

the Bishop and Prior of Norwich *and their villeins*, by the Bishop and Prior of Ely *and all their villeins*, by the Lord Roger de Bigod *and his villeins*, and by other noblemen and knights and their *villeins*. But these seem to have been cases of non-residents in the borough. There is a remarkable stipulation respecting the villeins of some of the privileged persons whom this Inquisition mentions. It is declared that *if the villeins are merchants*, they are to pay their custom towards the king for their merchandise. This seems to prove that in John's time some villeins were permitted by their lords to traffic on their own account: as was often the case with slaves in ancient Rome. The gains of the merchant-villein would be strictly "*Peculium*." See the Ipswich Inquisition in Merewether and Stephens' "History of Boroughs," vol. i. p. 396. See also the 38th chapter in Britton, "De Purchas de Villeyns."

* "It is highly probable that from the time of the Conquest till the reign of Edward III., England was little troubled with either vagrant beggars or paupers. The 'patrimony of the poor' was found in the possessions of the church, and each lord maintained his serfs or villeins, much as each proprietor of a West India sugar plantation in more recent times has maintained his slaves. It is not till after Edward III.'s wars in France, and after the industry and wealth of towns came into existence, that we first notice traces of any considerable class of free labourers."—*Pashley*, p. 161.

cattle; and such freemen as became destitute found relief from the Church; the ample endowments of which continued, after the Conquest, as before it, to provide means for the maintenance of the afflicted and distressed, aided by the alms of the laity, which the clergy received and administered: the clergy being in those days the overseers and guardians of the poor.

As has been already stated, County Courts and the Hundred Courts were preserved by the Anglo-Norman kings: and the subdivision of the freemen of each hundred into decennas, and the old Saxon regulations respecting frankpledge were also in full vigour in the reign of John. The poorest free peasant was so far vested with political functions, as to have the capacity and to be under the obligation of being enrolled in a decenna; and he co-operated with his brother decennaries in preserving the peace and being bail for each other. He also attended as a member of the court of the Hundred (the court-leet as it was now termed), and participated in the numerous active duties of local self-government that were there performed. The presidents of the Hundred Courts had now, with very few exceptions, ceased to be elective. Frequently the right of presiding in the Hundred Court had become annexed to the lordship of one of the principal manors of the district. In other cases, the lordship of the Hundred (or the lordship of the leet, as it is more often called) had been granted by the Crown to some favourite baron, the office being lucrative by reason of the fines and forfeitures that accrued to its holder. But every freeman was eligible to serve the minor offices of local self-government, so far as the tithing and the hundred were concerned; and, as a "free and lawful man," he also acted on the inquests or juries, on which (as we shall see hereafter) the king's judges frequently summoned the hundredors.

When we direct our attention to the state of the upper and middle classes at this period (exclusively of the inhabitants of the towns), we shall find the various incidents of the several Anglo-Norman feudal tenures of land so frequently requiring allusions and explanations, that it is best to direct our attention to them in the first instance.

It is to be remembered that the king was and is supreme feudal lord of all the land in the kingdom.

There were three principal tenures by which the subjects of John held their land, either immediately of him, or immediately of some other subject, and so mediately of the king. These were, 1st, tenure in chivalry, sometimes called military tenure, or tenure by knight's service; 2nd, tenure in free socage, the original of our modern freehold tenure; 3rd, tenure in villeinage, the original of our modern copyhold tenure.*

Tenure in chivalry was the most honourable; it was that by which the barons and other chief land-owners held their lands of the Crown, and by which they frequently made sub-grants of land to their own military followers. But the burdens of this tenure were numerous and severe. They require particular attention, in order that we may comprehend the oppressions at the hand of the sovereign to which the barons, who gained the Great Charter, were exposed, and which caused them to become the chiefs of a great national movement on behalf of the liberty of England. Not that we would deny or disparage the renown justly due to them for the magnanimous and far-sighted spirit in which they obtained protection for the rights of others besides their own; but we must observe that a community in suffering led to

* Tenure by chivalry included tenure by grand and petit serjeantry. For more full information on these points, see Reeve's "History of the English Law," vol. i. p. 38. Stephens' "Blackstone," vol. i. p. 174.

their community in action with the other freemen of the realm, when those primary constitutional guarantees against arbitrary oppression were obtained, which are frequently designated in English history by the title of the Baronial reforms.

The king, as feudal lord of his barons, and other military tenants, had a right to exact from them military service, or a pecuniary payment in lieu thereof: and it seems to have become optional with the king to claim the money, whether the vassal wished to serve in person or not; and even to exact both money and personal service. This war-tax was called "escuage," or "scutage;" and the constant wars and troubles of the times always furnished a ready pretext for demanding it. Other exactions of money-payments, under the title of *aids*, were continually practised. Besides these, the heir, on succeeding to his estate, was required to pay a sum of money to the lord, under the title of a "*relief*." If the heir was a minor, the lord took possession of the land as guardian, and used or abused it as he pleased, till the heir attained his majority. And even then the heir was obliged to pay a fine on suing out his livery, that is, on obtaining the delivery of the land from his guardian to him. The lord also had the right of nominating and tendering a wife to his male ward, or a husband to his female ward. And if the ward declined to marry the person so selected, the ward forfeited to the lord such a sum of money as the alliance was considered worth. The lord was entitled to a fine upon alienation; that is, if the tenant disposed of the land or any portion of it to any third party. If the tenant died without heirs, the land reverted to the lord. This was termed Escheat; and, as the right of devising real property did not exist in England after the Conquest till Henry the VIIIth's time, escheats must have been numerous. The lord also claimed to take back the land whenever the tenant committed any of a numerous list of crimes or acts of feudal misconduct. Such criminality or misconduct on the tenant's part was held to work a *forfeiture;* a doctrine which was made peculiarly severe in England, where, "by attainder of treason or felony, the tenant not only forfeited his land, but his blood was held to be corrupted or stained; whereby every inheritable quality was entirely blotted out and abolished, so that no land could thereafter be transmitted from him or through him in a course of descent."* The king's military tenants *in capite* were also subject to the peculiar burden of *primer seisin,* which did not apply to those who held of inferior or mesne lords. *Primer seisin* was a kind of extra *relief;* and under it the king, on the death of any of his military tenants in chief, took of the heir (if of full age) a whole year's profits of the lands.

The landholders of inferior rank, who held their lands, not by military, but by socage tenure, and whom we might correctly speak of by a modern term as the yeomanry of England, were not liable to so many exactions from their feudal lord as were the military tenants. The tenant in free socage was subject to the payment of aids for knighting the lord's son, and providing a portion for the marrying his eldest daughter. *Relief* was due on this tenure; but its amount was fixed and limited to one year's rent of the land. Escheat and forfeiture were incident to socage tenure, and fines were due upon alienation. The lord had no right of wardship or marriage over his socage tenants.

The holders of land by villein tenure were originally villeins on the domain of feudal lords of manors, whom the indulgence of the lords permitted to remain in the occupation of their little strips of ground so

* Stephens' "Blackstone," vol. i. p. 181.

long as they duly rendered the customary service. When villeins were emancipated, they often continued to reside on the lord's estate and on the same holdings, and they still rendered the sold service to the lord, which were no longer variable at his will. Sometimes, also, men who were freeborn took lands which had been previously held by villeins, and became bound to continue the services which the lord had usually received from the servile occupants of such lands. By degrees the customary expectation, which such holders of manorial lands naturally felt that they and their heirs would not be removed so long as they paid the customary rent and performed their customary duties, ripened into the legal title of our modern copyholders; but it is not probable that any considerable number of freemen occupied land by villein tenure so early as the reign of John.*

William the Conqueror had kept among his own share of the spoil nearly all the considerable cities and towns in England. Some few had been granted by him to favourite Norman lords. By no class was the effect of the Conquest felt more severely than by that of the citizens and burgesses. Their Norman lord required of them an annual rent, and various dues and customs. He commonly farmed these out to the highest bidder; who, under the title of Bailiff, became the chief local ruler of the oppressed citizens, instead of their own old elected port-reeve or borough-reeve. By degrees they bought back some of their old liberties. Their Norman lords found that they could not extort so much by force, as the burgesses would voluntarily pay, for the sake of getting rid of the obnoxious petty tyranny of the bailiff, and recovering their own local self-government. This led the

* For further explanation of tenure in villeinage, see Stephens' "Blackstone," vol. i. p. 175; Reeve's "Hist. Law," vol. i. p. 269; and Scriven on "Copyholds."

king and other lords of towns to farm them to the burgesses themselves, who paid a fixed rent, and were thenceforth said to hold their town in fee-farm, or by burgage tenure. They also obtained charters entitling them to elect their own chief officer, who generally took the Norman title of Mayor. Other privileges were similarly purchased; for, a fine of money was almost invariably the consideration on which a charter was granted; and the cupidity of the lords made them seek pretexts for declaring that a borough had forfeited its charter, in which case another fine for a re-grant was exacted.

Besides these liabilities to the king, or other lord of the city or land, the burgesses were liable to be *tallaged;* that is, to have special contributions of money levied on them for the lord's behalf, in the same way that *aids* were exacted by him of his tenants of land.

The political rights (in judicial and other matters) of the middle and upper classes, the powers of the sovereign, and the general legal system of the age, will be most conveniently considered when we discuss the terms of the Great Charter and its supplements. We may at present best proceed to a view of the circumstances under which Magna Carta was gained from John; how it was renewed under Henry III.; and how its powers were extended and confirmed by the final charter of Edward I.

## CHAPTER X.

Evil Character of King John.—Its Importance to our History.—Fortunate Loss of Normandy.—John's Quarrels with his Clergy and with the Pope.—The Interdict. —The Excommunication.—John's abject Submission to the Pope.—Return of Archbishop Langton to England.—His patriotic Character.—He checks the King.—King's Oath to redress Wrongs.—His repeated Acts of Tyranny.—Council of the Barons.—Archbishop Langton produces the Charter of Henry I.—Nature of this Charter, and its Value.—Demands of the Barons on the King.—Vain Intervention of the Pope.—Firmness of Archbishop Langtou.—Strength of the National Party. Runnymede.—Articuli Cartæ.—The Grant of the Great Charter.

THE Father of History sums up the evil qualities of a Despot in these words: "He subverts the laws and usages of the country, he violates women, and he puts people to death without trial."*

The character and conduct of King John exemplify every word of this emphatic definition. The feudal law of England (as it has been described in the preceding chapters) gave him oppressively strong powers over his barons and other subjects; but the savage tyranny of John was exercised over every class, high and low, often without the semblance, and in open defiance of the law. Several of his predecessors had solemnly promulgated charters, which tended to restrain the abuses of feudal rule. These charters

* *Νόμαιά τε κινεῖ πάτρια, καὶ βιᾶται γυναῖκας, κτείνει τε ἀκρίτους.*—HERODOTUS, *Thalia*, lxxx.

The old chronicler, the Waverley annalist, says of John, that the old laws and free customs of the realm "Maxime suo tempore corruptæ nimis et aggravatæ fuerant; nam quosdam absque judicio parium suorum exhæredebat, nonnullos morte durissimâ condemnabat. Uxores filiasque eorum violabat; et ita pro lege ei erat tyrannica voluntas."—P. 181.

usually contained also general promises to respect ancient rights, to cease to follow evil practices, and to maintain the old liberties of the people. The kings who gave them often violated them; but they were recognitions (though vague and imperfect ones) of rights that ought to limit the royal will: and none even of the most arbitrary of the six first Anglo-Norman kings professed to govern without regard to legal rules and restrictions.*

The seventh set at nought every restraint of law, either human or divine; and what was afterwards said of Henry VIII. might, with more truth, have been affirmed of John, that he spared neither woman in his lust, nor man in his revenge. But John was utterly destitute of such high abilities and resolute will as signalized the haughty Tudor. John mingled all the qualities that inspire contempt with those that provoke hatred. His portrait has been thus truly as well as powerfully drawn by Lingard:—"He stands before us polluted with meanness, cruelty, perjury, and murder; uniting with an ambition, which rushed through every crime to the attainment of its object, a pusillanimity which often, at the sole appearance of opposition, sank into despondency. Arrogant in prosperity, abject in adversity, he neither conciliated affection in the one nor esteem in the other. His dissimulation was so well known, that it seldom deceived; his suspicions served only to multiply his enemies, and the knowledge of his vindictive temper contributed to keep open the breach betwixt him and those who had incurred his displeasure."

A few only of the specific instances of the tyranny of this bad, but not bold man, may be cited here; besides referring to his murder of his nephew Arthur,

* See Guizot's "History of Representative Government," part 2, lecture vi., on the Charters of William the Conqueror, Henry I., Stephen, and Henry II.

which he was believed by his contemporaries to have perpetrated with his own hand.* William de Braosse, one of his nobles, had offended him and escaped to Ireland. John, in 1211, got into his power De Braosse's wife, Matilda, their son William, and their son's wife. The king then gratified his fiendish malignity by sending these three prisoners to Windsor Castle, where he had them shut up in a dungeon and starved to death.† In the next year, one of his clergy, Geoffry of Norwich, whom the old chronicler terms a loyal, learned, and accomplished man, came under the capricious displeasure of the king. John had him seized and carried off to Nottingham Castle, where he put him to death with refined and subtle tortures.‡

Under his tyranny there was no more safeguard for property than for person. His exactions were often made with open and undisguised violence,§ though they were also often practised in the form of judicial fines which John levied upon men and women on the most trivial and insulting pretexts.|| The grossness and the frequency of his outrages on the honour of private families almost surpass belief; and Eustace de Vesci was but one of many, who, when

* See for the various narratives of the manner in which John committed this murder, the "Pictorial History of England," vol. i. p. 519.

† Matthew Paris, 230. Roger de Wendover, "Chron.," vol. iii. p. 235.

‡ Matthew Paris, 232. "Fecit pœnâ excogitatâ usque ad mortem torqueri:" according to another chronicler, John had him wrapped in a cope of lead and left to die of starvation.

§ For instance, in 1203, he forced from his subjects, clerical as well as lay, a seventh part of their moveables. See Roger de Wendover, vol. iii. p. 173, who names the "hujus rapinæ executores." In 1205, he extorted from them a sum which the chronicler terms "infinite."—Ib. 182.

|| The Bishop of Winchester paid a tun of good wine for not reminding the king (John) to give a girdle to the Countess of Albemarle; and Robert de Vaux five best palfreys that the same king might hold his peace about Henry Pinel's wife. Another paid four marks for leave to eat (pro licentiâ comedendi)."—*Hallam's Middle Ages*, vol. ii. p. 317. Citing from "Madox's History of the Exchequer."

they rose against John as the public enemy of the country, were animated also by the fiercest indignation for the wrongs that had been offered them as husbands or as fathers, by the brutal licentiousness of the king.*

I have dwelt on the subject of the character of John, because that character had a most important effect on our constitutional history. Had he been less vicious and cruel, it is probable that the barons would not have leagued with the inferior freemen of England against their Norman king. Had he been less imbecile, it is probable that the national league would have been crushed by him. Even the foreign events of John's reign (I mean those which more immediately affected the continental provinces of the Plantagenet princes) were of infinite moment in determining the future destinies of England. The shames of the sovereign proved the sources of the country's glory and freedom.

Foremost amongst these we may place the fortunate loss of Normandy. Philip Augustus, the able sovereign of France, took advantage of John's murder of his nephew Arthur, to cite him as Duke of Normandy, and a feudal vassal of the crown of France, to take his trial before the high peers of France on the charge of having murdered an *arrière* vassal and homager of the French king. John scoffed at the summons, but the French Court passed sentence on him of forfeiture of all the lands which he held in France by homage, and Philip Augustus carried that sentence into speedy execution. All the provinces north of the Loire which John's ancestors had bequeathed to him, were wrested from him, but he

* See Walter de Hemingburg, 249. According to tradition, John had caused the daughter of another great baronial chief to be poisoned, in revenge for her having resisted his dishonourable solicitations. See the legends respecting Marian Fitzwalter, in Thomson's "Magna Carta," p. 505.

succeeded in retaining Guienne, Poitou, and a small portion of Touraine.

Both the amount of what he lost, and the amount of what he retained, were important to the constitutional history of England. After the annexation of the duchy of Normandy to the actual dominions of the French king, our barons' only homes were in England. Henceforth we find them proud of the name of Englishman, the application of which to a man of Norman race, had once been the deadliest of insults. The Saxon now no more appears in civil war against the Norman, the Norman no longer scorns the language of the Saxon, or refuses to share with him in the common love for a common country. No part of the community think themselves foreign to another part. They feel that they are all one people, and they have learned to unite their efforts for the common purpose of protecting the rights and promoting the welfare of all.

And, while the loss of Normandy thus happily tended to promote the union of all the inhabitants of this land, John's partial success in preserving Guienne and Poitou from the conquering arms of Philip Augustus, aided materially in completing the same result. From these provinces he drew large bands of mercenary soldiers, whose support emboldened him to defy the remonstrances and discontent of his English barons; and trusting to whom, he took no pains to form or preserve any party for himself among the nobility of his kingdom. The rapacity and the violence which these hireling cut-throats and brigands from beyond the seas were licensed by their sovereign to practise throughout England, came home to the middle and lower orders of the English, and made them eagerly co-operate with the barons against the Crown. In the rural districts also the oppressive cruelties of the forest-laws, which John carried to a worse pitch than had been the case even under the most arbitrary of his predecessors, tended still further to exasperate the people against the Government; and filled the forests with bands of adventurers, who were ready to join in any enterprise against the tyranny which had driven them beyond the pale of the law.

John had made himself the enemy of the powerful body of the English clergy, as fully as he had drawn on himself the hostility of his lay subjects. He levied pecuniary contributions on his ecclesiastics as arbitrarily and as rapaciously as he pillaged the rest of the nation. A dispute which broke out in 1205, respecting the election to the see of Canterbury,* involved John in dissension with Innocent III., who refused to consecrate the nominee of John. The Pope caused Cardinal Langton to be elected by some of the Canterbury monks, who had been deputed to Rome, and, after a vain attempt to obtain the English king's consent, he consecrated Langton at Viterbo in Italy, as Primate of England.

Stephen de Langton, to whom we are more deeply indebted than to any other individual for the obtaining of the Great Charter, was an Englishman by birth, but had been chiefly educated in the University of Paris, where he acquired the highest reputation for learning and piety. Pope Innocent III. had invited him to Rome, and conferred on him the dignity of Cardinal; and he now sought to place him at the head of the Church of England. John fiercely refused to permit Langton to set foot in England; and wreaked his vengeance on the Canterbury monks, by seizing their lands and possessions, and driving them all out of England. The Pope in return placed Eng-

* The conflicting claims and rights of the Augustine monks at Canterbury, of the suffragan bishops, of the king, and of the pope in this election, are very fairly stated by Lingard, vol. iii., p. 19, et seq.

land under an interdict, on which John confiscated all the ecclesiastical property in the kingdom. When the interdict had lasted a year, the Pope pronounced sentence of excommunication against John: and finally, in 1213, Pope Innocent assumed and exercised the right of deposing John, and solemnly exhorted all Christian princes and barons to unite in dethroning him as an impious and unworthy king.*

These spiritual thunders of papal Rome were (like the Amphictyonic decrees in ancient Greece, and the edicts of the modern German diets) of little effect, when those against whom they were levelled maintained vigorous union at home, and were threatened by the arms of no formidable foe from abroad: but they were truly terrible when there was disunion in the State which was the mark of their operation; and when a powerful and ambitious prince, like Philip of Macedon in the classic ages, or Philip Augustus in John's time, was ready to undertake the execution of the sentence for the secret purposes of his own aggrandizement. King John found himself menaced with invasion from France; and though he assembled an army of 60,000 men ("sufficient," says the old historian, "to have defied all the powers of Europe had they been animated with love for their sovereign"), John knew that all his subjects hated him with a hate which he had richly earned, and there was in the vast host around him scarcely a man on whose fidelity he could depend. The ruffian in his disposition now suddenly was changed into the craven. He had an interview at Dover with the Pope's confidential Nuntio, Pandulph, and signed a deed (May 13, 1213) whereby he consented to admit Langton as Archbishop of Canterbury, to restore the refugees

* See "Lingard," vol. iii., notes at pp. 16 and 35, for the grounds of these temporal pretensions of the popes. See generally on the subject, Hallam's chapter on "The Ecclesiastical Power during the Middle Ages."

both of his clergy and laity to their possessions and offices, to liberate those whom he had imprisoned, and to make full restitution for the injuries which he had wantonly inflicted. On condition of the king's doing this, the sentences of interdict and excommunication were to be revoked.

Had John's submission ended here, there would have been nothing in the terms to censure, whatever we might think of the motives which caused him to make it. But, rushing from arrogant defiance of the Roman pontiff into abject servility, on Ascension Eve, Wednesday, May 15, 1213, the king, by a formal deed, gave up his kingdom to the Pope, to take it back as the Pope's vassal, and under the obligation of paying a yearly tribute of 1000 marks. By this mean betrayal of his duty towards the State, of which he was the kingly head, John won for himself the partizanship of the Pope, but he increased the alienation and disgust of his subjects, ecclesiastics as well as laymen. Hallam* has truly observed that we are deeply indebted to the English clergy for their zeal in behalf of liberty during the reign of John's successor; and the same remark may be made with reference to the exertions of our churchmen in the nation's cause in the time of John himself. Cardinal Langton is the most illustrious example of patriotism and wisdom that the history of the Charter supplies. On this prelate's return to England, and installation in his archbishopric, in 1214, he showed immediately that, though he was one of the Pope's cardinals, he was no mere emissary of an Italian priest, but a true-hearted Englishman, to whom his country's honour and his country's freedom were most dear, and one whom no threats of either temporal or ecclesiastical superiors could deter from the path of duty. Before

* "Middle Ages," vol. ii. p. 327.

he would grant absolution to the king at their first meeting, he compelled him to swear that he would abolish all illegal customs; that he would restore the good laws of his predecessors, especially King Edward's; that he would give just and true judgment to all men, and that he would restore to all their rights.* A council was also convened at St. Albans, at which Fitz-Peter, the chief justiciary, presided on behalf of the king. Proclamations were then issued in the king's name, ordering the observance of the laws granted by Henry I., and denouncing the punishment of death against all sheriffs, officers of the royal forests, and other ministers of the crown, who should exceed the strict limits of their authority. The mention here of the laws of Henry I., instead of those of Edward the Confessor, is somewhat remarkable. Possibly it was made out of deference to the prejudices of some of the Anglo-Norman barons, who may have preferred the name of a Norman lawgiver to that of a Saxon one, and who may not yet have learnt the necessity of merging all differences of race between themselves and their fellow inhabitants of this island. The laws referred to may have been those which we now read in the collection entitled the laws of Henry I.,† which, though not compiled and issued by that monarch, is an unquestionably ancient collection, and is believed to have been formed by

* "It became the favourite cry to demand the laws of Edward the Confessor; and the Normans themselves, as they grew dissatisfied with the royal administration, fell into these English sentiments. But what these laws were, or more properly, perhaps, these customs subsisting in the Confessor's age, was not very distinctly understood. So far, however, was clear, that the rigorous feudal servitude, the weighty tribute upon the poorer freemen had never prevailed before the Conquest. In claiming the laws of Edward the Confessor, our ancestors meant but the redress of grievances, which tradition told them had not always existed."—*Hallam's Middle Ages*, vol. ii. p. 321.

† See this collection in the first volume of "The Ancient Laws and Institutes of England," p. 504, et seq.

some judge or lawyer during the reign of the sovereign whose name it bears. It consists principally of extracts from the laws of various Saxon kings. One of its provisions deserves special notice; it is that which ordains that "every man is to be tried by his peers."*

While this council was being held, John had sailed on an expedition against France. Incensed at the refusal of his barons to follow him, he returned to England, and began to avenge himself upon them according to his custom by leading the armed force of foreign mercenaries, which he had brought back with him, through the parts of his own kingdom where his barons' estates lay, as if it had been an enemy's country, and pillaging and burning without mercy. He had marched up from the south coast as far as Northampton, when the archbishop met him and rebuked him to his face. "This barbarous violence," said the prelate, "is a direct breach of your oath. Your barons must be judged and tried by their peers, and not subjected to military execution." John fiercely answered, "Rule you the Church, and leave me to govern the State.' He proceeded on his vindictive career as far as Nottingham, where Langton again braved his wrath and commanded him to desist. The archbishop accompanied his rebuke by threatening to excommunicate every follower of John who should dare to draw his sword again in such impious warfare. John now gave way, and for the sake of appearance summoned those whom he had accused to appear before him, or his justices, in his Court.

Langton and the barons knew John's character too well to believe that this submission to legal restraint on the king's part would be permanent; and on the 25th of August, 1213, at the great council of the prelates and the barons, which was held at St.

* Ibid. 534.

Paul's, in London, the archbishop took measures for forming an effective confederacy for curbing the power of the oppressor.

The ostensible purpose of the council was to settle the amount of compensation which the king was to pay to those who had been exiled during the late troubles, and whose possessions the king had despoiled; but Langton addressed them on the subject which they all had most at heart—the obtaining of some security against the tyranny of John for the future. The archbishop told them that he had discovered a charter of King Henry I. which they might force the king to re-establish, and thereby regain their liberties. They answered with joyous acclamations, and the archbishop administered an oath to them, by which each bound himself to strive for their liberties, if need were, even to the death.

This charter of Henry I. had been granted by that sovereign when he first seized the crown to the exclusion of his elder brother Robert, and when he was desirous to win the favour of the Saxon as well as of the Norman inhabitants of England. It contains specific provisions against the abuse of the right of wardship, against the abuse of the right of claiming aids, and against other of the chief feudal oppressions to which the military tenants of the crown were liable at the hands of the king. It gives also a general promise to observe the good laws of Edward the Confessor.* Copies of this charter had been deposited in the principal monasteries; and Blackstone† has doubted the possibility of its having become so generally unknown in John's time that its discovery by the archbishop should have been such a matter of tri-

* See this charter in the first volume of the "Statutes of the Realm," and in the note to Blackstone's "History of the Charters," p. 8 of the Introduction.

† Ibid. p. 8, et seq.

umph and novelty as the old chroniclers relate. If, however, we call to mind the devastations that took place throughout England during Stephen's reign, and the negligence often shown by ecclesiastical bodies with regard to the preservation of even their own muniments, we may readily understand that copies of the charter of Henry I. may have become scarce, and almost inaccessible, in the lapse of a century. If we recollect also how few laymen had even enough education to read, we shall not be surprised at the general ignorance which prevailed in 1213 as to the contents of the ancient charter which Archbishop Langton spoke of.

By admitting the truth of the old narrative respecting this charter of Henry I., we by no means detract from the original value of the Great Charter of John. The older instrument bears no comparison with the latter, with regard either to explicitness, to fulness, or to comprehensiveness, in providing for the rights of all classes of freemen. But still the charter of Henry I. applied specifically to many of the feudal grievances under which John's barons smarted; it furnished them with a legal authority to appeal against the king; and it gave to the archbishop, and the other chiefs of the great movement in behalf of the national liberties, an invaluable moral basis for their operations. There is in the minds of most civilized men a natural, a laudable reluctance to advance their interests, or even to defend themselves, by the introduction of mere political novelties: but the same men will act cheerfully and zealously when they have the sanction of ancient ordinance on their side. The Restorer has a lighter task and a lighter conscience than the Innovator: at least it is so at the commencement of his task; though, in order to restore with effect, it frequently becomes necessary to add, to alter, and to reorganize. Langton, and other leading spirits of the baronial party, may have early foreseen the necessity of doing much more than revive the decayed legal safeguards of a former century; but, for the mass of their party, the demand for the restoration of the laws and liberties of Henry I. was an effective rallying cry, till it was changed at Runnymede for a fuller and a nobler strain.

During the greater part of the next year John was engaged in unsuccessful warfare on the Continent; and in the autumn he returned to England, soured with disappointment, and bent on wreaking on his domestic enemies the vindictiveness and the malice which had been baffled and humiliated abroad. He had brought back some bands of soldiers of fortune from France; and with these "alien knights, cross-bow-men, and hired followers, who came with arms and horses to molest England" (as the Great Charter afterwards expressively described them), John recommenced his old course of spoliation and outrage. His chief justiciary, Fitz-Peter, one of the very few ministers who exercised any control over John, had died during the last year. John, who had stood in some awe of this man, exclaimed with joy when he heard of his death, "It is well. Fitz-Peter will now shake hands again with our late Archbishop Hubert in hell, for assuredly he will find him there. By God's teeth I am now for the first time true lord and king of England." He showed, on his return to England in the autumn of 1214, what he meant by true lordship and kingship. Plunging, without restraint or shame, into the Bacchanalia of despotism, the king continued to pillage, to banish, and to slay, and to perpetrate, with every aggravation of ribald insolence, those violations of domestic honour, by which far tamer spirits than those of our Anglo-Norman barons have oft been goaded into insurrection.

On the 20th of November, St. Edmund's day,

1214, the earls and barons of England met again at St. Edmund's Bury. Archbishop Langton, who was the guiding spirit of the assembly, came among them. The primate of England stood at the high altar ; and thither advanced each peer according to seniority, and, laying his hand on the altar, swore solemnly that if the king would not consent to acknowledge the rights which they claimed, they would withdraw their fealty and make war upon him till, by a charter under his own seal, he should confirm their just demands. "And at length," says the old chronicler,* "it was agreed that, after the nativity of our Lord, they should come to the king in a body, to desire a confirmation of the liberties before-mentioned ; and that in the meantime they were to provide themselves with horses and arms in the like manner, that if the king should perchance break through that which he had specially sworn (which they well believed), and recoil by reason of his duplicity, they would instantly, by capturing his castles, compel him to give them satisfaction."

Accordingly, in the beginning of the following year, the barons appeared before the king, fully prepared both to state and to enforce the national will. The same old historian thus narrates the scene :—

"The Demand for the Liberties
"of England made by the Barons."

"In the year of grace one thousand two hundred and fifteen, which is the seventeenth year of King John, the same king held his court, for the space of one day, at Worcester, where he had been at the feast of the Birth of our Lord. Thence he came with all haste to London, and was received at New Temple

* Matthew Paris, p. 176.

Inn. Here, then, came to the king the aforesaid great barons, in a very resolute guise, with their military garb and weapons, insisting on the liberties and laws of King Edward, with others for themselves, the kingdom, and the Church of England, to be granted and confirmed according to the Charter of King Henry the First. They asserted, moreover, that at the time of the king's absolution at Winchester, those ancient laws and liberties were promised, and that he was bound to observe them by especial oath. But the king finding the barons so resolute in their demands, was much concerned at their impetuosity. When he saw that they were furnished for battle, he replied, that it was a great and difficult thing which they asked, from which he required a respite until after Easter, that he might have space for consideration; and if it were in the power of himself or the dignity of his crown, they should receive satisfaction. But at length, after many proposals, the king unwillingly consented that the Archbishop of Canterbury, the Bishop of Ely, and William Marshal should be made sureties, and that by reason of their intercession, on the day fixed he would satisfy all."*

During the interval which he had thus gained, John sought to strengthen himself by detaching the clergy from the barons. He granted (Jan. 15, 1215) a charter to the Church of England, by which he secured to her the free election of the bishops, and ordained that when a bishop had been thus elected and presented to the king, the king's consent should not be refused unless lawful reasons could be assigned for the refusal. He took another measure, which shows how much the influence of the yeomanry and the other freemen of England below the rank of the barons had increased, and how conscious John was

* Matthew Paris, p. 176. Thomson's "Essay on Magna Charta," p. 24, and notes.

that they also were ready to act against him. He ordered the sheriffs to summon the freemen of each shire and tender to them a new oath of allegiance. He confessed at the same time how little he had a right to rely on the loyalty of his subjects, by seeking the special protection which the church gave in those ages to the person and the property of Crusaders. John took the cross on the 2nd February, 1215, and vowed to lead an army into Palestine for the recovery of the Holy Sepulchre from the Infidels.

None of these manœuvres was successful. The national union against him was firm; and his pretence for preparing for the Crusades only revived the contemptuous hatred of those who remembered his lion-hearted brother Richard, and John's treasonable practices against that true Crusader. Nor did he gain any advantage in this time of need from his ignominious subjection to the Pope. John applied to Innocent for help against his barons, and the pontiff openly sided with his vassal king. A peremptory and vehement letter came from Rome to Archbishop Langton, wherein the Pope directed his cardinal to support John in upholding the rights of the crown, and to reconcile the barons to their sovereign. In another letter the Pope censured the violence of the barons, and ordered them to act towards their sovereign with humility. But neither the English primate nor the English barons succumbed to this intervention of Rome. Langton continued to advise the barons; they continued their preparations; and when Easter approached, the confederates fixed their muster-place at Stamford, in Lincolnshire. The time within which the king was to answer their demands was now on the point of expiring; and in Easter week the barons assembled at Stamford with a force of 2000 armed knights to receive or to enforce the king's ratification of the liberties which they claimed. John was at

Oxford. He did not summon the barons thither, nor did he venture to go to them, but he sent William Marshal, Earl of Pembroke, the Earl Warenne, and Archbishop Langton to Brackley, in Northamptonshire (whither the barons had marched), to demand a more specific account of those laws and liberties which were so earnestly desired. The confederates delivered a schedule containing the articles of their claims. The deputies returned with this to Oxford, and, when Langton was explaining to the king what was demanded of him, John broke out into one of his fits of impotent phrenzy—"And why do they not demand my crown also ?" exclaimed he, with his customary blasphemous oath—"By God's teeth I will not grant them liberties that will make me a slave." He sent back his deputies to the barons' camp with orders to offer an appeal to the Pope, as feudal lord of England. The barons refused it. Pandulph, the papal legate, was in England at the king's court, and he now called on Archbishop Langton to excommunicate the barons as mutineers against the Holy See. Langton calmly replied that he was better acquainted than Pandulph was with the pontiff's real purposes, and added, that unless John instantly dismissed his foreign mercenaries, he, the archbishop, would excommunicate them. John now threw himself into the Tower of London, and endeavoured to secure the possession of the capital. The barons acted as if open war had commenced. They proclaimed themselves the army of God and Holy Church, and elected Robert Fitzwalter, Earl of Dunmore, as their general. Their numbers increased rapidly ; and the middle classes of England, both the yeomanry in the country and the burghers in the towns, now actively aided them, and rendered their success certain. It was no longer a rising of one order of the community, but a movement of all the freemen of the land. John seems to have felt the formidable importance which it thus assumed, and he endeavoured to detach the barons from the national cause, by offering special terms in favour of themselves and their immediate retainers.* But the baronial chiefs felt their true position as champions of a nation's rights, and disregarded the insidious offers of the king. The army of God and the Holy Church moved first against Northampton Castle, which was garrisoned by some of John's foreign mercenaries. The garrison refused to capitulate; and the national army, unprovided with engines for a regular siege, moved upon Bedford, where they were gladly received. Thence they marched to the Metropolis, where they arrived on the 24th of May—the gates were open to them—the citizens eagerly welcomed them as national deliverers, and the Mayor of London took his position in the army as one of the principal leaders. John had fled from the Tower, and was now at Odiham, in Hampshire, whither only seven knights had followed him. He now in despair sent the Earl of Pembroke to London to inform the confederates that he was ready to comply with their petitions, and to desire that a place and time might be named for a conference. The barons answered, "Let the day be the 9th of June,—the place, Runnymede."

This Holy Land of English liberty is about halfway from Odiham to London, and it is a grassy plain, of about 160 acres, on the south bank of the Thames, between Staines and Windsor. Various derivations are given for the name: that of the antiquary Leland affirms it to have been so called from the Saxon word *Rune*, or council, and to mean the council meadow, having been used, in the old Saxon times, as a place

* See his letters patent, dated the 10th of May, which are extant in the rolls in the Tower, and which are cited by Blackstone in the note at p. xxxi of the introduction to Blackstone's tract on the Charter.

of assembly. No column or memorial marks the spot where the primary triumph of the English Constitution was achieved; but the noble lines of Akenside should be present to the mind of all who tread the plain of Runnymede.

INSCRIPTION FOR A COLUMN AT RUNNYMEDE.

"Thou, who the verdant plain dost traverse here
While Thames among his willows from thy view
Retires; O stranger, stay thee, and the scene
Around contemplate well. This is the place
Where England's ancient barons, clad in arms
And stern with conquest, from their tyrant king
(Then render'd tame) did challenge and secure
The Charter of thy freedom. Pass not on
Till thou hast bless'd their memory, and paid
Those thanks which God appointed the reward
Of public virtue. And if chance thy house
Salute thee with a father's honoured name,
Go, call thy sons; instruct them what a debt
They owe their ancestors; and make them swear
To pay it, by transmitting down entire
Those sacred rights to which themselves were born."

On the 8th of June, the day before that named for the conference at Runnymede, the king came to Merton, in Surrey. But the conference was adjourned to the 15th, the Monday following, and the king in the meantime proceeded to Windsor; thence, on the last appointed day, being Trinity Monday, A. D. 1215, the king, with his scanty train of personal followers, came to Runnymede, where the barons and their host were now encamped.

On the part of John stood only eight bishops, fifteen noblemen and knights, and Pandulph, the papal legate: even of these many were only seemingly his adherents, or, as the old chronicler expressively phrases it, they stood "*Quasi ex parte Regis.*"* The opposite side of the plain, that nearest

* W. de Hemingburg.

to where the town of Egham now stands, was white with the tents of an army, which the old chronicler terms a host above all price.* "It is needless," says another old writer, "to enumerate the barons who composed the army of God and the Holy Church; they were the whole nobility of England." Negotiations were formally opened and continued for several days, during which it is probable that the chief managers of the conference on either side may have retired to the little island a short distance higher up the river, which still bears the name of Magna Carta Island, and which tradition points to as the scene of these memorable deliberations.

The conference was not concluded till Friday, the 19th of June. Articles or heads of agreement were first drawn up, which were afterwards regularly embodied in the form of a Charter. These "Articuli Magnæ Cartæ" are still preserved, and deserve attentive comparison with the Charter for which they served as the rough draft, but which does not always strictly accord with them. When the Charter itself was prepared, the royal seal was solemnly affixed to it before the Congress at Runnymede, and it bears date as of the first day of that conference, the 15th June, in the year of our Lord 1215, being 149 years after the Norman Conquest, and seven centuries and a half after the reputed era of the landing of the first of our Saxon ancestors in this island.

* "Exercitum inæstimabilem confecere." Matthew Paris, p. 253.

# CHAPTER XI.

**Magna Carta.—General Distribution of its Clauses.—Text of the Great Charter, and Comments.**

BEFORE setting out the text of the Great Charter, it may be useful to premise some general summary of its contents. A very little attention is necessary to show how unjust it is to speak of it as a mere piece of class-legislation, obtained by the barons for their own especial interests. Guizot* well asks, "How is it possible that at least a third of the provisions of the Charter should have related to promises and guarantees made on behalf of the people, if the aristocracy had only aimed at obtaining that which would benefit themselves? We have only to read the Great Charter in order to be convinced that the rights of all three orders of the nation are equally respected and promoted."

By the three orders which Guizot here speaks of are meant the clergy, the nobility, and the general commonalty of the freemen of the realm. It will be seen, also, that the serfs are not wholly neglected in it. And inasmuch as the serfs were always capable of being raised into freemen, and the process of their emancipation was continually, though gradually, going forward, the Great Charter, by providing for the

* "History of Representative Government," pt. ii. lect. 7.

rights of all freemen, provided in effect for the rights of all the inhabitants of the land.

Part of the Great Charter consists of clauses relating to the clergy. These are not numerous, as the charter granted by John in the preceding February had provided for ecclesiastical interests. The Great Charter confirms these provisions.

With respect to the rights of the laity, the Great Charter determines with careful precision the amount of feudal obligation to which the barons and other immediate tenants of the crown should be thenceforth subject. Involved in those provisions is the all-important article about convening the great council of the realm. It will be seen also that the Charter binds the barons to allow their sub-vassals the same mitigations of the feudal burdens which the barons acquired for themselves from the king. In behalf of members of the rest of the free community, special clauses will be found by which the ancient customs and liberties of cities and boroughs are secured, and by which protection for the purposes of commerce is given to foreign merchants. Thus far the Charter legislates specially for the interests of separate classes, though several of the clauses of this kind, besides redressing an immediate and partial wrong, contain also the germ of a permanent and national right. But the Great Charter is also rich with clauses which have for their object the interests of the nation as a whole. It provides for the pure, the speedy, the fixed, and uniform administration of justice. It prohibits arbitrary imprisonment and arbitrary punishment of any kind. It places the person and the property of every freeman under the solemn and sacred protection of free and equal law.

Lastly, it contains clauses of a temporary character for the redress of the immediate evils of the time, as by directing the removal of the king's foreign mercenaries from England, and it provides guarantees for King John adhering to its obligations, by appointing a baronial council who were to be the guardians of the Charter, and who were to be armed with the most ample powers for redressing any infraction of it which the king or his ministers might attempt.

The translation of the Great Charter, which will now be laid before the reader, is accompanied by explanatory notes; but full comment on its most important passages is reserved until we shall have seen the form which the Charter assumed, as adopted and ratified by Henry III. and subsequent monarchs, and until we shall have also examined the confirmation which it received from Edward the First.

## Magna Carta.

JOHN, by the grace of God King of England, Lord of Ireland, Duke of Normandy, Aquitaine, and Count of Anjou, to his Archbishops, Bishops, Abbots, Earls, Barons, Justiciaries, Foresters, Sheriffs, Governors, Officers, and to all Bailiffs, and his lieges, greeting. Know ye, that we, in the presence of God, and for the salvation of our soul, and the souls of all our ancestors and heirs, and unto the honour of God and the advancement of Holy Church, and amendment of our Realm, by advice of our venerable Fathers, STEPHEN, Archbishop of Canterbury, Primate of all England and Cardinal of the Holy Roman Church, HENRY, Archbishop of Dublin, WILLIAM of London, PETER of Winchester, JOCELIN of Bath and Glastonbury, HUGH of Lincoln, WALTER of Worcester, WILLIAM of Coventry, BENEDICT of Rochester, Bishops; of Master PANDULPH, Sub-Deacon and Familiar of our Lord the Pope, Brother AYMERIC, Master of the Knights-Templars in England; and of the

Noble Persons, William Marescall, Earl of Pembroke, William, Earl of Salisbury, William, Earl of Warren, William, Earl of Arundel, Alan de Galloway, Constable of Scotland, Warin Fitz Gerald, Peter Fitz Herbert, and Hubert de Burgh, Seneschal of Poitou, Hugh de Neville, Matthew Fitz Herbert, Thomas Basset, Alan Basset, Philip of Albiney, Robert de Roppell, John Mareschal, John Fitz Hugh, and others our liegemen, have, in the first place, granted to God, and by this our present Charter confirmed, for us and our heirs for ever:

1. That the Church of England shall be free, and have her whole rights, and her liberties inviolable; and we will have them so observed, that it may appear thence, that the freedom of elections, which is reckoned chief and indispensable to the English Church, and which we granted and confirmed by our Charter, and obtained the confirmation of the same from our Lord the Pope Innocent III., before the discord between us and our barons, was granted of mere free will; which Charter we shall observe, and we do will it to be faithfully observed by our heirs for ever. 2. We also have granted to all the freemen of our kingdom, for us and for our heirs for ever, all the underwritten liberties, to be had and holden by them and their heirs, of us and our heirs for ever: If any of our earls, or barons, or others, who hold of us in chief by military service, shall die, and at the time of his death his heir shall be of full age, and owes a relief,* he shall have his inheritance by the ancient relief; that is to say, the heir or heirs of an earl, for a whole earldom, by a hundred pounds; the heir or heirs of a baron, for a whole barony, by a hundred pounds; the heir or heirs of a knight, for a whole

* Explanations of the feudal terms in this and the six next clauses will be found at pp. 71–76, supra.

knight's fee, by a hundred shillings at most; and whoever oweth less shall give less, according to the ancient custom of fees. 3. But if the heir of any such shall be under age, and shall be in ward when he comes of age, he shall have his inheritance without relief and without fine. 4. The keeper of the land of such an heir being under age, shall take of the land of the heir none but reasonable issues, reasonable customs, and reasonable services, and that without destruction and waste of his men and his goods; and if we commit the custody of any such lands to the sheriff, or any other who is answerable to us for the issues of the land, and he shall make destruction and waste of the lands which he hath in custody, we will take of him amends, and the land shall be committed to two lawful and discreet men of that fee, who shall answer for the issues to us, or to him to whom we shall assign them: and if we sell or give to any one the custody of any such lands, and he therein make destruction or waste, he shall lose the same custody, which shall be committed to two lawful and discreet men of that fee, who shall in like manner answer to us as aforesaid. 5. But the keeper, so long as he shall have the custody of the land, shall keep up the houses, parks, warrens, ponds, mills, and other things pertaining to the land, out of the issues of the same land; and shall deliver to the heir, when he comes of full age, his whole land, stocked with ploughs and carriages, according as the time of wainage shall require, and the issues of the land can reasonably bear. 6. Heirs shall be married without disparagement, and so that before matrimony shall be contracted those who are near in blood to the heir shall have notice. 7. A widow, after the death of her husband, shall forthwith and without difficulty have her marriage and inheritance; nor shall she give anything for her dower, or her marriage, or her inheritance, which her husband

and she held at the day of his death; and she may remain in the mansion house of her husband forty days after his death, within which term her dower shall be assigned. 8. No widow shall be distrained to marry herself, so long as she has a mind to live without a husband; but yet she shall give security that she will not marry without our assent, if she holds of us; or without the consent of the lord of whom she holds, if she hold of another.* 9. Neither we nor our bailiffs shall seize any land or rent for any debt, so long as the chattels of the debtor are sufficient to pay the debt; nor shall the sureties of the debtor be distrained so long as the principal debtor is sufficient for the payment of the debt; and if the principal debtor shall fail in the payment of the debt, not having wherewithal to pay it, then the sureties shall answer the debt; and if they will they shall have the lands and rents of the debtor, until they shall be satisfied for the debt which they paid for him, unless the principal debtor can show himself acquitted thereof against the said sureties. 10. If any one have borrowed anything of the Jews,† more or less, and die before the debt be satisfied, there shall be no interest paid for that debt, so long as the heir is under age, of whomsoever he may hold; and if the debt fall into our hands we will only take the chattel mentioned in the deed. 11. And if any one shall die indebted to the Jews, his wife shall have her dower and pay nothing of that debt; and if the deceased left children under age,

* By the old law, grounded on the feudal exactions, a woman could not be endowed without a fine paid to the lord, neither could she marry again without his licence, lest she should contract herself, and so convey part of the feud to the lord's enemy. This licence the lords took care to be well paid for, and, as it seems, would sometimes force the dowager to a second marriage in order to gain the fine.—2 *Bl. Com.* 135.

† Some curious information respecting the position of the Jews in England at this and other early periods will be found in Tovey's "Anglia Judaica." Oxford, 1738.

they shall have necessaries provided for them, according to the tenement of the deceased ; and out of the residue the debt shall be paid, saving however the service due to the lords ; and in like manner shall it be done touching debts due to others than the Jews. 12. *No scutage or aid shall be imposed in our kingdom, unless by the general council of our kingdom ; except for ransoming our person, making our eldest son a knight, and once for marrying our eldest daughter ; and for these there shall be paid a reasonable aid. In like manner it shall be concerning the aids of the City of London.* 13. *And the City of London shall have all its ancient liberties and free customs, as well by land as by water : furthermore we will and grant, that all other cities and boroughs, and towns and ports, shall have all their liberties and free customs.* 14. *And for holding the general council of the kingdom concerning the assessment of aids, except in the three cases aforesaid, and for the assessing of scutages, we shall cause to be summoned the archbishops, bishops, abbots, earls, and greater barons of the realm, singly by our letters. And furthermore we shall cause to be summoned generally by our sheriffs and bailiffs, all others who hold of us in chief, for a certain day, that is to say, forty days before their meeting at least, and to a certain place ; and in all letters of such summons we will declare the cause of such summons. And summons being thus made, the business of the day shall proceed on the day appointed, according to the advice of such as shall be present, although all that were summoned come not.** 15. We will not for the future grant to any one that he may take aid of his own free tenants, unless to ransom his body, and to

* Ful. comments on these important clauses will be found in chapter 13, where the origin of our Parliament is discussed.

make his eldest son a knight, and once to marry his eldest daughter; and for this there shall be only paid a reasonable aid. 16. No man shall be distrained to perform more service for a knight's fee, or other free tenement, than is due from thence. 17. Common pleas shall not follow our court, but shall be holden in some place certain.* 18. Assizes of novel disseisin, and of mort d'ancestor, and of darrien present-

* By the ancient Saxon constitution there was only one superior court of justice in the kingdom, and that court had cognizance both of civil and spiritual causes, viz. the *witenagemote* or general council, which assembled annually, or oftener, wherever the king kept his Christmas, Easter, or Whitsuntide, as well to do private justice as to consult upon public business. At the Conquest the ecclesiastical jurisdiction was diverted into another channel, and the Conqueror established a constant court in his own hall, thence called by Bracton and other ancient authors *aula regia* or *aula regis*. This court was composed of the king's great officers of state resident in his palace, and usually attendant on his person; such as the lord high constable and lord mareschal, who chiefly presided in matters of honour and of arms, determining according to the law military and the law of nations. Besides these, there were the lord high steward and lord great chamberlain, the steward of the household, the lord chancellor, whose peculiar business it was to keep the king's seal, and examine all such writs, grants, and letters as were to pass under that authority, and the lord high treasurer, who was the principal adviser in all matters relating to the revenue. These high officers were assisted by certain persons learned in the laws, who were called the king's justiciars or justices, and by the greater barons of Parliament, all of whom had a seat in the *aula regia*, and formed a kind of court of appeal, or rather of advice, in matters of great moment and difficulty; all these in their several departments transacted all secular business both criminal and civil, and likewise the matters of the revenue; and over all presided one special magistrate, called the chief justiciar, or *capitalis justiciarius totius Angliæ*, who was also the principal minister of state, the second man in the kingdom, and, by virtue of his office, guardian of the realm in the king's absence; and this officer it was who principally determined all the vast variety of causes that arose in this extensive jurisdiction; and from the plenitude of his power grew at length both obnoxious to the people and dangerous to the government which employed him.

This great universal court being bound to follow the king's household in all his progresses and expeditions, the trial of common causes therein was found very burthensome to the subject; wherefore King John, who dreaded also the power of the justiciar, very readily consented to that article which now forms the above chapter of Magna Charta.—3 *Bl. Com.* 38. See also Lord Campbell's "Lives of the Chief Justices of England," vol. i. c. i.

ment, shall not be taken but in their proper counties, and after this manner: We, or, if we should be out of the realm, our chief justiciary, shall send two justiciaries through every county four times a year, who, with four knights, chosen out of every shire by the people, shall hold the said assizes, in the county, on the day, and at the place appointed. 19. And if any matters cannot be determined on the day appointed for holding the assizes in each county, so many of the knights and freeholders as have been at the assizes aforesaid, shall stay to decide them, as is necessary, according as there is more or less business.* 20. A

* The legal term, "assize," means strictly the jury of twelve knights, whom Henry II. appointed as "assessors" to the judges on certain trials of questions of fact respecting real property. Thence the word came to mean the trial itself; and the term "assizes" has long been popularly used for the trials, both civil and criminal, which are held before the judges on their circuits. The three actions (or assizes) which are spoken of in the text, had long been obsolete before they were formally abolished about 20 years ago. The two first related to the trial of title and possessory rights to real property; the last related to disputes as to the rights to advowson. Actions of this nature were obliged to be commenced in the king's court. "But because few, comparatively speaking, could have recourse to so distant a tribunal as that of the king's court, and perhaps also on account of the attachment which the English felt to their ancient trial by the neighbouring freeholders, Henry II. established itinerant justices to decide civil and criminal pleas in each county. Justices in Eyre (or, as we now call them, of assize) were sometimes commissioned in the reign of Henry I., but do not appear to have gone their circuits regularly before 22 Hen. II. (1176.) We have owed to this excellent institution the uniformity of our common law, which would otherwise have been split, like that in France, into a multitude of local customs; *and we still owe to it the assurance, which is felt by the poorest and most remote inhabitant of England, that his right is weighed by the same incorrupt and acute understanding upon which the decision of the highest questions is reposed.* The justices of assize seem originally to have gone their circuits annually; and as part of their duty was to set tallages upon all royal towns, and superintend the collection of the revenue, we may be certain that there could be no long interval. This annual visitation was expressly confirmed by the twelfth section of Magna Charta, which provides also, that no assize of novel disseisin, or mort d'ancestor, should be taken except in the shire where the lands in controversy lay. Hence this clause stood opposed on the one hand to the encroachments of the king's court, which might otherwise, by drawing pleas of land to itself, have defeated the suitor's right to a jury from the vicinage; and, on the other, to those of the feu-

freeman shall not be amerced for a small fault, but after the manner of the fault; and for a great crime according to the heinousness of it, saving to him his contenement; and after the same manner a merchant, saving to him his merchandise. And a villein* shall be amerced after the same manner, saving to him his wainage, if he falls under our mercy; and none of the aforesaid amerciaments shall be assessed but by the oath of honest men in the neighbourhood. 21. Earls and barons shall not be amerced, but by their peers, and after the degree of the offence. 22. No ecclesiastical person shall be amerced for his lay tenement, but according to the proportion of the others aforesaid, and not according to the value of his ecclesiastical benefice.† 23. Neither a town nor any tenant shall be distrained to make bridges or banks, unless that anciently and of right they are bound to do it. 24. No sheriff, constable, coroner, or other our bailiffs, shall hold pleas of the Crown.‡ 25. All

dal aristocracy, who hated any interference of the Crown to chastise their violation of law, or control their own jurisdiction."—*Middle Ages*, vol. ii. p. 334. I have drawn these remarks of Hallam's partly from his text, and partly from a note. It may be doubtful how far the passage, which I have italicised, is still applicable, since the introduction and extension of the new county courts.

* See an explanation of villeinage, p. 85, supra.

† Blackstone describes the meaning of these clauses to be, that no man should have a larger amercement imposed upon him than his circumstances or personal estate would bear; saving to the landholder his contenement or land, to the trader his merchandise, and to the countryman his wainage or team, and instruments of husbandry.

‡ The object of this enactment was, that all criminal charges, which exposed the party accused to the peril of heavy punishment, should be tried before judges of learning and experience in the laws of the realm, and not before inferior, and probably incompetent officers. (See Coke, 2 Inst. 30.)

"*Pleas of the Crown*" mean those judicial processes, which are carried on in the sovereign's name against criminal offenders, because (as Blackstone observes) "in him centres the majesty of the whole community, and he is supposed by the law to be the person injured by every infraction of the public rights belonging to that community, and is therefore in all cases the proper prosecutor for every public offence." At the time of counties, hundreds, wapentakes, and tythings, shall stand at the old rents, without any increase, except

the grant of the Great Charter, the crimes of theft (see Reeves, Hist. Law," vol. i. p. 281), forgery, coining false money, and other acts coming within the definition of the *crimen falsi*, were held to be pleas of the Crown, as well as treason, murder, manslaughter, robbery, and other graver atrocities (see Reeves, vol. i. p. 200). So that the effect of this clause of the Charter was to put an end entirely to the most important functions of the criminal branch of the county court, and of the other inferior and local tribunals of the country. This prohibition was, however, held only to apply to hearing and determining pleas of the Crown, and sheriffs continued to take (but not to try) indictments of felonies and misdemeanors, and coroners continued to take (but not to try) appeals, till forbidden by a statute of Edward IV. Coroners still take inquisitions whereby parties are charged of murder or manslaughter, and on which they are tried by the judges, who have commissions of oyer and terminer and gaol delivery.

(For the duties and powers which the courts of the tourn and the leet still retained as to frankpledge and other matters, see *post*, the note on the provision respecting it, which was introduced into the Great Charter as issued by Henry III.)

The present clause of the Great Charter mentions specifically sheriffs, constables, coroners, and bailiffs; but it has been held to prohibit all persons from trying and determining criminal cases, unless they have a special commission from the Crown for that purpose, such as the commissions of oyer and terminer and of gaol delivery, which are given to the judges on each circuit, or such as are included in the commission given to the justices of the peace in their respective counties. "Some explanation may be useful of the four degrees of the royal officers who are specified in the text of the Charter, and forbidden thenceforth to try pleas of the Crown as by their general authority. Sheriffs were the chief officers under the king in every county, deriving their title from the two Saxon words 'shire' and 'reeve,' the bailiff or steward of the division. They are called in the Latin text of the Great Charter, *vivecomes*, which literally signifies 'in place of the earl of the county,' who anciently governed it under the king, as Lord Coke observes in his Commentary on the first statute of Westminster, chap. 10, enacted in 1274, the third of Edward I. The next officer mentioned in this chapter of Magna Charta is *constabularius*, or *constable*, which is sometimes derived from the Saxon, but other authorities have conceived it more truly to come from the Latin *comes stabuli*, a superintendent of the imperial stables, or master of the horse. This title, however, began in the course of time to signify a commander, in which sense it was introduced into England. In the present instance, the word is put for the constable, or keeper of a castle, frequently called a Castellan. They were possessed of such considerable power within their own precincts, that previously to the present Act they held trials of crimes, properly the cognizance of the Crown, as the sheriffs did within their respective bailiwicks; and sealed with their own effigies on in our demesne manors.* 26. If any one holding of us a lay-fee die, and the sheriff, or our bailiffs, show

horseback. The English fortresses to which these officers belonged, in the time of King Henry II. amounted in number to 1115; and it was held that there should be one in every manor, bearing the name of that manor, wherein the constable had equal rule. As prisons were considered to be an important part of all ancient castles, these officers are sometimes called constables of fees, which signifies those who were paid for keeping prisons. In this part of their duty, they appear often to have been guilty of great cruelty; since in the fifth year of Henry IV., 1403, chap. 10, it is enacted, the justices of peace shall imprison in the common gaol, 'because,' says the passage, 'that divers constables of castles within the realm of England be assigned to be justices of peace by commission from our Lord the King, and by colour of the said commissions they take people to whom they bear ill-will, and imprison them within the said castles, till they have made fine and ransom with the said constables for their deliverance.' This statute, observe Jacob and Tomlins, seems to have put an end to them. The title of *Coroner* implies that he was an officer to the Crown, to whom, in certain cases, pleas of the Crown in which the king is more immediately concerned, are properly belonging; and in this sense the Lord Chief Justice of the King's Bench is the principal coroner of the kingdom. Previously to this chapter of Magna Charta, a coroner might not only receive accusations against offenders, but might try them; but his authority was afterwards in general reduced to the inquiry into violent and untimely death, on sight of the body; although by custom in some places he might make inquisition of other felonies. By the first statute of Westminster, chap. 10, his power was somewhat more positively explained, since it was there ordained that the coroner should attach pleas of the Crown, and present them to the justices, but he can proceed no further. The last rank of great officers mentioned in this chapter, is that of *bailiffs*, whose name is derived from the old French word Bayliff, the keeper of a province; but in the present instance, in this term, says Coke, 'are comprehended all judges or justices of any court of justice;' by all which specifications it is evident, according to a rule cited by the same author, that 'the pleas of our Lord the King shall be especially reserved, that by none now in the kingdom can pleas be had or held, after the confirmation of the aforesaid charter is made, without a special commission.'"—*Thomson's Magna Charta*, p. 204.

* The Anglo-Norman kings used to make a regular profit out of the appointment of sheriffs to counties, and of the officers to other districts. Sometimes they were farmed out to the highest bidder. The effect of this, of course, was to produce great oppression of the people, as the officials who paid thus largely for their places, strove to indemnify themselves by exacting immoderate fees, by unjust confiscations, by imposing excessive fines, and every other species of extortion.

This clause of John's Charter is not repeated in the Charter as confirmed by Henry III.

our letters patent, of summons for debt which the dead man did owe to us, it shall be lawful for the sheriff or our bailiff to attach and inroll the chattels of the dead, found upon his lay-fee, to the value of the debt, by the view of lawful men, so as nothing be removed until our whole clear debt be paid; and the rest shall be left to the executors to fulfil the testament of the dead, and if there be nothing due from him to us, all the chattels shall go to the use of the dead, saving to his wife and children their reasonable shares. 27. If any freeman shall die intestate, his chattels shall be distributed by the hands of his nearest relations and friends, by view of the church; saving to every one his debts which the deceased owed to him.* 28. No constable or bailiff of ours shall take corn or other chattels of any man, unless he presently give him money for it, or hath respite of payment by the good-will of the seller.† 29. No

* For an account of the ancient law as to a man's right to bequeath his personal property by will, the functions of executors, the mode in which personal property was distributed when a man died intestate, the claims of the church, the duties of administrators, and the right of creditors, see Williams on Executors, or Stephens' "Blackstone," vol. ii. See also, as to the precise meaning of these clauses of the Great Charter, 1 Reeve, 244, and Thomson's "Magna Charta," p. 208.

† "The profitable prerogative of purveyance and pre-emption was a right enjoyed by the Crown of buying up provisions and other necessaries, by the intervention of the king's purveyors, for the use of his royal household, at an appraised valuation, in preference to all others, and even without the consent of the owner; and also of forcibly impressing the carriages and horses of the subject to do the king's business on the public roads in the conveyance of timber, baggage, and the like, however inconvenient to the proprietor, upon paying him a settled price; a prerogative which prevailed pretty generally throughout Europe during the scarcity of gold and silver, and the high valuation of money consequential thereupon. In those early times the king's household (as well as those of inferior lords) were supported by specific renders of corn and other victuals from the tenants of the respective demesnes; and there was also a continual market kept at the palace gate to furnish viands for the royal use; and this answered all purposes in those ages of simplicity, so long as the king's court continued in any certain place. But when it removed from one part of the kingdom to another (as was formerly very frequently done),

constable shall distrain any knight to give money for castle guard, if he himself will do it in his person, or by another able man in case he cannot do it through any reasonable cause. And if we lead him, or send him in an army, he shall be free from such guard for the time he shall be in the army by our command.* 30. No sheriff or bailiff of ours, or any other, shall take horses or carts of any freeman for carriage, but by the good-will of the said freeman.† 31. Neither shall we nor our bailiffs take any man's timber for our castles or other uses, unless by the consent of the owner of the timber.† 32. We will retain the lands of those convicted of felony only one year and a day, and then they shall be delivered to the lord of the fee.‡ 33. All wears for the time to come shall be

it was found necessary to send purveyors beforehand to get together a sufficient quantity of provisions and other necessaries for the household; and, lest the unusual demand should raise them to an exorbitant price, the powers before-mentioned were vested in these purveyors, who, in process of time, very greatly abused their authority, and became a great oppression to the subject, though of little advantage to the Crown; ready money in open market (when the royal residence was more permanent and specie began to be plenty) being found upon experience to be the best proveditor of any; wherefore by degrees the power of purveyance having fallen into disuse during the suspension of monarchy, King Charles at his restoration consented to resign entirely these branches of his revenue and powers."—1 *Bl. Com.*, 287; *Greening's Magna Charta*, p. 17.

* According to Lord Coke, the common law was, that he who held by castle-guard, that is, by the service of keeping a tower, or a gate, or the like, of a castle in time of war, might do it either by himself, or by any sufficient deputy; and that if such tenant were by the king led or sent to his hosts in time of war, he was excused and quit of his service for keeping of the castle either by himself or by another during the time he so served the king.—2 *Coke's Inst.*, 34; *Greening's Magna Charta*, p. 18.

† See note to c. 28.

‡ The word *convict* here means attainted (2 Coke's Inst., 37), although it generally has a very different signification. The difference between a man attainted and convicted is, that a man is said to be convicted before he hath judgment, as if a man be convicted by verdict or confession; and when he hath his judgment upon the verdict or confession, then he is said to be attainted (1 *Inst.* 390 *b*), that is to say, his blood is become (*attinctus*) *tainted*, stainted, or corrupted; insomuch that, by the common law, in cases of treason or capital felony, his children or other kindred

put down in the rivers of Thames and Medway, and throughout all England, except upon the sea-coast.*

could not inherit his estate, nor his wife claim her dower; the same could not be restored or saved but by Act of Parliament, and therefore, in divers instances before the 54 Geo. 3, there was a special provision by Act of Parliament that such or such an attainder should not work corruption of blood, loss of dower, or disherison of heirs.—1 *Inst.* 391 *b.* And by the common law, all lands of inheritance whereof the offender was seised in his own right, and also all rights of entry to lands in the hands of a wrong-doer, were forfeited to the king by an attainder of high treason; and to the lord of whom they were immediately holden by an attainder of petit treason or felony.—2 *Haw. P. C.* c. 49, s. 1. But the lord could not enter into the lands holden of him upon an escheat for petit treason or felony without a special grant, till it appeared by due process that the king had had his prerogative of the year, day, and waste. —2 *Haw. P. C.* c. 49, s. 3.

But by the statute 54 Geo. 3, c. 145, intituled, "An Act to take away corruption of blood, save in certain cases," it is enacted, "That no attainder for felony which shall take place from and after the passing of that Act, save and except in cases of the crime of high treason, or of the crimes of petit treason or murder, or of abetting, procuring, or counselling the same, shall extend to the disinheriting of any heir, nor to the prejudice of the right or title of any person or persons other than the right or title of the offender or offenders, during his, her, or their natural lives only; and that it shall be lawful to every person or persons to whom the right or interest of any lands, tenements, or hereditaments, after the death of any such offender or offenders, should or might have appertained, if no such attainder had been, to enter into the same." And by the 3 & 4 Will. 4, c. 106, s. 10, it is further enacted that "when the persons from whom the descent of any land is to be traced shall have had any relation who, having been attainted, shall have died before such descent shall have taken place, then such attainder shall not prevent any person from inheriting such land who would have been capable of inheriting the same, by tracing his descent through such relation, if he had not been attainted, unless such land shall have escheated, in consequence of such attainder, before the 1st day of January, 1834."—*Greening*, p. 18. The personal property of a convicted felon is still forfeited to the Crown.

* The intent of this was to prevent any person from appropriating to himself a fishery of any part of a public river. Every public river or stream, says Lord Coke, is the king's highway, which cannot be privately occupied. It was accordingly held to be illegal to erect any obstruction, such as a weir, across a public river. The peculiar kind of weirs mentioned in the text, and called Kidelli, were dams having a loop or narrow cut in them, and furnished with wheels and engines for catching fish.—*Thomson's Notes on the Great Charter*, p. 214. For further information as to the king's right to the soil, &c., of the sea-shore, and of navigable rivers, and so to the rights of highway and fishery which the public have in them, see Jerwood on Rights to the Sea-shore, &c.

34. The writ which is called *præcipe*, for the future, shall not be made out to any one, of any tenement, whereby a freeman may lose his court.* 35. There shall be one measure of wine and one of ale through our whole realm; and one measure of corn, that is to say, the London quarter; and one breadth of dyed cloth, and russets, and haberjeets, that is to say, two ells within the lists; and it shall be of weights as it is of measures. 36. Nothing from henceforth shall be given or taken for a writ of inquisition of life or limb, but it shall be granted freely, and not denied.† 37. If any do hold of us by fee-farm, or by socage, or by burgage, and he hold also lands of any other by knight's service, we will not have the custody of the heir or land, which is holden of another man's fee by

* This clause was designed to protect, to some extent, the local jurisdiction of the courts baron. When the tenant of lands, who was not a tenant *in capite* of the Crown, was dispossessed, he was required first to sue for their recovery in the court baron of the inferior lord, of whom he held them. It was only when the inferior lord resigned his privilege of jurisdiction, that the tenant was entitled to sue out in the king's court the writ of right for the recovery of the lands, which was called a *præcipe in capite.*

† The object of this clause was, to prevent the long imprisonment of a person charged with a crime without inquiring into his guilt or innocence. For the proper purpose of imprisoning such is, as Lord Coke says, only for securing that they may be duly tried. The writ of inquisition mentioned in the text was called a writ *de odio et atiâ*, and was one of the great securities of personal liberty in those days. It was a rule that a person committed to custody on a charge of homicide should not be bailed by any other authority than that of the king's writ; but to relieve such a person from the hardship of lying in prison till the coming of the justices in eyre, this writ used to be directed to the sheriff, commanding him to make *inquisition*, by the oaths of lawful men, whether the party in prison was charged through malice, *utrum rettatus sit odio et atiâ;* and if it was found that he was accused *odio et atiâ*, and that he was not guilty, or that he did the fact *se defendendo* or *per imfortunium*, yet the sheriff had no authority by this writ to bail him, but the party was then to sue a writ of *tradas in ballium*, directed to the sheriff, and commanding him that if the prisoner found twelve good and lawful men of the county who would be mainprize for him, then he should deliver him in bail to those twelve.—See *Reeve's Hist. Com. Law*, 258; *Thomson's Magna Charta.*

reason of that fee-farm, socage, or burgage; neither will we have the custody of such fee-farm, socage, or burgage, except knight's service was due to us out of the same fee-farm. We will not have the custody of an heir, nor of any land which he holds of another by knight's service, by reason of any petty serjeanty that holds of us, by the service of paying a knife, an arrow, or the like.* 38. No bailiff from henceforth shall put any man to his law upon his own bare saying, without credible witnesses to prove it.†

39. NULLUS LIBER HOMO CAPIATUR, VEL IMPRISONETUR, AUT UTLAGETUR, AUT EXULETUR, AUT ALIQUO MODO DESTRUATUR; NEC SUPER EUM IBIMUS, NEC SUPER EUM MITTEMUS, NISI PER LEGALE JUDICIUM PARIUM SUORUM, VEL PER LEGEM TERRÆ. 40. NULLI VENDEMUS, NULLI NEGABIMUS, AUT DIFFEREMUS RECTUM AUT JUSTITIAM.

39. NO FREEMAN SHALL BE TAKEN OR IMPRISONED, OR DISSEISED, OR OUTLAWED, OR BANISHED, OR ANY WAYS DESTROYED, NOR WILL WE PASS UPON HIM, NOR WILL WE SEND UPON HIM, UNLESS BY THE LAWFUL JUDGMENT OF HIS PEERS, OR BY THE LAW OF THE LAND. 40. WE WILL SELL TO NO MAN, WE WILL NOT DENY TO ANY MAN, EITHER JUSTICE OR RIGHT.‡

* For explanation of socage tenure, knight's service, fee-farm, and burgage tenure, see Chapter IX., *supra*. "Petit serjeanty," as defined by Littleton, "consists in holding lands of the king by the service of rendering to him annually some small implement of war, as a bow, a sword, a lance, or an arrow, or the like."—2 *Bl. Com.*

† See 1 *Reeves* p. 248, as to the meaning of this disputed clause. It is generally understood as referring to the modes of trial in which a party charged was allowed to prove that a criminal charge or a civil claim made against him was unfounded, by pledging his own oath, and bringing others to swear with him to that effect. This mode of defence was called in criminal cases a trial by compurgators (and will be hereafter referred to when the origin of trial by jury is discussed); in civil cases it was called Wager of law, and has only been entirely abolished in the last reign (see 3 & 4 Will. 4, c. 42, s. 13.)

‡ These clauses are the crowning glories of the Great Charter. Mr. Hallam (*Midd. Ag.* ii. 324) calls them its "essential clauses," being those

41. All merchants shall have safe and secure conduct, to go out of, and to come into England, and to

which "protect the personal liberty and property of all freemen, by giving security from arbitrary imprisonment and arbitrary spoliation." The same high authority observes that these words of the Great Charter, "interpreted by any honest court of law, convey an ample security for the two main rights of civil society. From the era, therefore, of King John's Charter, it must have been a clear principle of our constitution that no man can be detained in prison without trial. Whether courts of justice framed the writ of habeas corpus in conformity to the spirit of this clause, or found it already in their register, it became from that era the right of every subject to demand it. That writ, rendered more actively remedial by the statute of Charles II., but founded upon the broad basis of Magna Charta, is the principal bulwark of English liberty; and if ever temporary circumstances, or the doubtful plea of political necessity, shall lead men to look on its denial with apathy, the most distinguishing characteristic of our constitution will be effaced."

Before commenting further on these clauses of the Great Charter of John, it may be convenient to observe that they are formed into one chapter in the Charter as issued by Henry III., and confirmed by subsequent kings, and that some words are added to one of the provisions, for the purpose apparently of making the meaning more explicit. The chapter of Henry III.'s Charter is as follows:—"Nullus liber homo capiatur, vel imprisonetur, aut disseisietur *de aliquo libero tenemento suo vel libertatibus vel liberis consuetudinibus suis*, aut utlagetur, aut exulet, aut aliquo *alio* modo destruatur, nec super eum ibimus, nec super eum mittemus nisi per legale judicium parium suorum vel per legem terræ. Nulli vendemus, nulli negabimus, aut defferemus rectum aut justitiam." This chapter is translated in our common edition of the Statutes as follows:—"No freeman shall be taken or imprisoned, or be disseised of his freehold, or liberties, or free customs, or be outlawed or exiled, or any otherwise destroyed, nor will we pass upon him, nor condemn him, but by lawful judgment of his peers, or by the law of the land. We will sell to no man, we will not deny or defer to any man, either justice or right."

These are all words which should be carefully read over and over and again, for, as Lord Coke quaintly observes, in his comments on them, "As the gold-finer will not out of the dust, shreds, or shreds of gold, let passe the least crum, in respect of the excellency of the metal; so ought not the learned reader to passe any syllable of this law, in respect of the excellency of the matter."

The first words of this chapter of the Charter (for it is convenient to follow the arrangement and the wording of Henry III.'s version) express the extent of its applicability. It is not a piece of class legislation, but its benefits apply to all the freemen of the land; and all freemen are equal in the eye of this great law. "*Nullus liber homo capiatur*"—*no freeman* shall be taken, &c. Lord Chatham's eulogium on the public spirit shown in this respect by the barons who signed the Great Charter is no less just than eloquent. "My lords," said that great statesman to the House of Peers, in his speech on the 9th of January, 1770, "it is to *your* stay there, and to pass as well by land as by water, for buying and selling by the ancient and allowed cus-

ancestors, my lords,—it is to the English barons, that we are indebted for the laws and constitution we possess. Their virtues were rude and uncultivated, but they were great and sincere. Their understandings were as little polished as their manners, but they had hearts to distinguish right from wrong; they had heads to distinguish truth from falsehood; they understood the rights of humanity, and they had spirit to maintain them.

"My lords, I think that history has not done justice to their conduct, when they obtained from their sovereign that great acknowledgment of national rights contained in Magna Carta; they did not confine it to themselves alone, but delivered it as a common blessing to the whole people. They did not say, These are the rights of the great barons, or these are the rights of the great prelates. No, my lords; they said, in the simple Latin of the times, *nullus liber homo*, and provided as carefully for the meanest subject as for the greatest. These are uncouth words, and sound but poorly in the ears of scholars; neither are they addressed to the criticism of scholars, but the hearts of free men. These three words, *nullus liber homo*, have a meaning which interests us all; they deserve to be remembered—they deserve to be inculcated in our minds—they are worth all the classics." The force of this noble panegyric will be doubly felt if we call to mind the insidious attempt made by John, about a month before the congress at Runnymede, to detach the barons from the general national interest, by offering to them and their immediate retainers, as privileges, those rights which the barons claimed and secured for every freeman of the land (see p. 114, *supra*). It is true that at the time of the grant of the Charter a large part of the population was not free; but it is to be remembered that the villeins were always capable of being raised, and were constantly rising into freemen, so that the ultimate effect of this chapter was to give and to guarantee full protection for property and person to every human being who breathes English air.

In Lord Coke's detailed commentary on this chapter of Magna Carta, he points out that the evils from which the laws of the land are to protect each person are recited in the order in which they most affect him; as, first, loss of liberty—"*No freeman shall be taken or imprisoned*," because the freedom of a man's person is more precious to him than all the succeeding particulars; and the word "*taken*," which occurs in this clause, signifies also being restrained of liberty by petition or suggestion to the king or his council. Secondly, the chapter declares that none "*shall be disseised of his free tenement, his liberties, or his free customs;*" meaning that neither the king nor others shall seize upon any of his possessions, and that a man shall not be put from his livelihood without answer. The word "*liberties*" has several significations, as the laws of the realm, privileges bestowed by the king, and the natural freedom possessed by the subjects of England; for which cause monopolies in general are against the enactments of the Great Charter.

The present chapter ordains, thirdly, that none shall be *outlawed, exiled, or in any way destroyed.* By *outlawry*, is signified the ejection of a person, by three public proclamations, from the benefit of the law, which, from toms, without any evil tolls; except in time of war, or when they are of any nation at war with us. And

the time of Alfred until long after the reign of William I., could be done for felony only, for which the penalty was death; and therefore an outlaw, being considered as a wolf, might be slain by any man. In the beginning of the days of King Edward III., however, it was enacted that none but the sheriff should put an outlaw to death; or else that they should be considered guilty of felony, unless he was slain in an attempt to take him. The expression, being *exiled*, signifies to be banished, or forced to abjure the realm against an individual's consent. For this cause, Sir Edward Coke observes that the king cannot send any subject of England into foreign parts on pretence of service, as an ambassador, deputy of Ireland, &c., unless he be willing to go.

The chapter next declares that none shall be "*in any manner destroyed contrary to the law of the land*," which Sir Edward Coke interprets to signify being "fore-judged of life or limb, disinherited, or put to torture or death." He also observes, that the words "*in any manner*" are added to the expression "*destroyed*," and to no other in the sentence, because they prohibit any means being used by which this destruction may be brought about; thus, if an individual be accused or indicted of felony, his goods or lands can neither be seized into the king's hands, nor granted, nor even promised to another, before his attainter. For, until he be attainted, he ought to derive his substance from his own possessions; and when they have been previously granted, it often followed that more undue means and violent prosecutions were used for private interest, than the ordinary course of the law would justify. (See Coke's Second Institute, and Thomson's *Magna Charta.*)

The next words in the original Latin of the Charter are, "*Nec super eum ibimus nec super eum mittemus.*" These are translated in the ordinary edition of the Statutes: "*Nor will we pass upon him, nor condemn him,*" a version neither accurate nor sufficiently expressive. Lord Coke says, that the words signify that none shall be condemned [that is, except after lawful trial, as next mentioned] at the king's suit, either before the king in his bench, where the pleas are supposed to be held in his presence, or before any judge or commissioner whatever. Dr. Lingard has pointed out that these words specially refer to the outrages which John had been accustomed to commit. He had hitherto been in the habit of *going* with an armed force or *sending* an armed force on the lands and against the castles of all whom he knew or suspected to be his secret enemies, without observing any form of law.

Then follow the words of the Great Charter, which specify the lawful trial which each freemen is to be entitled to before he can suffer aught at the hands of the executioner. He is to suffer none of the abovementioned things, "*nisi per legale judicium parium suorum vel per legem terræ,*" *unless by the lawful judgment of his peers or by the law of the land.* The full meaning of these important words will be found discussed in the text (*infra*, p. 217, *et seq.*) when we investigate how far Magna Carta recognises trial by jury as a principle of our constitution. For the present, it if there be found any such in our land, in the beginning of the war, they shall be attached, without damage to their bodies or goods, until it be known unto us or our chief justiciary, how our merchants be treated in the nation at war with us; and if ours be safe there, the others shall be safe in our dominions.* 42. It shall be lawful, for the time to come, for any one to go out of our kingdom, and return safely and securely, by land or by water, saving his allegiance to us; unless in time of war, by some short space, for the common benefit of the realm, except prisoners and outlaws, according to the law of the land, and people in war with us, and merchants who shall be in such condition as is above mentioned.† 43. If any man hold of any escheat, as of the honour of Wal-

may be observed, that this part of the Great Charter establishes the general right of the subject to have his guilt or innocence of any criminal charge that may be preferred against him, determined by the free voice of his equals, and not by the sovereign or any nominee of the sovereign. And the same general principle is established as to all civil suits by which he may be affected, so far as their determination may depend upon the decision of the issues of fact.

The conclusion of this chapter of Henry's Charter (being the 40th clause of that of John), ordains, "*We will sell to no man, we will not deny or delay to any man, justice or right.*" One immediate object of this was to put an end to the fines which John and his predecessors had been accustomed to extort from suitors in their courts (see p. 101, *supra*). But it contains a general principle also. Lord Coke observes, that these words are spoken in the person of the king, who is supposed to be present in all his courts of law, wherefore all his subjects, of every profession and degree, and for all kinds of injuries, are entitled to have immediate and perfect justice.

* Montesquieu has justly eulogized our English ancestors for having thus "made the protection of foreign merchants an article of their national liberty." This generous and foresighted enactment in favour of commerce ought alone to have prevented any English writer from speaking (as some have done) of the struggle for Magna Carta as a selfish squabble of the barons against the king.

† This clause is only to be found in the Charter of John. The sovereign has the prerogative of restraining, by the writ "Ne exeat regno," any subject from quitting the kingdom. The reason given for this power is, that every man ought, if required, to defend the king and the realm. It was not, however, limited to time of war. In practice it is now only

lingford, Nottingham, Boulogne, Lancaster, or of other escheats which be in our hands, and are baronies, and die, his heir shall give no other relief, and perform no other service to us, than he would to the baron, if it were in the baron's hand; we will hold it after the same manner as the baron held it.* 44. Those men who dwelt without the forest, from henceforth shall not come before our justiciaries of the forest, upon common summons, but such as are impleaded, or are pledges for any that are attached for something concerning the forest.† 45. *We will not make any justices, constables, sheriffs, or bailiffs, but of such as know the law of the realm and mean duly to observe it.*‡ 46. All barons who have founded ab-

used as part of the process of the Court of Chancery to prevent a party to a suit in equity from improperly withdrawing his person and property from the jurisdiction of the court before the end of the suit.—See *Bowyer's Commentary on the Constitution of England.*

* The general purpose of this clause was that the tenant of an inferior lord (or baron) should not have his feudal burdens increased if the lord's estate (or barony) lapsed to the Crown, and the tenant thereby became the king's tenant. For an explanation of the special terms, see 1 *Reeves*, p. 238.

† This and the 47th, 48th, and part of the 53rd clauses in John's Charter, are all that relate to the mitigation of the oppressions caused by the forest laws, and the abuses perpetrated under colour of them. These evils were afterwards more specifically redressed by the Carta de Forestâ of Henry III. See *Blackstone's Introduction to the Charters*, pp. xxii. xli.

‡ This clause only appears in John's Charter. It is said to have been specially required at the time, in consequence of the misconduct and incompetency of some of the judicial officers whom John had lately appointed.

The principle on which it is founded ought to be permanently remembered both by those who confer and those who accept judicial appointments; especially the important station of justice of the peace, an office that was indeed created after the time of John, but which comes fully within the spirit of this clause of the Great Charter. Wilful or corrupt perversion of the law by county or borough magistrates is almost unknown in modern times; but the gross ignorance of the laws of the realm in which many of them venture to administer those laws, is equally discreditable to themselves and mischievous to the community. Lord Coke truly said that "*ignorantia judicis fit sæpenumero calamitas innocentis.*" And those who mount the judgment-seat without qualifying themselves by beys, and have the kings of England's charters of advowson, or the ancient tenure thereof, shall have the keeping of them, when vacant, as they ought to have. 47. All forests that have been made forests in our time, shall forthwith be disforested; and the same shall be done with the banks that have been fenced in by us in our time. 48. All evil customs concerning forests, warrens, foresters and warreners, sheriffs and their officers, rivers and their keepers, shall forthwith be inquired into in each county, by twelve sworn knights of the same shire, chosen by creditable persons of the same county; and within forty days after the said inquest, be utterly abolished, so as never to be restored: so as we are first acquainted therewith, or our justiciary, if we should not be in England. 49.* We will immediately give up all hostages and

knowledge as well as by property, may well be reminded of an anecdote of the great Alfred. That king used earnestly to watch and examine the mode in which those who administered justice under him discharged their duty. When any of their decisions which were erroneous were observed by him or reported to him, he used to summon them to his presence, his principal object being to discover whether they had done wrong through ignorance or evil intention. "It sometimes happened that the justices admitted their ignorance; but Alfred then earnestly represented to them their folly, and said, 'I wonder at your great rashness, that you, who have taken from God and myself the office and dignity of Wise Men, should have entirely neglected the studies and conduct of the wise. Therefore either resign your temporal power, or exercise yourselves, as I desire, more zealously in the study of wisdom.'"—See *Paulli's Life of Alfred.*

* The remainder of the Great Charter of John (except the 54th chapter) is not repeated in the subsequent Charters. It consists of provisions of a temporary nature rendered necessary by the recent events, and which sufficiently explain themselves. The 61st and 62nd chapters deserve more particular attention. Guizot remarks on them,—"It is not enough that rights should be recognised and promises made, it is further necessary that these rights should be respected, and that these promises should be fulfilled. The 61st and last article of the Great Charter is intended to provide this guarantee. It is there said that the barons shall elect twenty-five barons by their own free choice, charged to exercise all vigilance that the provisions of the Charter may be carried into effect; the powers of these twenty-five barons are unlimited. If the king or his agents allow themselves to violate the enactments of the Charter in the smallest particular, the barons will denounce this abuse before the king,

writings delivered unto us by our English subjects, as securities for their keeping the peace, and yielding us faithful service. 50. We will entirely remove from our bailiwicks the relations of Gerard de Atheyes, so that for the future they shall have no bailiwick in England; we will also remove Engelard de Cygony, Andrew, Peter, and Gyon, from the Chancery; Gyon de Cygony, Geoffrey de Martyn and his brothers; Philip Mark, and his brothers, and his nephew, Geoffrey, and their whole retinue. 51. As soon as peace is restored, we will send out of the kingdom all foreign soldiers, cross-bowmen, and stipendiaries, who are come with horses and arms to the prejudice of our people. 52. If any one has been dispossessed or deprived by us, without the legal judgment of his peers, of his lands, castles, liberties, or right, we will forthwith restore them to him; and if any dispute arise upon this head, let the matter be decided by the five-and-twenty barons hereafter mentioned, for the preservation of the peace. As for all those things of which any person has, without the legal judgment of his peers, been dispossessed or deprived, either by King Henry our father, or our brother King Richard, and which we have in our hands, or are possessed by others, and we are bound to warrant and make good, we shall have a respite till the term usually allowed the crusaders; excepting those things about which there is a plea depending, or whereof an inquest hath been made, by our order, before we undertook the crusade, but when we return from our pilgrimage, or if perchance we tarry at home and do not make our

and demand that it be instantly checked. If the king do not accede to their demand, the barons shall have the right, forty days after the summons has been issued by them, to prosecute the king, to deprive him of his lands and castles (the safety of his person, of the queen, and of their children being respected), until the abuse has been reformed to the satisfaction of the barons." He points out also the effect of this in centralizing the council of barons.

pilgrimage, we will immediately cause full justice to be administered therein. 53. The same respite we shall have (and in the same manner about administering justice, disafforesting the forests, or letting them continue) for disafforesting the forests, which Henry our father, and our brother Richard have afforested; and for the keeping of the lands which are in another's fee, in the same manner as we have hitherto enjoyed those wardships, by reason of a fee held of us by knight's service; and for the abbeys founded in any other fee than our own, in which the lord of the fee says he has a right; and when we return from our pilgrimage, or if we tarry at home, and do not make our pilgrimage, we will immediately do full justice to all the complainants in this behalf. 54. No man shall be taken or imprisoned upon the appeal* of a

* An *appeal*, in the sense wherein it is here used, does not signify any complaint to a superior court of an injustice done by an inferior one, which is the general use of the word; but it here means an *original* suit at the time of its first commencement. An appeal, therefore, when spoken of as a criminal prosecution, denotes an accusation by a private subject against another for some heinous crime, demanding punishment on account of the particular injury suffered, rather than for the offence against the public.

This private process for the punishment of public crimes had probably its origin in those times when a private pecuniary satisfaction, called a *weregild*, was constantly paid to the party injured, or his relative, to expiate enormous offences. As, therefore, during the continuance of this custom a process was certainly given for recovering the weregild by the party to whom it was due, it seems that when these offences by degrees grew no longer redeemable, the private process was still continued, in order to insure the infliction of punishment upon the offender, though the party injured was allowed no pecuniary compensation for the offence.—4 *Bl. Com.*, 312.

An appeal of *felony* might have been brought for crimes committed, either against the parties themselves or their relations. The crimes against the parties themselves were, larceny, rape, and arson, and for these, as well as for mayhem, the persons robbed, ravished, maimed, or whose houses were burnt, might have instituted this private process. The only crime against one's relation for which an appeal could be brought was that of *killing* him by either murder or manslaughter. But this could not be brought by every relation, but only by the wife for the death of her husband, or by the heir male for the death of his ancestor, which woman, for the death of any other than her husband. 55. All unjust and illegal fines made by us, and all amerciaments imposed unjustly and contrary to the law of the land, shall be entirely given up, or else be left to the decision of the five-and-twenty barons hereafter mentioned for the preservation of the peace, or of the major part of them, together with the aforesaid Stephen, archbishop of Canterbury, if he can be present, and others whom he shall think fit to take along with him; and if he cannot be present, the business shall notwithstanding go on without him; but so that if one or more of the aforesaid five-and-twenty barons be plaintiffs in the same cause, they shall be set aside as to what concerns this particular affair, and others be chosen in their room, out of the said five-and-twenty, and sworn by the rest to decide the matter. 56. If we have disseised or dispossessed the Welsh, of any lands, liberties, or other things, without the legal judgment of their peers, either in England or in Wales, they shall be immediately restored to them; and if any dispute arise upon this head, the matter shall be determined in the marche by the judgment of their peers; for tenements in England according to the law of England, for tenements in Wales according to the law of Wales, for tenements of the marche according to the

heirship was also confirmed by an ordinance of King Henry the First to the four nearest degrees of blood. It was given to the wife on account of the loss of her husband; therefore, if she married again before or pending her appeal, it was lost and gone; or if she married after judgment, she could not demand execution. The heir must also have been heir male, and such a one as was the next heir by the course of the common law at the time of the killing of the ancestor. But this rule had three exceptions: first, if the person killed left an innocent wife, she only, and not the heir could have the appeal; secondly, if there were no wife, and the heir were accused of the murder, the person who next to him would have been heir male should have brought the appeal; thirdly, if the wife killed her husband, the heir might appeal her of the death.—See further, 4 *Bl. Com.*, 315.

law of the marche; the same shall the Welsh do to us and our subjects. 57. As for all those things of which a Welshman hath, without the legal judgment of his peers, been disseised or deprived of by King Henry our father, or our brother King Richard, and which we either have in our hands, or others are possessed of, and we are obliged to warrant it, we shall have a respite till the time generally allowed the crusaders; excepting those things about which a suit is depending, or whereof an inquest has been made by our order, before we undertook the crusade: but when we return, or if we stay at home without performing our pilgrimage, we will immediately do them full justice, according to the laws of the Welsh and of the parts before mentioned. 58. We will without delay dismiss the son of Llewellin, and all the Welsh hostages, and release them from the engagements they have entered into with us for the preservation of the peace. 59. We will treat with Alexander, King of Scots, concerning the restoring his sisters and hostages, and his right and liberties, in the same form and manner as we shall do to the rest of our barons of England; unless by the charters which we have from his father, William, late King of Scots, it ought to be otherwise; but this shall be left to the determination of his peers in our court. 60. All the aforesaid customs and liberties, which we have granted to be holden in our kingdom, as much as it belongs to us, towards our people of our kingdom, as well clergy as laity shall observe, as far as they are concerned, towards their dependents. 61. And whereas, for the honour of God and the amendment of our kingdom, and for the better quieting the discord that has arisen between us and our barons, we have granted all these things aforesaid; willing to render them firm and lasting, we do give and grant our subjects the underwritten security, namely, that the barons may choose five-and-twenty barons* of the kingdom, whom they think convenient; who shall take care, with all their might, to hold and observe, and cause to be observed, the peace and liberties we have granted them, and by this our present charter confirmed; so that if we, our justiciary, our bailiffs, or any of our officers, shall in any circumstance fail in the performance of them, towards any person, or shall break through any of these articles of peace and security, and the offence be notified to four barons chosen out of the five-and-twenty before mentioned, the said four barons shall repair to us, or our justiciary, if we are out of the realm, and, laying open the grievance, shall petition to have it redressed without delay: and if it be not redressed by us, or if we should chance to be out of the realm, if it should not be redressed by our justiciary, within forty days, reckoning from the time it has been notified to us, or to our justiciary, (if we should be out of the realm,) the four barons aforesaid shall lay the cause before the rest of the five-and-twenty barons; and the said five-and-twenty barons, together with the community of the whole kingdom, shall distrain and distress us in all possible ways, by seizing our castles, lands, possessions, and in any other manner they can, till the grievance is redressed according to their pleasure; saving harmless our own person, and the persons of our queen and children; and when it is redressed, they shall obey us as before. And any person whatsoever in the kingdom, may swear that he will obey the orders of the five-and-twenty barons aforesaid, in the execution of the premises, and will distress us, jointly with them, to the utmost of his power; and we give public and free liberty to any one that shall please to swear to this, and never will hinder any person from taking the same oath. 62. As for all

* See note at p. 156, *supra.*

those of our subjects who will not, of their own accord, swear to join the five-and-twenty barons in distraining and distressing us, we will issue orders to make them take the same oath as aforesaid. And if any one of the five-and-twenty barons dies, or goes out of the kingdom, or is hindered any other way from carrying the things aforesaid into execution, the rest of the said five-and-twenty barons may choose another in his room, at their discretion, who shall be sworn in like manner as the rest. In all things that are committed to the execution of these five-and-twenty barons, if, when they are all assembled together, they should happen to disagree about any matter, and some of them, when summoned, will not, or cannot, come, whatever is agreed upon, or enjoined, by the major part of those that are present, shall be reputed as firm and valid as if all the five-and-twenty had given their consent; and the aforesaid five-and-twenty shall swear, that all the premises they shall faithfully observe, and cause with all their power to be observed. And we will not, by ourselves, or by any other, procure anything whereby any of these concessions and liberties may be revoked or lessened; and if any such thing be obtained, let it be null and void; neither shall we ever make use of it, either by ourselves or any other. And all the ill will, indignations, and rancours that have arisen between us and our subjects, of the clergy and laity, from the first breaking out of the dissensions between us, we do fully remit and forgive: moreover all trespasses occasioned by the said dissensions, from Easter in the fifteenth year of our reign, till the restoration of peace and tranquillity, we hereby entirely remit to all, both clergy and laity, and as far as in us lies do fully forgive. We have, moreover, caused to be made for them the letters patent testimonial of Stephen, lord archbishop of Canterbury, Henry, lord archbishop of Dublin, and the bishops aforesaid, as also of master Pandulph, for the security and concessions aforesaid. 63. Wherefore we will and firmly enjoin, that the Church of England be free, and that all the men in our kingdom have and hold all the aforesaid liberties, rights, and concessions, truly and peaceably, freely and quietly, fully and wholly to themselves and their heirs, of us and our heirs, in all things and places, for ever, as is aforesaid. It is also sworn, as well on our part as on the part of the barons, that all the things aforesaid shall be observed *bonâ fide* and without evil subtilty. Given under our hand, in the presence of the witnesses above named, and many others, in the meadow called Runingmede, between Windsor and Staines, the 15th day of June, in the 17th year of our reign.

## CHAPTER XII.

**Renewals of the Great Charter in Henry the Third's Reign.—The Charter as confirmed by Edward I. and subsequent Kings.—The Statute Confirmatio Cartarum.—All Taxation without consent of Parliament made illegal.**

JOHN died soon after the grant of the Great Charter, leaving England torn by civil war and foreign invasion, both of which had been caused by his perfidy and tyranny. The first act of the great Earl of Pembroke, as Protector of the Kingdom on the accession of Henry III., was to renew the Great Charter, but with several changes, the most important of which was the omission of the provisions concerning the manner and reason of levying scutages. It assigned as a reason for the omission of this and other weighty matters, that the prelates and barons had agreed to respite the consideration of them till further deliberation could be had, when they and such other things as *pertained to the welfare of all* should be most fully reviewed and set right. The stipulations in John's Charter, which were of a temporary nature, and referred to the troops and allies of that king and his barons respectively, were of course not copied into Henry's Charters. And the provisions for empowering the twenty-five chosen barons to redress violations of the Charter, were not renewed. A duplicate of the Charter was forthwith transmitted to Ireland, for the benefit of the king's subjects there; and writs were sent to the sheriffs of the several English counties, commanding them to cause the Charter of Liberties to be publicly read in full County Court, and to see that its ordinances were fully observed within their several jurisdictions. In the next year, after the French Dauphin had been driven out of the kingdom, and the malcontent English who had fought under him had returned to their allegiance, the Charter of Liberties was granted again, and on this occasion some words of infinite value were added to the clause by which the King binds himself to respect the property and the personal rights of his subjects. The Charter was again renewed by Henry in the ninth year of his reign, at which same time the Charter of the Forest was granted, whereby many of the most atrocious iniquities of the primitive game-laws were redressed. The two Charters were five times renewed between this period, and Henry's death. At some of these renewals temporary variations were introduced; but it is in the form in which it was promulgated in the ninth year of Henry's reign that the Great Charter was solemnly confirmed by his successor, and in that form it appears at the head of our statute book, where (as before mentioned) it is printed from the *inspeximus* and confirmation of it by Edward I.

---

## Magna Carta.

## THE GREAT CHARTER,

(TRANSLATED AS IN THE STATUTES AT LARGE,)

MADE IN THE NINTH YEAR OF KING HENRY THE THIRD, AND CONFIRMED BY KING EDWARD THE FIRST, IN THE FIVE-AND-TWENTIETH YEAR OF HIS REIGN.

**EDWARD**, by the grace of God, King of England, Lord

of Ireland, and Duke of Guyan: to all archbishops, &c. We have seen the Great Charter of the Lord Henry, sometimes King of England, our Father, of the Liberties of England in these words:

"HENRY, by the grace of God, King of England, Lord of Ireland, Duke of Normandy and Guyan, and Earl of Anjou: To all archbishops, bishops, abbots, priors, earls, barons, sheriffs, provosts, and officers, and to all bailiffs and other our faithful subjects, which shall see this present Charter, greeting: Know ye that We, unto the honour of Almighty God, and for the salvation of the souls of our progenitors and successors, kings of England, to the advancement of Holy Church and amendment of our realm, of our mere and free will have given and granted to all archbishops, bishops, abbots, priors, earls, barons, and to all freemen of this our realm, these liberties following, to be kept in our kingdom of England for ever."

## CHAPTER I.

*A Confirmation of Liberties.*

"FIRST, we have granted to God, and by this our present Charter have confirmed for us and our heirs for ever, that the Church of England shall be free, and shall have all her whole rights and liberties inviolable. We have granted also, and given to all the freemen of our realm, for us and our heirs for ever, these liberties, under-written, to have and to hold to them and their heirs, of us and our heirs for ever."

## CHAPTER II.

*The Relief of the King's Tenant of full Age.*

[Same as 2nd Chapter of John's Charter.]

## CHAPTER III.

*The Wardship of the Heir within Age. The Heir a Knight*

[Similar to 3rd Chapter of John's Charter.]

## CHAPTER IV.

*No waste shall be made by a Guardian in waste lands.*

[Same as 4th Chapter of John's Charter.]

## CHAPTER V.

*Guardians shall maintain the Inheritance of Wards. Of Bishoprics, &c.*

[Similar to 5th Chapter of John's Charter, with addition of like provisions against the waste of ecclesiastical possessions while in the king's hand during a vacancy in the see, &c.]

## CHAPTER VI.

*Heirs shall be Married without Disparagement.*

[Similar to 6th Chapter of John's Charter.]

## CHAPTER VII.

*A Widow shall have her Marriage, Inheritance and Quarantine. The King's Widow, &c.*

[Similar (with additions) to the 7th and 8th Chapters of John's Charter.]

## CHAPTER VIII.

*How Sureties shall be charged to the King.*

[Same as 9th Chapter of John's Charter.]

## CHAPTER IX.

*The Liberties of London and other Cities and Towns confirmed.*

[Same as 13th Chapter of John's Charter.]

## CHAPTER X.

*None shall distrain for more service than is due.*

[Same as 16th Chapter of John's Charter.]

## CHAPTER XI.

*Common Pleas shall not follow the King's Court.*

[Same as 17th Chapter of John's Charter.]

## CHAPTERS XII. AND XIII.

*When and before whom Assizes shall be taken. Adjournment for Difficulty. Assizes of Darrien Presentment.*

[Analogous to 18th and 19th Chapters of John's Charter.]

### CHAPTER XIV.

*How men of all sorts shall be amerced, and by whom.*

[Same as 20th and 21st Chapters of John's Charter.]

### CHAPTERS XV. AND XVI.

*Making and defending of Bridges and Banks.*

[Similar to 23rd Chapter of John's Charter.]

### CHAPTER XVII.

*Holding Pleas of the Crown.*

[Same as 24th Chapter of John's Charter.]

### CHAPTER XVIII.

*The King's Debtor dying, the King shall be first paid.*

[Same as 26th Chapter of John's Charter.]

### CHAPTERS XIX., XX., AND XXI.

*Purveyors for a Castle. Doing of Castle-ward. Taking of Horses, Carts, and Woods.*

[Same as 28th, 29th, 30th, and 31st Chapters of John's Charter.]

### CHAPTER XXII.

*How long Felons' Land shall be holden by the King.*

[Same as 32nd Chapter of John's Charter.]

### CHAPTER XXIII.

*In what places Wears shall be put down.*

[Same as 33rd Chapter of John's Charter.]

### CHAPTER XXIV.

*In what case a Præcipe in Capite is grantable.*

[Same as 14th Chapter of John's Charter.]

### CHAPTER XXV.

*There shall be but one Measure through the Realm.*

[Same as 35th Chapter of John's Charter.]

### CHAPTER XXVI.

*Inquisition of Life and Member.*

[Same as 38th Chapter of John's Charter.]

## CHAPTER XXVII.

*Tenure of the King in Socage, and of another by Knight's Service. Petit Serjeanty.*

[Same as 37th Chapter of John's Charter.]

## CHAPTER XXVIII.

*Wager of Law shall not be without witness.*

[Same as 38th Chapter of John's Charter.]

## CHAPTER XXIX.

*None shall be condemned or injured in property, person, or liberty, without Trial. Justice shall not be sold or deferred.* *

NULLUS LIBER HOMO CAPIATUR VEL IMPRISONETUR, AUT DISSEISIATUR DE ALIQUO LIBERO TENEMENTO SUO VEL LIBERTATIBUS VEL LIBERIS CONSUETUDINIBUS SUIS, AUT UTLAGETUR AUT EXULET AUT ALIQUO ALIO MODO DESTRUATUR; NEC SUPER EUM IBIMUS, NEC SUPER EUM MITTEMUS, NISI PER LEGALE JUDICIUM PARIUM SUORUM VEL PER LEGEM TERRÆ. NULLI VENDEMUS, NULLI NEGABIMUS, AUT DIFFEREMUS RECTUM VEL JUSTITIAM.

NO FREEMAN SHALL BE TAKEN, OR IMPRISONED, OR BE DISSEISED OF HIS FREEHOLD, OR LIBERTIES, OR FREE CUSTOMS, OR BE OUTLAWED OR EXILED, OR ANY OTHERWISE DESTROYED; NOR WILL WE PASS UPON HIM NOR CONDEMN HIM, BUT BY LAWFUL JUDGMENT OF HIS PEERS, OR BY THE LAW OF THE LAND. WE WILL SELL TO NO MAN, WE WILL NOT DENY OR DEFER TO ANY MAN, EITHER JUSTICE OR RIGHT.

## CHAPTER XXX.

*Merchant Strangers coming into this Realm shall be well used.*

[Same as 41st Chapter of John's Charter.]

## CHAPTER XXXI.

*Tenure of a Barony coming into the King's hands by Escheat.*

[Same as 43rd Chapter of John's Charter.]

## CHAPTER XXXII.

*Lands shall not be Aliened to the Prejudice of the Lord's Service [i. e. Lord of the Fee].*

* See 39th and 40th chapters of John's Charter, and notes at p. 134, *supra*. See also p. 149, *supra*.

## CHAPTER XXXIII.

*Patrons of Abbeys shall have the custody of them in time of Vacation.*

[Same as 46th Chapter of John's Charter.]

## CHAPTER XXXIV.

*In what cases only a Woman shall have an Appeal of Death.*

[Same as 51st Chapter of John's Charter.]

## CHAPTER XXXV,

*At what time shall be kept a County Court, a Sheriff's Tourn, and a Leet.*

"No county court shall from henceforth be holden but from month to month: and where a greater term has been used, it shall be greater. Neither shall any sheriff or his bailiff keep his tourn in the hundred but twice in the year; and nowhere but in due and accustomed place, that is to say, once after Easter, and again after the Feast of Saint Michael. And the view of frank-pledge shall be likewise at Saint Michael's term, without occasion; so that every man may have his liberties, which he had and was accustomed to have in the time of King Henry our grandfather, or which he hath purchased since. The view of frank-pledge shall be done so, that our peace may be kept, and that the tything be wholly kept as it hath been accustomed; and that the sheriff seek no occasions, and that he be content with so much as the sheriff was wont to have for his view-making, in the time of King Henry our grandfather." *

* The sheriff's tourn is (or rather was) the county court for criminal matters, and for the preservation of the peace; and that officer used to hold it in the respective hundreds of the county by rotation. The courts leet are minor local courts of the same character as that of the tourn, having the same jurisdiction, but being limited to smaller districts. According to Lord Coke (2 Inst. 70), the courts leet were carved out of the courts of the tourn, "for the ease of the people, that they should have justice done them at their own doors." It is more probable that they are the original hundred courts of the Saxon times, though the area of a manor often became the area of their jurisdiction, instead of the old area of a hundred. The right of holding a court leet was often granted to the lord of a manor, partly for the benefit of his tenants, resident in the manor, and partly for the benefit of the lord himself; who, besides the judicial authority and dignity which he gained, derived pecuniary advantages

## CHAPTER XXXVI.

*No Land shall be given in Mortmain.**

"It shall not be lawful from henceforth to any to give his lands to any religious house, and to take the same land again to hold of the same house. Nor shall it be lawful to any house of religion to take the lands of any, and to lease the same to him of whom he received it: if any from henceforth give his lands to any religious house, and thereupon be convict, the gift shall be utterly void, and the land shall accrue to the lord of the fee."

from the fines and fees of court; generally also when the leet continued to be held for a particular hundred, some neighbouring lord received from the Crown the right of presiding in it personally, or by his steward. The criminal jurisdiction both of the tourn and the leet was reduced within very narrow limits after the 24th clause of the Great Charter (see *supra*, p. 127) respecting the holding pleas of the Crown. But these courts still continued to be of practical importance in many matters of local self-government. Besides the important duty of the view of frankpledge (see *supra*, p. 45), the assembled inquest or jury of the leet inquired and made presentments respecting persons of notorious evil fame; respecting cheats, especially with regard to the vendors of unwholesome provisions; respecting escapes from prisons, breaches of the peace, public nuisances, and many other subjects. The court of leet (or tourn) could impose a fine or amerciament on any person who was presented as an offender in any of these respects, and such fine or amerciament could be levied by distress. Headboroughs or constables for the hundred were also chosen at the court leet, and many other local officers. The tourn had become obsolete before Lord Coke's time. Courts leet are still held for the appointment of constables in some hundreds, but they practically exercise no other functions. For further information as to these courts, see Coke's second "Institute," p. 69. Scriven on "Copyholds," vol. ii., and Comyns's "Digest," title Leet. With regard to the local criminal jurisdiction exercised in particular places in England by special charter or usage, see an excellent note in the second volume of Hallam's "Middle Ages," p. 347.

* Alienation in *mortmain, in mortua manu*, is an alienation of lands or tenements to any corporation, sole or aggregate, ecclesiastical or temporal. But these purchases having been chiefly made by religious houses, in consequence whereof the lands became perpetually inherent in one dead hand, this hath occasioned the general appellation of mortmain to be applied to such alienations, and the religious houses themselves to be principally considered in forming the statutes of mortmain.—See 2 *Bl. Com.* 268.

## CHAPTER XXXVII.

*A Subsidy in Respect of this Charter and the Charter of the Forest, granted to the King.*

"Escuage from henceforth shall be taken like as it was wont to be in the time of King Henry our grandfather; reserving to all archbishops, bishops, abbots, priors, templars, hospitalers, earls, barons, and all persons as well spiritual as temporal, all their free liberties and free customs, which they have had in time passed. And all these customs and liberties aforesaid, which we have granted to be holden within this our realm, as much as appertaineth to us and our heirs, we shall observe. And all men of this our realm, as well spiritual as temporal (as much as in them is), shall observe the same against all persons in like wise. And for this our gift and grant of these liberties and of other contained in our Charter of liberties of our forest, the archbishops, bishops, abbots, priors, earls, barons, knights, freeholders, and other our subjects, have given unto us the fifteenth part of all their moveables. And we have granted unto them, for us and our heirs, that neither we nor our heirs shall procure or do anything, whereby the liberties in this Charter contained shall be infringed or broken. And if anything be procured by any person contrary to the premises, it shall be had of no force nor effect. These being witnesses, Lord B. Archbishop of Canterbury, E. Bishop of London, I. Bishop of Bath, P. of Winchester, H. of Lincoln, R. of Salisbury, W. of Rochester, W. of Worcester, J. of Ely, H. of Hereford, R. of Chichester, W. of Exeter, Bishops: the Abbot of St. Edmonds, the Abbot of St. Albans, the Abbot of Bello, the Abbot of St. Augustines in Canterbury, the Abbot of Evesham, the Abbot of Westminster, the Abbot of Bourgh St. Peter, the Abbot of Reding, the Abbot of Abindon, the Abbot of Malmsbury, the Abbot of Winchcomb, the Abbot of Hyde, the Abbot of Certesy, the Abbot of Sherburn, the Abbot of Cerne, the Abbot of Abbotebir, the Abbot of Middleton, the Abbot of Seleby, the Abbot of Cirencester: H. de Burgh, Justice, H. Earl of Chester and Lincoln, W. Earl of Salisbury, W. Earl of Warren, G. de Clare Earl of Gloucester and Hereford, W. de Ferrars Earl of Derby, W. de Mandeville Earl of Essex, H. de Bygod Earl of Norfolk, W. Earl of Albemarle,

H. Earl of Hereford, J. Constable of Chester, R. de Ros, R. Fitzwalter, R. de Vyponte, W. de Bruer, R. de Muntefichet, P. Fitzherbert, W. de Aubenie, J. Gresly, F. de Breus, J. de Monemue, J. Fitzallen, H. de Mortimer, W. de Beauchamp, W. de St. John, P. de Mauly, Brian de Lisle, Thomas de Multon, R. de Argenteyn, G. de Nevil, W. Mauduit, J. de Balun and others."

"We, ratifying and approving these gifts and grants aforesaid, confirm and make strong all the same for us and our heirs perpetually; and by the tenor of these presents do renew the same, willing and granting for us and our heirs, that this Charter, and all and singular its articles forever shall be steadfastly, firmly, and inviolably observed. Although some articles in the same Charter contained yet hitherto peradventure have not been kept, we will, and, by authority royal, command, from henceforth firmly they be observed. In witness whereof we have caused these our letters patent to be made. Witness Edward, our Son, at Westminster, the twelfth day of October, in the twenty-fifth year of our reign."

Magna Carta, in this form, has been solemnly confirmed by our kings and parliaments upwards of thirty times; but in the twenty-fifth year of Edward I. much more than a simple confirmation of it was obtained for England. As has been already mentioned, the original Charter of John forbad the levying of *escuage* save by consent of the Great Council of the land; and although those important provisions were not repeated in Henry's Charter, it is certain that they were respected. Henry's barons frequently refused him the subsidies which his prodigality was always demanding. Neither he nor any of his ministers seems ever to have claimed for the Crown, the prerogative of taxing the landholders at discretion: but the sovereign's right of levying money from his towns and cities under the name of tallages was constantly exercised during Henry III.'s reign and during the earlier portion of his son's. But, by the statute of Edward I., intituled *Confirmatio Chartarum,* all private property was secured from royal spoliation and placed under the safeguard of the great council of *all* the realm.

King Edward had committed several violent and arbitrary measures in order to raise the moneys which his wars required. The details of these transactions will be found in Guizot's "History of Representative Government," and in Blackstone's "Introduction to the Charter," as well as in the regular Histories of England. Providentially for this nation, wise and fearless patriots were still to be found among our barons,* who led the national opposition to these royal aggressions. But Edward, like Elizabeth in after ages, was a prince of sagacity as well as of spirit, and yielded to the popular feeling.† While he was in Flanders, in 1297, his son (who presided as regent in the English Parliament) passed, in the king's name, the statute usually called "Confirmatio Chartarum," in the then usual form of a charter. It was sent over to King Edward, and signed by him at Ghent; ‡ and was afterwards (after some attempts at evasion) solemnly confirmed by him in a parliament held by himself in person in the year 1300.

The material portions of this Statute, or Charter, are as follows :—

* See Hallam's just eulogy on the earls of Hereford and Essex, "Hist. Mid. Ages," vol. iii., p. 2, note.

† "To know when to yield in government is at least as necessary as to know when to lose in trade; and he who cannot do the first, is so little likely to govern a kingdom well, that it is more than probable he would govern a shop ill."—*Bolingbroke.*

‡ See Blackstone's "Introduction," p. xcv.

## "CONFIRMATIO CHARTARUM.

ANNO VICESIMO QUINTO EDV. I.

### CAP. V.

"And for so much as divers people of our realm are in fear that the aids and tasks which they have given to us beforetime, towards our wars and other business, of their own grant and good will (howsoever they were made), might turn to a bondage to them and their heirs because they might be at another time found in the rolls, and likewise for the prises taken throughout the realm, in our name, by our ministers; we have granted for us and our heirs that we shall not draw such aids, tasks, nor prises, into a custom for anything that hath been done heretofore, be it by roll or any other precedent that may be founden.

### CAP. VI.

"Moreover, we have granted for us and our heirs, as well to archbishops, bishops, abbots, priors, and other folk of holy church, as also to earls, barons, and to all the commonalty of the land, that for no business from thenceforth we *shall take such manner of aids, tasks, nor prises, but by the common consent of all* * *the realm, and for the common* profit thereof, saving the ancient aids and prises due and accustomed." †

* "Par commun assent de *tut* le roiaume." The version in our statute book omits the important word "All."

† Lord Coke says the ancient aids *pour file marier*, &c., (see *supra*, p. 124), are here meant: and the ancient takings or seizures are here intended, such as waifes, strays, the goods of felons and outlaws, deodands, and the like.—*Second Institut.* p. 529.

## CHAPTER XIII.

The Principles of the Constitution traced in the Charter.—Kingship in England.—Its powers and limitations.—Parliament.—Origin of the House of Peers.—Of the two branches of the House of Commons.—Trial by Jury.—Writ of Habeas Corpus.—Origin and value of these Constitutional Rights.

HAVING now examined the text of Magna Carta and its Supplement, we may pause and consider how far they recognize or establish those great primary principles of our constitution, which have been defined in the first chapter of this work, and which may conveniently be repeated here.

The government of the country by an hereditary sovereign, ruling with limited powers, and bound to summon and consult a parliament of the whole realm comprising hereditary peers, and elective representatives of the commons.

That without the sanction of parliament no tax of any kind can be imposed, and no law can be made, repealed, or altered.

That no man be arbitrarily fined or imprisoned, that no man's property or liberties be impaired, and that no man be in any way punished, except after a lawful trial.

Trial by jury.

That justice shall not be sold or delayed.

In the first place, with regard to the government of the country, the Great Charter and its supplements clearly recognize the authority of an hereditary sovereign. The repeated expressions in them of the king *granting for himself and his heirs* the various popular privileges, which they secure, are themselves sufficient to prove this. It would not be difficult to point out in them recognitions of the king being the fountain of honour,* of the king being the fountain of justice,* of the inviolability of the royal person,* and of other rules respecting English royalty, which will hereafter be more fully noticed. But, without resorting to literal criticism, no one can read the Charter without feeling perfectly certain that royalty is a fundamental portion, and the primary governing power of our political system. Indeed, not only in England, but throughout Europe, during the middle ages, the existence of a "permanent suzerain, vested with large rights of a mixed personal and proprietary character over his vassals, though subject also to certain obligations towards them," was always presumed as indispensably necessary for the existence of political society.† "The rights of the chief were always conceived as constituting a *Status* apart, and neither conferred originally by the grant, nor revocable at the pleasure of those over whom they were exercised. This view of the essential nature of political authority was a point in which all the three great elements of modern European society—the Teutonic, the Roman,‡ and the Christian, concurred, though each in a different way and with different modifications." Thus in England we find the nation constantly striving to

* See sections 14, 39, 36, 45, and 61 of John's Charter and notes in the last chapter.

† See Grote's "History of Greece," vol. iii., p. 13, *et seq.*; the reflections on the discontinuance of Kingship in Hellas, compared with its preservation in Mediæval Europe, deserve an attentive perusal.

‡ *i. e.* the *Imperial* Roman. The influence of Republican Rome, when her history and literature were first made familiar to Europe by the revival of classical studies, was certainly not monarchical.

regulate and temper, by solemn compact and laws, the power of its royal chief, but never attempting, in early times, to dispense with the existence of kingly chiefdom. Even when the oppressiveness and proved perfidy of individual monarchs induced the nation to take away practical power from them, and to choose an executive board, who should rule in their name, such provisions, however necessary, were always considered and designed to be of a temporary nature. Nor even when kings were solemnly deposed, as in the cases of the second Edward and the second Richard, was kingship ever assailed. A new sovereign was instantly placed in the room of the deposed one, in order that the nation might not be deprived for a moment of the monarchical head, that was reckoned politically indispensable.

The peaceable and undisputed accession of Edward I., though he was far distant from England at the time of the death of Henry III., established not only that the crown was hereditary in the royal family, but also that it was hereditary according to the principles of descent which regulate a private inheritance.*

It appears with equal clearness from the Charter, that the royal power which forms part of our constitution, is a limited power. The king's Council sanctions the royal will. The very charters purport in their preambles to be granted by the advice of the great spiritual and lay councillors of the Crown. We shall have occasion to consider the importance of this

* The form of popular consent expressed at the coronation was long considered necessary to complete the royal title. The heir to the throne had an inchoate right immediately on his predecessor's death, but his reign dated from his coronation. Such was the case till Edward I.'s reign, which dated from the day (four days after Henry III.'s death) when the barons swore fealty to him in his absence, and his peace was proclaimed.—See *Hallam's Middle Ages*, vol. ii. p. 342.

more fully, when we examine the origin of our parliaments. But the great principle which emphatically distinguishes a constitutional from an absolute monarchy—the principle that the Crown is subject to the law—requires our present attention, and it is fully established by the Great Charter. A king, who avows that he is bound to inflict no punishment, save according to the law of the land,* and that he cannot, save by the authority of the law, touch a freeman's property or person, or control his freedom of action; a king, who by a public instrument surrenders all fines and amerciaments which he has imposed contrary to the law of the land,†—completely admits the supremacy of law over royal power. And in fact, although the government of our Anglo-Norman kings was often extremely arbitrary, they never were supposed, either by others or by themselves, to be absolute irresponsible lords of the lives and properties of their subjects, like the despots of the Eastern World. But, though by common understanding the king was bound to consult his Great Council before he made new laws or exacted fresh taxes, and though the very essence of feudalism involved a reciprocity of duties between lord and vassal, the checks on royal caprice and royal oppression were always vague, and generally ineffectual before the epoch of the Great Charter. From that time forward the limitations of the royal prerogative were unmistakable and undeniable, and "Sub lege Rex" became a sure constitutional maxim, though forensic sycophants in after ages were sometimes found who whispered its converse.‡

* Magna Carta, sec. 39, and notes thereon, *supra*, p. 134.

† Sec. 55, *supra*, p. 143.

‡ See Hallam's "Middle Ages," vol. ii. p. 431, for the proofs found in Bracton, a judge at the end of Henry III.'s reign, of the limitations of prerogative by law. "The king can do nothing but what he can do by law," &c. See, also, Guizot on "Representative Government," part 2, lect. 1, *ad fin.* The volume of "Ancient English Political Songs," published by

Next let us trace the great principle of the sovereign of England being bound to summon and consult a parliament of the whole realm, comprising hereditary peers and elective representatives of the commons. This important topic requires consideration under several aspects. We must first ascertain the existence of such a body as a Great Council of the realm, or Parliament; and next examine of whom and how it was composed. This will lead us to examine the origin of each of the two Houses of Parliament; and with regard to the Lower House, we shall have to trace separately the growth of its two branches, its knights of the shire, and its representatives of cities and boroughs. Together with the general principle of the authority of parliament, and its composition, we may conveniently consider the maxims relating to legislation and taxation,—and the important fact that we have had one parliament for all England, and not separate parliaments for separate provinces.

Among all the nations of the Gothic stock, whether of its Scandinavian or of its Teutonic branch, and in all the kingdoms founded by them out of conquered Roman provinces, councils or assemblies of some form existed, whose consent the ruling chief was

the Camden Society, also gives good proof of how the clergy and educated part of the laity in the 13th century reasoned on this topic. The fine poem on the baron's war, in Henry III.'s reign, (which must have been written after the battle of Lewes, 1264, before the battle of Evesham, 1265,) contains many spirited passages as to the necessary restrictions of royal power. The patriotic poet says: "It is a vulgar error to assert that the course of law depends on the king's will. The truth is the reverse; for the king may fail, but the law stands firm. The law rules even the royal dignity:—

> Dicitur vulgariter ut rex vult, lex vadit,
> Veritas vult aliter; nam lex stat, rex cadit.
> * * * *
> Legem quoque dicimus regis dignitatem
> Regere," &c.

An excellent condensation of the best passages of this remarkable poem will be found in Mr. Blaauw's "History of the Barons' War," one of the best historical monographs that we possess.

bound to obtain, in order to legalize important measures of State. We have already drawn attention to the assemblies of the *principes*, and the general assemblies of freemen among the primitive Germans,* and to the Tings of the primitive Danes.† The student may also here usefully refer to what has been said respecting the witenagemotes of the Anglo-Saxons.‡ At least he must bear in mind that it was only with the sanction of this witan that an Anglo-Saxon king could make new laws or impose new taxes; that the prelates and the great nobles and thanes attended these assemblies; and that the inferior class, the ceorls, though not directly represented there, yet were not without protectors and advocates; inasmuch as certain of the magistrates, whom the men of every borough and township regularly elected from among themselves for the purpose of local self-government, might be present at the witan, for the purpose of obtaining redress for any wrong which might have been committed, and for the redress of which the ordinary tribunals were inadequate. When once present at the witan, though ostensibly only for the purpose of remedial justice, the ceorl magistrates must also have had some influence in other matters: inasmuch as the cheerful co-operation of the bulk of the community in carrying any particular measure into effect, never can be thought immaterial, even by those who have the power of enforcing sullen obedience. The Anglo-Saxon polity was overthrown by the conquering Normans; but the recollection of this virtual though indirect system of representation, must have survived among the bulk of the population; and may have greatly facilitated the adoption and insured the good working of the subsequent parliamentary representation of the Commons.

* See *supra*, p. 17

† See *supra*, p. 34.

‡ Chapter iv. *supra*, p. 48.

It has also been pointed out* that though we have no authority for minute details of the polity of the Normans in Normandy, prior to the conquest of this country by Duke William, thus much is certain, that there was a council of the Norman barons which the dukes were obliged on all important occasions to summon and consult. It was not likely that they, by whose help William won the crown of this country, and to whom he parcelled out its lands as rewards, would consent to forego in their new abodes the political rights which they had enjoyed in their old homes across the Channel. The Anglo-Norman king summoned and consulted his great Council, as he had done while merely a Norman duke.† All who held land by military tenure immediately of the Crown, had a right to attend, and were expected to attend the king's court on the solemn days of council, and all these were originally styled the king's barons.‡ Besides these, the prelates, and the heads of the chief abbeys and priories formed here, as in every country of Christendom, an essential part of the Great Council. No other persons of any class whatever had the right to appear there, either in person, or by any sort of representative, to take part in the proceedings; though petitioners for justice still flocked thither, as to the highest court of the realm.

Many among the large number of the tenants-in-chief, by reason of their comparative poverty, the distance of their estates from the cities where the Council was usually convened, and other causes, soon ceased to attend as regularly as the more powerful and wealthy nobles. These last were soon termed the greater barons, and ultimately, the titles of

* See *supra*, p. 55.

† See Hallam's "Middle Ages," vol. ii. p. 319, and vol. iii. p. 4, *et seq*. Guizot on "Representative Government," part ii. lect. 4.

‡ See Hallam's "Middle Ages, vol. iii. p. 6, *et seq*.

"peer" and "baron," which had first been common to all the king's immediate tenants, were, in speaking of the kingdom generally, exclusively applied to the heads of a few great houses, who, largely endowed with lands, and constant members of the Great Council, were clearly distinguishable in rank and in circumstances from the mass of the inferior tenants-in-chief. Traces of the distinction appear earlier than John's reign, but in that king's Great Charter the line is drawn decisively and broadly between these two bodies, which we may safely call, in modern phraseology, the nobility and the gentry of the realm. By the 14th chapter of John's Charter, the king binds himself in order to constitute the General Council for the grant of pecuniary aids, that it shall be summoned thus— "We shall cause the archbishops, bishops, abbots, earls* and greater barons to be separately summoned by our letters. And we shall cause our sheriffs and bailiffs to summon generally all others who hold of us in chief."

With respect to the spiritual lords no particular comment here is necessary. We principally direct our attention to the origin of the temporal peers. Altogether we see in the words of the Charter, which have just been quoted, the clear original of our Upper House of Parliament, consisting of lords spiritual and temporal. And, as the temporal peerage was thus a body originally composed of the most powerful landowners in the kingdom, it naturally became an hereditary peerage without any express enactment to that effect. This will appear clear, if we call to mind that the power of devising real estates did not exist

* The title "Earl," under the first Anglo-Norman kings, meant that its holder was governor of a county or province. By degrees it became a mere titular distinction. The title of duke was first granted to a peer in Edward III.'s reign; that of marquis in Richard II.; that of viscount in Henry VI.

for many ages after the grant of the Great Charter; and, although alienation with the consent of the lord, and upon paying him a fine, was permitted by law, the entire transfer of large estates by such means could seldom or never have occurred, for the simple and obvious reason, that there were no wealthy capitalists to come forward, and buy the whole lands of a mighty but impoverished baron at a single bargain. As, therefore, the estates of the great barons descended generally from heir to heir, and as each heir on coming into possession had the same right as his predecessor to be treated as a great baron of the realm, the idea of hereditary descent became gradually associated with the *status* of a peer. And this theory of the descent of peerage at last prevailed so far as to be extended to a new species of peers: to men who held no baronial possessions, but whom our kings summoned by writ to meet and consult among the prelates, and magnates, and the chief men of the realm. This mode of creating peers by writ is said to have been first practised in Edward I.'s reign; and it appears to have been established as early as Richard II.'s reign, that such a writ of summons to parliament, and the fact of having sat there by virtue of such a writ, gave an hereditary right to the descendants of the person so summoned. The modern form of the sovereign creating a peer by letters patent dates from the reign of Richard II. By an almost invariable usage, the letters patent creating a peer, direct its hereditary descent. Whether in default of such words the peerage would be only a peerage for life, and whether it is in the power of the Crown to grant a peerage that shall not be hereditary, are interesting questions on which high authorities differ.*

* See Bowyer's "Commentaries on the Constitutional Law of England," p. 461.; and see generally, as to the early English peerage, Hallam's "Middle Ages," vol. iii. p. 123, and supplemental note at p. 234.

We next come to the rise and progress of our Commons House of Parliament; and it will be convenient to deal separately with its two branches—the knights of the shire, and the borough members.

The 14th clause of the Great Charter of John, after providing that the prelates and great barons shall be summoned individually, ordains that the king shall, by his sheriffs and bailiffs, summon generally all others who hold of the king in chief. There is nothing said here about any two or any other number in each county being elected to sit as representatives of the rest. But if we can satisfy ourselves that the idea and the practice of representation were at this period becoming familiar to the English, we can readily understand that the practice of representation in this instance also might be tacitly annexed to this provision of the Great Charter; and, then, if we consider that, by virtue of the 14th clause, the mass of inferior tenants-in-chief in each county would, at the summons of their sheriff, elect certain individuals of their body to represent them in the Great Council of the realm, we see a clear recognition of that part of the supreme assembly, which now consists of the county members of the House of Commons, and we find the principle of representation also.

From the very first establishment of the Normans in this country we find traces of the representative system. The causes why this system of government was so seldom and so unsuccessfully attempted by the classic States of Greece and Rome, and why it grew and throve in mediæval Europe, are most interesting to investigate, but the discussion would occupy undue space in this work.* Feudalism favoured, and to

* See Newman's "Contrasts between Ancient and Modern History," and Guizot on "European Civilization," lect. 2. The most remarkable instances of representative government in purely classic times are the Achæan League, and the system adopted by the Italian Allies in the Social

some extent involved, Representation. The lord who attended his sovereign's council was supposed to vote, and make grants of money on his own behalf and on behalf of his vassals also. The abbots (who as spiritual lords formed a considerable part of the councillors of every sovereign in Christendom) were more completely the elected representatives of the whole body of the members of their respective monasteries or abbeys. And the Church did much to diffuse the idea of representative action by councils, her synods, and other assemblies, "all of which were formed on the principle of a virtual or express representation, and had a tendency to render its application to national assemblies more familiar." *

Specific instances of election of individuals from each county for purposes connected with the administration of government, even before the date of John's Charter, can be proved; and it is reasonable to believe that very many more must have taken place which no chronicler has thought it necessary to mention, and of which no documentary proof has survived. Thus, four years after the Conquest, we find William directing twelve persons to be chosen for each county, to inform him rightly of the laws and customs of England.† Writs are extant by which King John, in 1214, the year before the grant of the Great Charter, ordered the sheriffs of each county to send to a general assembly at Oxford "four chosen knights, in order to discuss with us the affairs of our kingdom." ‡ It is also deserving of attention, that

war. It is curious to speculate what Italica would have been if it had conquered Rome.

* See Hallam's "Mid. Ages," p. 11, and Guizot on "European Civilization," lect. 2.

† Hoveden, 343.

‡ "Quatuor discretos milites ad loquendum nobiscum de negotiis regni nostri." See Güizott's remarks on these writs in his "History of Representative Government," lect. 11.

another clause of John's Charter (the 48th) very explicitly requires an election of knights of the shire in each county for a very important purpose. It directs that "all evil customs concerning forests, &c., shall be forthwith inquired into in each county by twelve sworn knights of the same shire, chosen by creditable persons of the same county." Moreover, the practice of knights being chosen from each district, who, in behalf of the whole body of the county, made presentments of crimes before the king's judges on their circuits, must have materially aided in habituating the freeholders of each county, especially the knights, to representative action. This practice was certainly as old as the reign of Henry the Second, and was probably based on a still more ancient Anglo-Saxon custom.* An ordinance of Richard the First had regulated the procedure for about twenty years before the date of Magna Carta. Four knights were chosen for each county, who then proceeded to choose others for each hundred or wapentake.

We must also, in examining the 14th clause of John's Charter, respecting the summoning of the mass of tenants-in-chief to the Great Council, bear in mind who the officer was by whom the summons was to be given. The officer specially mentioned in the Great Charter for this purpose is the sheriff. The sheriff would naturally execute this duty at the county court, of which he was the presiding officer, and at which the mass of the tenants-in-chief, like other freeholders, were bound to attend. It may be taken for certain that it was at the county court that the twelve knights, under section 48 of the Charter, were to be elected; that it was there that the four knights were chosen for the presentment of offences, under Richard the First's ordinance; and it was there that the selections of knights for any purpose (such as that

* See Forsyth's "History of Trial by Jury," p. 187.

which had occurred in 1214) were made. It would naturally follow that the assembled tenants-in-chief, who heard at the county court a general summons from the sheriff to the Great Council of the Realm, would follow their usual course, and appoint some of their number to act for them. They may not have intended to waive the abstract right which each possessed of attending in person; but it is improbable that on the receipt of a mere general summons they should have recommenced a practice which they had laid aside as burdensome.* But it would be requisite to pay some kind of obedience to the royal summons, and the mode of doing so would naturally be by electing some of their number to attend and act for the whole body.

The clauses of John's Charter respecting the manner of granting aids and escuages, and the summonses to the Great Council, were not repeated in the charter as issued under Henry the Third. But it is clear that the prohibition against levying these imposts without consent was considered to be still binding; † nor did Henry, though he tallaged the royal towns without mercy, venture to take escuages or aids by the mere exercise of royal power.

As the records of the long reign of this Prince proceed, we find the proofs of county representation in parliament becoming more numerous and more clear. Thus, during the earlier years of Henry the Third, we find repeated instances of elections of knights of the shire, for the purpose of presenting grievances, and for assessing on each individual his

* See *supra*, p. 166.

† See Hallam's "Middle Ages," p. 327. It will be observed on reading the conclusion of the Great Charter as issued by Henry in the twenty-fifth year of his reign (see p. 156, *supra*), that he there acknowledges a grant from his subjects.

fair proportion of a voted subsidy.* In 1245 we find Henry, in the very terms of the Great Charter of John, summoning the great barons singly, and the other tenants-in-chief generally, by writs to the sheriffs of each county. To a Great Council summoned in 1246, the title of Parliament is for the first time given by the old chronicler, which had previously been applied to any kind of conference, but thenceforth in England became restricted to the Great Council of the nation. In 1254 Henry directs a parliament to be convened at London, to which the sheriff of each county is to cause to be elected in the county court two good and discreet knights of the shire whom the men of the shire shall have chosen for this purpose, in the stead of all and each of them, to consider along with the knights of other counties what aid they will grant the king

Finally, in 1265, in the celebrated parliament summoned by De Montfort in Henry's name, at which the representation of the boroughs was created, the representation of the counties was undoubtedly placed or confirmed on its permanent basis, as the writs are still extant by which each sheriff is directed to return two lawful, good, and discreet knights for his shire.

The date cannot be exactly given of the important feature in county representation, of all the freeholders of the county voting in the election of knights of the shire, and not merely those who held their land directly of the Crown by military tenure. It is obvious that this extension of the franchise arose from the circumstance of the knights being elected at the county courts, at which all the freeholders of the shire did suit and service. And although opinions vary as to the precise time and mode in which it was

* Hallam's "Middle Ages," p. 13. Guizot's "History of Representative Government," part ii. lect. 11.

effected, it is clear that at a very early period, certainly during Henry III.'s reign, the county members of England were elected by all the freeholders, without regard to their holding by military or by socage tenure, and without reference to their being or not being immediate tenants of the Crown. Subsequently, a statute of Henry VI. limited the county franchise to such freeholders only as possessed free tenements of the clear annual value of forty shillings.

For the commencement of the other branch of our House of Commons, the representatives of cities and boroughs, we must take a date subsequent to the Great Charter of John. Those who obtained that Charter, had designed to give the citizens and burghers of England the same protection from royal rapacity which they exacted from the landholders. This is evident from the "Articuli Magnæ Cartæ," * the rough draft of the barons' stipulations laid before King John at Runnymede, and to which he assented under seal. In the 32nd of these articles, after the provision against the levy of scutages or aids, save by consent of the General Council of the realm, were added the important words, "And in like manner be it done respecting the talliages and aids of and from the city of London and other cities." Through some unexplained neglect or manœuvre, these important words were omitted when the Charter was formally drawn up ; and the cities and towns were left exposed to the exactions of their feudal oppressors, without any protection in the national Council. Simon De Montfort was the first statesman who perceived and fully appreciated the growing importance of the commercial middle classes in England. The instances sometimes asserted of borough representation before his time are both scanty and spurious ; but to the

* See them at length in Blackstone on the Charter, p. 1, *et seq.*

parliament summoned by him in Henry's name, after the battle of Lewes, 1264, two burgesses were returned for every borough in each county, the writs for which are still preserved. De Montfort soon perished in the vicissitude of civil war; but his reform measure perished not with him. The victorious royalists felt the policy of enfranchising the trading community of the land. Parliaments continued to be summoned on De Montfort's plan; and when at length the Confirmatio Chartarum, in the 25th year of Edward I., by the enactments which have above been quoted, made the consent of parliament necessary to the levy of talliages, of subsidies, and, in effect, of all taxes, the presence of the burgesses in the parliaments of England became thenceforward essential and indispensable.

Had our kings been less wasteful and warlike, it is probable that parliaments including the burgesses would seldom have been convened; and it is certain that the House of Commons never would have grown into a great governing organ of the constitution. There was an essential difference in the origin of the two branches of the Lower House. The presence of the knights of the shire in parliament sprung from the old Anglo-Norman right of each immediate military tenant of the king to be present at the king's Great Council. Councils might have therefore long continued to be called at which the prelates, the great barons, and the knights, would attend and take part in legislation and the deliberations of State affairs, but in which the burgesses would have no place. Councils of this nature were in fact frequently convened at intervals in Edward the First's reign, after the introduction of what we should term full parliaments of peers, knights of the shire, and burgesses.*

* Two kinds of parliament appeared under Edward I. The one kind was composed only of the higher barons, and seemed to form the Grand

But the ample domains with which the Conqueror had fortified the Crown, were diminished rapidly by the lavish generosity and costly campaigns of his successors. Our kings were in constant need of money, and the money granted by the burgesses was an important consideration. The frequent convention of parliaments, therefore, at which the burgesses attended, became indispensable; and the gradual strengthening of the parliament on which the Crown was thus dependent for supplies was equally inevitable. As it has been pithily said, the power of the purse drew after it other power. The representatives of cities and boroughs acquired and exercised equal rights with the knights of the shire; and both these bodies, by uniting together, gained the needful authority for their country's good which neither could have singly maintained.*

Council of the king; in the other, deputies from counties and boroughs had a seat.

No legal and fixed distinction existed between these assemblies; their attributes were almost identical, and they often exercised the same powers. However, the meetings of those parliaments which were composed only of the higher barons were very frequent; they took place regularly four times a year. The other parliaments, on the contrary, were only convened on extraordinary occasions, and when it was necessary to obtain from the freeholders, either of the counties or of the towns and boroughs, some general impost.

This, however, was not the only motive which could lead to the convocation of this last-mentioned assembly, which, in truth, alone deserves the name of parliament. Whenever business arose of so great importance that the concurrence of a great number of interests were judged necessary, the great parliament was assembled, and by this cause its range of deliberation became more extended, and it assumed a greater consistency.—*Guizot.*

* It is very instructive to compare the growth and durability of English liberty with the fate of that at Castile. The Castilian cities sent deputies to the cortes long before the English towns were represented in parliament. These popular members of the early cortes were fully equal in spirit to the early members of our Commons House, and had much more power. But the inferior nobility, and the country landowners of Castile, were unrepresented. Hence the cortes of Castile, when the great struggle between them and the Crown, in the reign of Charles V. (Charles I. of Castile), came on in the 16th century, were overthrown, and the

The constitutional principle that the Crown should not tax the subject without the consent of parliament was undoubtedly the practical mainspring of parliamentary power. But it would be unjust to the men of the thirteenth century to suppose that they had no discernment of the general advantage which a State acquires when the exercise of political power is carried on from the amplest basis that is consistent with the due influence of intelligence, property, and rank. Sir William Temple has said that for a prince to govern all *by* all is the great secret of happiness and safety both for prince and people.* Gleams of the spirit of this precept appear in the political poem of Henry the Third's time, which has been already referred to. For example, the poet (probably a friend and adviser of De Montfort) bids that the Commons of the realm be consulted, and that the opinion of the whole body of the people be made known:—

> "Igitur communitas regni consulatur,
> Et quid universitas sentiat sciatur."

Then, too, we find an archbishop of Canterbury, in Edward the First's reign, in a letter to the Pope, asserting that it is the custom of the kingdom of England that, "in matters which regard the state of that kingdom, the advice of all those interested in the matter should be consulted." Guizot observes on this, that "there is no need that we should take this

cause of constitutional freedom in Spain fell with them. On the other hand, it is well to watch the fatal weakness of freedom in Poland, where a martial nobility and gentry had the fullest rights, but where the towns were allowed no political power. Kosciusko and his compatriots endeavored to reform this, but it was too late.

* Napoleon's maxim was the exact converse. "Everything *for* the people, nothing *by* them. The fate of Napoleon himself, and of France both under and after him, is the best proof of the superior wisdom of the English statesman.

principle in its most rigorous application; it is not the fact that all those who were interested in these matters were consulted about them; but the sentiment is still a witness of the progress which had already been made by the ideas of a free and public government."*

We have examined the respective origins of the elements of our parliament; next comes the very important subject of its division into two Houses, one consisting of the lords spiritual and the lords temporal, the other of the knights of the shire and burgesses. In the first place, the mere fact of the division of our parliament into *two* Houses, neither more nor less, has been of infinite importance in our constitutional history. We have escaped thereby the miseries, which the instability, the violence, and the impassioned temerity of a single legislative assembly, have ever produced, when that form of government has been attempted, as it often was in the Italian Republics of the middle ages, as it was for a short period in Pennsylvania and Georgia, and as it has been repeatedly essayed by revolutionary France, Spain, Naples, and Portugal, in our own time. The great political writers of the United States, Kent, Story, and Lieber,† have exhausted the arguments on this topic, and have completely proved how essential a guarantee for orderly and permanent liberty is "The Principle of Two Houses," or the "Bicameral System," as it has been phrased by Jeremy Bentham.‡

* "Hist. Represent. Gov.," part 2, lect. 13.

† See, also, the excellent remarks of a writer of our own country, Mr. Bowyer, on this subject, in his recent very learned work, on "Universal Public Law," p. 316.

‡ I gladly quote some of the observations on this important point which Professor Lieber makes at p. 157 of his great work on "Civil Liberty and Self-Government:"—"Practical knowledge alone can show the whole advantage of this Anglican principle, according to which we equally discard the idea of three and four estates, and of one House only. Both are

An increase of the number of Houses beyond two, gives no advantage which the bicameral plan does not afford, and introduces irreparable mischief, by the complicated dissensions, the vacillations, and the delays which are inevitable when there are three or more legislative councils. The facilities for corruption and intimidation by the sovereign or his ministers, are also fearfully augmented; and it becomes an easy matter for an adroit and ambitious politician to gain an ascendancy in one weak House out of many, and thereby to destroy the general free action of the political body. It is useful to compare, in this respect, the primary institutions of our own country with the different forms assumed by the national assemblies of other European nations in early times. For example, we shall find in mediæval Sweden four estates in four Houses; in mediæval Spain and France, three estates in three Houses. And we shall find that of all the early free institutions of Europe, our own alone have been permanent.*

The division of our parliament into two Houses is foreshadowed in the distinction drawn by John's Charter between the great barons and the inferior

equally and essentially un-Anglican. Although, however, practice alone can show the whole advantage that may be derived from the system of two Houses, it must be a striking fact to every inquirer in distant countries, that not only has the system of two Houses historically developed itself in England, but it has been adopted by the United States in all the thirty-one States, as well as the six now existing territories, and by all the British Colonies, where local Legislatures exist. We may mention even the African State of Liberia. The bicameral system accompanies the Anglican race like the common law, while no one attempt at introducing the uni-cameral system in larger countries has succeeded. France, Spain, Naples, Portugal—in all these countries it has been tried, and everywhere it has failed. The idea of one House flows from that of the unity of power so popular in France. The bicameral system is called, by the advocates of democratic unity of power, an aristocratic institution. This is an utter mistake. In reality, it is a truly popular principle to insist on the protection of a Legislature, divided into two Honses."

* See Sir J Mackintosh's Memoirs, vol. ii. p. 188.

tenants-in-chief, and the nature of the division which took place, when our parliament was fully constituted by the addition of borough members, has been most momentous for the liberty of England. If the representatives of the inferior military tenants-in-chief had been admitted to the chamber of the great barons, or if they had sat apart from the burgesses, the same violent distinctions of class and caste must have grown up in England, that have been so pernicious in the continental kingdoms. But, providentially for England, the knights of the shire coalesced in parliament with the borough representatives; and though some time elapsed before any certain system was maintained, they became the joint representatives of the Commons of England, leaving the great barons to form together with the prelates a separate senate and a separate order. The benefits of this to England have been incalculable. She has had the advantage of a nobility, and has not been cursed with a noblesse. One of the proud deficiencies of our language is, that the term "roturier" is untranslatable into English. As Hallam truly and eloquently remarks, "from the reign of Henry III. at least, the legal equality of all ranks [of freemen] below the peerage was to every essential purpose as complete as at present." * * * * * * What is most particular, is that the peerage itself confers no privilege, except on its actual possessor. The sons of peers, as we well know, are commoners, and totally destitute of any legal right beyond a barren pre-eminence. There is no part of our constitution so admirable as this equality of civil rights, this *isonomia*, which the philosophers of ancient Greece only hoped to find in democratical government. From the beginning our law has been no respecter of persons. It screens not the gentleman of ancient lineage from the judgment of an ordinary jury, nor from ignominious punishment. It confers not, it never did confer, those unjust immunities from public burdens which the superior orders arrogated to themselves upon the Continent. Thus, while the privileges of our peers, as hereditary legislators of a free people, are "incomparably more valuable and dignified in their nature, they are far less invidious in their exercise than those of any other nobility in Europe. It is, I am firmly persuaded, to this peculiarly democratical character of the English monarchy that we are indebted for its long permanence, its regular improvement, and its present vigour. It is a singular, a providential circumstance, that in an age when the gradual march of civilization and commerce was so little foreseen, our ancestors, deviating from the usages of neighbouring countries, should, as if deliberately, have guarded against that expansive force which, in bursting through obstacles improvidently opposed, has scattered havoc over Europe."*

There is yet another important characteristic of our parliament, which requires attention. Our nation has had *one* parliament for all England, and not separate legislative and taxing assemblies for separate counties or separate provinces. We have thus enjoyed the blessings of "a national representative Government—of a representative system, comprehending the whole State, and throwing liberty over it broadcast."† Without this centralization of parliamentary power, our sovereigns never could have been kept under parliamentary control, and within the limited scope of action which alone is open to a constitutional king. The remarks on this point, of the noble and learned author of the "History of England and France under the House of Lancaster" deserve attention. According to him, the great diversity in the ultimate result

* "Middle Ages," vol. ii. p. 343.

† Lieber, "Civil Liberty and Self Government," p. 137.

of the English struggles for a free, that is, a rational and stable mixed constitution, and those of the French barons and towns during the fourteenth and fifteenth centuries for the same purpose, was caused by England having one central Government and one parliament acting for the whole, whereas in France, the various great provinces of the kingdom (such as Normandy) had each its provincial states in parliament, the assembling of the States General being only occasional.* Professor Lieber similarly remarks, that wherever popular bodies, like the estates of mediæval France, have existed, no matter how great their privileges were, or how zealously they have defended them, civil liberty has not been firmly established; on the contrary, it has been lost in the course of time, unless the estates have become united in some central representative system. He also acutely observes, that in our own time we find that those Governments, which can no longer resist the demand of liberty by the people, yet are bent on yielding as little as possible, always have tried as long as possible to grant provincial estates only.†

The last great principles of our Constitution guarantee the security of person and property from arbitrary violence, and the due administration of justice. They are these three:

That no man be arbitrarily fined or imprisoned, that no man's property or liberties be impaired, and that no man be in any way punished, except after a lawful trial.

Trial by jury.

That justice shall not be sold or delayed.

This last maxim needs no comment. We have, and our ancestors for more than six centuries have

* See the LXVth and LXVIth Supplemental Notes to this excellent historical work.

† P. 137.

had, in the words of the Great Charter, the solemn declaration and covenant of the sovereign—"We will sell to no man, we will not deny or delay to any man, either justice or right." Would that we could boast that it had been carried out in practice as fully as it has been acknowledged in theory. "*The law's delay*" still, as in Shakspeare's time, forms one of the curses of human life, to an extent never contemplated at Runnymede; and our modern law-reformers would do well to consider how far the practice of making suitors pay for judicial writs, and exacting court-fees on trials, is in accordance with the great constitutional canon. The security from arbitrary imprisonment, and the other great constitutional principle, that of trial by jury, claim our most earnest attention, both on account of their universally practical importance,* and by reason of the tendency now shown in many quarters to disparage and discard that long-venerated system of trial.

The great words of the Great Charter—worth all the classics, to Lord Chatham's mind—which have protected for six centuries, and still protect the personal liberty and property of all freemen, have been already quoted, but never can be too often repeated. "No freeman shall be taken, or imprisoned, or be disseised of his freehold, or liberties, or free customs, or be outlawed or exiled, or any otherwise destroyed; nor will we pass upon him, nor send upon him, but by the lawful judgment of his peers, or by

* See the judicious comments of Lieber ("Civ. Lib. and Self Gov.," p. 54), on the value of a well-guarded penal trial as an element of constitutional liberty. He cites and comments on the dictum of Montesquieu, that, "It is upon the excellence of the criminal laws that chiefly the liberty of the citizen depends" ("Esprit des Lois," xii. 2): and the words with which Mittermaier concludes his recent work on the "Penal Process of England, Scotland, and the United States:"—"It will be more and more acknowledged how true it is that the penal legislation is the keystone of a nation's public law."

the law of the land. We will sell to no man, we will not deny or delay to any man, justice or right."

The value of these words of the Charter, as constitutional checks on royal power, has been already referred to. We are now viewing them as strictly applying to the administration of justice. They contain two great principles. First, that no man shall be imprisoned on mere general grounds of suspicion, or for an indefinite period, at the discretion or caprice of the executive power; but that imprisonment shall be only inflicted as the result of a legal trial and sentence, or for the purpose of keeping in safe custody, when necessary, an accused person on a definite charge, until he can be tried on that charge. Secondly, they provide that, as a general rule, every person accused of a criminal offence shall have the question of his guilt or innocence determined by a free jury of his fellow-countrymen, and not by any nominee of the Government.

The first of these principles is familiar to us by the term of an Englishman's right to a Habeas Corpus, if his personal liberty be interfered with. Some writers on our constitution have erroneously supposed that this safeguard of freedom dates only from the reign of Charles II., when the celebrated Habeas Corpus Act was passed. But its true foundation is the Great Charter; and from the earliest times of our law "no freeman could be detained in prison except upon a criminal charge, on conviction, or for a civil debt. In the former case it was always in his power to demand of the Court of King's Bench a suit of *habeas corpus ad subjiciendum* directed to the person detaining him in custody, by which he was enjoined to bring up the body of the prisoner with the warrant of commitment, that the court might judge of its sufficiency, and remand the party, admit him to bail, or discharge him, according to the nature of the charge. This writ issued of right, and could not be refused by the court." *

It is impossible to overvalue this great barrier against tyrannical power. Blackstone's eulogy on it, and his historical sketch of the Habeas Corpus Act,†

* Hallam's "Constitutional History,' vol. i. p. 16.

An imprisonment must either be by process "from a court of judicature, or by warrant from some legal officer having authority to commit to prison: which warrant must be under the hand and seal of the magistrate, and express the cause of the commitment, in order to be examined into, if necessary, upon a *Habeas Corpus.*" "The gaoler is not bound to detain the prisoner, if there be no cause of committal expressed in the warrant. And Sir Edward Coke observes that the law judges in this respect like Festus the Roman Governor,—that it is unreasonable to send a prisoner, and not to signify the crimes alleged against him."—*Bowyer's Commentaries on the Const. Law*, p. 425. *Coke's 2nd Inst.*, 52, 53.

† "The language of the Great Charter is, that no freeman shall be taken or imprisoned but by the lawful judgment of his equals, or by the law of the land. And many subsequent old statutes expressly direct that no man shall be thken or imprisoned by suggestion or petition to the king or his council, unless it be by legal indictment, or the process of the common law. By the petition of Right, 3 Car. II., it is enacted that no freeman shall be imprisoned or detained without cause shown, to which he may make answer according to law. By 16 Car. I. c. x., if any person be restrained of his liberty by order or decree of any illegal court, or by command of the king's majesty in person, or by warrant of the council-board, or of any of the privy council, he shall, upon demand of his council, have a writ of *habeas corpus*, to bring his body before the Court of King's Bench or Common Pleas: who shall determine whether the cause of his commitment be just, and thereupon do as to justice shall appertain. And by 31 Car. II. c. ii., commonly called the *Habeas Corpus* Act, the methods of obtaining this writ are so plainly pointed out and enforced, that so long as this statute remains unimpeached, no subject of England can be long detained in prison, except in those cases in which the law justifies and requires such detainer. And lest this Act should be evaded by demanding unreasonable bail or sureties for the prisoner's appearance, it is declared, by 1 Wm. and M. stat. 2, c. ii., that excessive bail ought not to be required. Of great importance to the public is the preservation of this personal liberty: for if once it were left in the power of any, the highest, magistrate to imprison arbitrarily whomever he or his officers thought proper, as in France it is daily practised by the Crown, there would soon be an end of all other rights and immunities. Some have thought, that unjust attacks, even upon life or property, at the arbitrary will of the magistrate, are less dangerous to the commonwealth than such as are made upon the personal liberty of the subject. To bereave a man of life, or by violence to confiscate his estate, without accusation or trial, would be so gross and notorious an act of despotism, as

deserve the earnest attention of every student of our constitution. And if we would satisfy ourselves by recent practical proofs of the fearful sufferings which a nation may undergo, when its rulers have power to arrest and imprison without trial, upon mere suspicion, we may usefully refer to Mr. Gladstone's narrative of the scenes which he witnessed in the Neapolitan prisons in 1849. If any one should suppose that such atrocities can exist only under unlimited monarchies, he may clear himself of that error by turning to the celebrated letters of the *Vieux Cordelier*, of Camille Desmoulins, in which that remorseful demagogue described the horrors that were caused in republican France during the first revolution, by making men's liberty or captivity dependent upon mere general suspicion.

We come now to the second great judicial principle contained in the clause of Magna Carta, which provides that a freeman is to have a free trial; that he is to suffer nought unless by the lawful judgment of his peers, or by the law of the land: in other

must at once convey the alarm of tyranny throughout the whole kingdom: but confinement of the person, by secretly hurrying him to gaol, where his sufferings are unknown or forgotten, is a less public, a less striking, and therefore a more dangerous engine of arbitrary government. And yet sometimes, when the State is in real danger, even this may be a necessary measure. But the happiness of our constitution is, that it is not left to the executive power to determine when the danger of the State is so great, as to render this measure expedient: for it is the parliament only, or legislative power, that, whenever it sees proper, can authorise the Crown, by suspending the *Habeas Corpus* Act for a short and limited time, to imprison suspected persons without giving any reason for so doing; as the senate of Rome was wont to have recourse to a dictator, a magistrate of absolute authority, when they judged the republic in any imminent danger. The decree of the senate, which usually preceded the nomination of this magistrate, "*dent operam consules, ne quid respublica detrimenti capiat*," was called the *senatus-consultum ultimæ necessitatis*. In like manner this expedient ought only to be tried in cases of extreme emergency; and in these the nation parts with its liberty for a while, in order to preserve it for ever."—*Commentaries*, vol. i. p. 145.

words, the principle of an Englishman's right to trial by jury.

The words of the Great Charter, *Legale judicium parium suorum*, "the lawful judgment of a man's peers," have for centuries been familiar to the nation as household words, and have been understood by Blackstone and most other commentators on our laws and institutions as referring to trial by jury. Some few writers, however, whose station and learning entitle them to attention, have treated this supposition as a mere vulgar error; and deny that the *judicium parium* has any reference whatever to trial by jury. The subject well deserves investigation; as it certainly involves not a mere point of legal archæology, but a constitutional question of the most solemn character.

Did trial by jury exist in England in John's time? and, if so, did the framers of the Great Charter mean trial by jury, when they spoke of the lawful judgment of a man's peers? These are the points on which an answer is to be given, and I believe that on each point the answer should be in the affirmative.

Before investigating the existence of trial by jury in the thirteenth century, we should be precise as to what we understand by the term. Some persons, when they speak of trial by jury, whatever be the period of our history that is referred to, are always thinking of a trial by jury, in all particulars resembling that which is now in actual practice in our courts. In a modern trial by jury we see a trial by twelve men, fairly taken from the general body of private citizens, with hardly any possibility of its being known beforehand who they will be, who are sworn to give a true verdict on a distinct question of fact before them; who act under the presidency of a professional judge, from whom they take directions in matters of law, and who must act according to their findings on matters of fact. All these are ancient characteristics of the institution; but there is also this other ingredient of modern jury trial, with which we are all practically familiar—that the juries give their verdict, not according to their own knowledge of the transaction, but according to the evidence which others lay before them. They act not as witnesses, but as critics of witnesses; as weighers, not as givers of proofs. Now, if we are to consider this last quality of a modern trial by jury to be necessarily involved in the term, we undoubtedly shall not find the trial by jury such as we seek, in John's time, nor shall we discover it for two centuries after his reign. If, on the other hand, when we speak of trial by jury as a safeguard of English liberty, we mean no more than the general principle, that the question of a man's guilt or innocence of a criminal charge is to be determined by a free and independent body of his fellow-citizens, and not by officers of the executive authority; we shall find that principle flourishing in the very earliest periods of our national existence; and we shall find it still earlier in the tribunals of the Germans, the Danes, and the Normans, that is to say, among three of the four elements of our race.

Something, however, more definite than this is fairly meant when trial by jury is spoken of. On the contrary, the first-mentioned idea of the essentials of trial by jury involves too much. Perhaps we may best express the fair signification of the phrase, by saying that when we speak of trial by jury, we mean a system whereby the judges, or public officers, who compose the court, and who are commissioned by the sovereign to administer the law, to put accused persons upon trial, to discharge them if innocent, and to pass sentence upon them if guilty, are not allowed to determine for themselves the question whether an accused person be innocent or guilty, but are required to be guided on this point by the opinion of a body of private individuals (usually twelve in number), fairly taken from among those who, in the eye of the law, are equals with the accused person, summoned to give, upon oath (*Jurati*), a True Saying (*Veredictum*) to the court, as to whether the party accused be guilty or not guilty; by means of which true saying the court may be enabled to pronounce a right judgment. We can readily understand, that in early times the simplest and shortest plan was followed, of summoning, as jurors, twelve men from the immediate neighbourhood, where the imputed crime was said to have been committed, who were to give the court a True Saying about it from their own knowledge. The well-working of this plan must have been greatly aided by the law of frankpledge,* which was, in those times, carried out in full practice, and which must have compelled the men of each neighbourhood to keep watch upon the conduct of each other. When the system of frankpledge became obsolete, when population increased, and the facilities of moving from place to place became greater, the personal knowledge which the twelve men from the neighbourhood would have respecting an imputed crime, must have become less full and less accurate. The custom, then, would naturally grow up of their hearing the evidence of others who happened to have actually seen the transaction in question, or who could testify, of their own knowledge, to any material fact, whence inferences of guilt or innocence might be drawn. The production before the jurors of documentary proof (where any existed) would be a still more natural step. The jurors would weigh the value of all this in giving their verdict, and thus, from being witnesses themselves, they would gradually become what they now are, the hearers of witnesses, and the deciders upon proof sup-

* See *supra*, p. 45.

plied by others. We see, however, that this last characteristic of modern trial by jury would be slowly and gradually established; and it need not be sought for as an essential part of trial by jury in its original existence.

Keeping in mind the third and last definition of trial by jury which we have been considering, both with respect to what the term necessarily implies, and what it does not necessarily imply, we may proceed to investigate its origin, and the recognition and sanction which it received from the Great Charter.

For the sake of brevity and clearness, I deal here almost solely with trial by jury in criminal cases. But it will be easily understood how the same mode of trying questions of fact would be practised in civil cases. I also limit the inquiry to the subject of the actual trial of guilt or innocence before the jury of twelve (which we now call the petty jury); that is to say, before the jury who give the verdict. The subject of the preliminary inquiry by the grand jury, who, in the name of the sovereign, make presentment to the court of the charge, is one of minor, though of considerable, importance, and can only be incidentally mentioned here.

Some writers have assigned to trial by jury a very specific and a very illustrious parentage. They have represented it as an institution established by the great Alfred, and as the peculiar gem of Anglo-Saxon freedom, which Norman tyranny could not destroy or dim. Others assign to it a still more remote and very general antiquity. They trace it in the ancient tribunals so generally prevalent among the Teutonic nations of the Continent, and also among the Scandinavian; in which "a select number of persons, often twelve, were taken from the community and appointed to try causes, but who did so in the capacity of judges," as well as in the capacity which we understand as the peculiar province of jurors, and "who, when satisfied as to the evidence, awarded, and pronounced the doom."* Such were the Norwegian Laugrettomen, the Swedish Nämbd, the Danish Nœvn, the Jutish Sandemœnd, the Germanic Scabini, and others. But, as Mr. Forsyth, in his excellent "History of Trial by Jury," has pointed out, the difference between all these tribunals and the English juries, is vital and essential. It is in England, and in England alone (unless Normandy should be added), that we find juries quite distinct from the judges who compose the court;—juries who are summoned for the sole purpose of giving a True Saying on a question of fact, and who have nothing to do with the sentence of the court which follows the delivery of their verdict. The same writer has well observed that it is to this peculiar characteristic of the English jury that we owe the preservation of jury trial in this country, while the ancient popular tribunals of Germany, France, and Scandinavia have perished.

"A court of justice where the whole judicial authority is vested in persons taken from time to time from amongst the people at large, with no other qualification required than that of good character, can only be tolerated in a state of society of the most simple kind. As the affairs of civil life become more complicated, and laws more intricate and multiplied, it is plainly impossible that such persons, by whatever name they are called, whether judges or jurors, can be competent to deal with legal questions. The law becomes a science which requires laborious study to comprehend it; and without a body of men trained

* Forsyth's "History of Trial by Jury." See chapters 2 and 3. Though differing from some of the doctrines advocated in this work, I bear willing testimony to the high merit which it displays, and gladly acknowledge my obligations to it for information on many important subjects.

to the task, and capable of applying it, the rights of all would be set afloat—tossed on a wide sea of arbitrary, fluctuating, and contradictory decisions.—Hence in all such popular courts as we are describing, it has been found necessary to appoint jurisconsults to assist with their advice, in matters of law, the uninstructed judges. These at first acted only as assessors, but gradually attracted to themselves and monopolized the whole judicial functions of the court. There being no machinery for keeping separate questions of law from questions of fact, the lay members felt themselves more and more inadequate to adjudge the causes that came before them. They were obliged perpetually to refer to the legal functionary who presided, and the more his authority was enhanced, the more the power of the other members of the court was weakened, and their importance lessened, until it was seen that their attendance might, without sensible inconvenience, be dispensed with altogether. And of course this change was favoured by the Crown, as it thereby gained the important object of being able, by means of creatures of its own, to dispose of the lives and liberties of its subjects under the guise of legal forms. Hence arose in Europe, upon the ruins of the old popular tribunals, the system of single judges appointed by the king and deciding all matters of fact and law, and it brought with it its odious train of secret process and inquisitorial examinations. But the result was inevitable. The ancient courts of Scandinavia and Germany carried in their very constitution the element of their own destruction, and this consisted in the fact that the whole judicial power was in the hands of persons who had no special qualifications for their office.

"Far otherwise has been the case in England. Here the jury never usurped the functions of the judge. They were originally called in to aid the court with information upon questions of fact, in order that the law might be properly applied; and this has continued to be their province to the present day. The utility of such an office is felt in the most refined as well as in the simplest state of jurisprudence. Twelve men of average understanding are at least as competent now as they were in the days of Henry II. to determine whether there is sufficient evidence to satisfy them, that a murder has been committed, and that the party charged with the crime is guilty. The increased technicality of the law does not affect their fitness to decide on the *effect* of proofs. Hence it is that the English jury flourishes still in all its pristine vigour, while what are improperly called the old juries of the Continent have either sunk into decay or been totally abolished."*

It is to be hoped that few educated men of the present day believe in the myth of trial by jury having been invented by Alfred. But some attention to the Anglo-Saxon criminal system is necessary in order to understand the rise and growth of trial by jury in England. The Anglo-Saxon system of criminal judicature had certainly the great principle of trying men publicly before a popular tribunal, and not permitting their fate to be dependent on the subserviency or caprice of any officer of the Crown. This principle is also an essential attribute of trial by jury, and the introduction of that system was without doubt facilitated by its being thus congenial to the old feelings and customs of the mass of the population. But according to the definition which has been above considered and adopted, much more is involved in the idea of trial by jury, which we shall vainly look for in Anglo-Saxon times. An Anglo-Saxon criminal trial did not take place before judges who summoned, as

* Forsyth, p. 9.

their informants on matters of fact, twelve sworn men, or any other definite number; but it took place in presence of all the assembled members of the hundred or the county court, the latter being the tribunal before which most criminal charges were determined. All the land owners of the county, under the presidency of the sheriff and bishop, formed this court. They were its "Sectatores," or suitors. They all took part, or had a right to take part, in a criminal trial, and they all *looked on* to see whether the stipulated proof of guilt or innocence was given. I say they *looked on*, for that term implies more accurately the functions of the county-court suitors in a Saxon criminal trial, than any word which involves the idea of giving and comparing testimony, or of arguing from apparent fact to inferential fact. This arose from the system of the Saxon jurisprudence making a trial, as Palgrave truly remarks,* "rather of the nature of an arithmetical calculation, or a chemical experiment, than what we now understand by the trial of a cause. A certain form was gone through, and according to its result, which was always palpable and decisive one way or the other, the accused person was found guilty or acquitted." This is in no degree an exaggerated account of the Anglo-Saxon system of trying offenders, either by the production of compurgators, or by the ordeal. In the first of these modes, the accused party was required to produce neighbours to swear to their belief in his innocence; and the effect of such neighbours' oaths was estimated not by the means of knowledge possessed by the deponents, or by their characters, or even by their number, but by their "worth" in the Anglo-Saxon scale of persons; according to which an eorl's oath was equal to the oaths of six ceorls, and so on. If the accused party produced

* See Palgrave's "History of the English Commonwealth."

the requisite amount of oath (which was in every case rigorously defined by a curiously-minute penal tariff), he was set free. If the aggregate value of the oaths of his compurgators fell below the prescribed sum, he was pronounced guilty. If the accused person put himself upon the trial by ordeal, the weight of the hot iron which he was to bear, or the depth to which he was to plunge his arm into the hot water, was scrupulously preappointed by the law. The assembly looked on. In trial by compurgation, they added up the amount of the oaths; in trial by ordeal, they watched the effect of the hot iron or hot water upon the culprit's skin, and that was all which they had to do.*

It has already been shown that the Danish Nævninger cannot be regarded as juries. We cannot look on either our Germanic or our Scandinavian ancestors as the founders of that mode of trial. How, then, did trial by jury arise in this country? There are two remaining theories, from one of which this question must be answered. According to one of these opinions, we are chiefly indebted for trial by jury to our Norman ancestors, who are supposed to have brought it hither from Normandy, where it had existed before the Conquest. This is the view of Reeves and of Serjeant Stephens, and was apparently taken by Sir Francis Palgrave when he wrote his "Rise and Progress of the English Commonwealth," though in his more recent "History of Normandy and England" he seems to have changed his judgment. Other

* See Palgrave, *ut supra.* It must not, however, be supposed that, in cases of flagrant guilt, the offender was allowed the chance of escaping through the perjury of compurgators, or the jugglery which was frequent in the ordeal. On the contrary, the slayer who was found near the bleeding corpse, or the thief who was taken on fresh pursuit in possession of the booty, *hond habend* and *back-barend*, was strung up to the nearest bough without ceremony.

writers, of very high eminence, consider that trial by jury first grew up in Anglo-Norman England, and that it was introduced into Normandy itself from England, while our kings were still dukes of that country. Those who hold this theory consider Henry II. and his justiciars as the founders of trial by jury, or rather as the first developers of jury trial out of the different processes and judicial customs which various races and rulers had imported into this island, or had created here. The choice between these two theories depends mainly on the opinion which we form respecting an old treatise called the "Grand Constumier," in which the laws and judicial usages of Normandy are minutely described. It is generally agreed, that the "Grand Constumier" was written before the separation of the Duchy from the English Crown, which we know to have been effected in John's time; but it is suggested that it may have been written after Henry II.'s time, and may only describe usages which had originated in England, and had been introduced from our courts into the Norman courts. But this is a mere hypothesis, without any evidence to uphold it; and it seems more reasonable to regard the law and customs described in the "Grand Constumier" as genuine primitive Norman, than as English importations. But I may remark, that even if we adopt the other view, and consider those Norman institutions as of English origin, it will only make us regard trial by jury as more exclusively and purely an English national institution. In Normandy (besides trial by battle, in which the accused and the accuser, or in some few cases their champions, settled their differences in mortal combat) criminal charges were tried as follows:—An inquest of twenty-four "good and lawful men" was summoned from the neighbourhood where the murder or the theft had been committed. These were the "Jurati" or "Juratores," so called from the oath they took to speak the truth. The officer is directed by the Norman law to select "those who are believed to be best informed of the truth of the matter, and how it happened." None were to be adduced who were known friends or declared enemies of either party. Before the culprit was put upon his trial, a preliminary inquest was taken by four knights, who were questioned concerning their belief of his guilt; and in their presence the officer afterwards interrogated the twenty-four jurors, not in one body, but separately from each other. They were then assembled and confronted with the culprit, who could challenge any one for lawful cause, and if the challenge was allowed, the testimony of that juror was rejected. The presiding officer or judge, then "recorded" the verdict of the jurors, in which twenty at least were required to concur.

The introduction into England of this jury trial, as well as of the trial by battle, was naturally favoured by the Norman judges who presided over the royal courts after the Conquest; and the king's itinerant courts, in which there was no assemblage of local members, soon assumed the functions of trying many of the cases which had previously been tried at the county courts. In all these courts, in the old Aula Regia, in the King's Bench, which sprung from it, and in the courts of the Justices in Eyre, the judges formed the court. They delivered judgment; they caused justice to be executed. But they did not themselves determine on the question of fact as to guilt or innocence. For the answer to that question the court looked to the event of the ordeal, or appeal of battle, or to the true saying of twelve sworn men summoned from the immediate neighbourhood. This was the original trial by jury, which by degrees superseded the other modes of trial. The Normans generally abolished trial by compurgators in criminal cases; and though the trial by ordeal long continued in force, men at length began to regard it in its true light, as an impious absurdity, and a not unfrequent engine of fraud. Henry II., by the laws in which he instituted the trial by twelve sworn knights, in certain civil causes, where real property was the subject of dispute, familiarized men's minds more and more with the theory and practice of jury trial; and the more it was known, the more it was valued. Repeated instances can be traced, in the reigns of his sons, of accused persons being tried by juries on criminal charges, for which mode of trial they paid a sum of money to the king, evidently regarding it as a valuable privilege. At length, in the year 1215, the year of the grant of Magna Carta, the Council of Lateran prohibited throughout Christendom the further continuance of trial by ordeal; and the adoption of trial by jury became unavoidably general in England, in order to dispose of the numerous class of cases, where the charge was preferred, not by an injured individual against the culprit in the form of an appeal, but by the great inquest of the county (our modern grand jury) in the form of a presentment. For, it was only where there was an accusing appellant, that the trial by battle was possible. Still, there was for a long time no mode of compelling a prisoner to put himself on the country, *i. e.* to commit the question of his guilt or innocence to twelve sworn men, summoned from the neighbourhood. Edward I.'s law, inflicting the "*Peine forte et dure,*" on prisoners who refused to plead, was passed to obviate this difficulty; which was not, however, completely got rid of till the reign of George III.

Trial by jury was originally, both in Normandy and here, an appeal to the knowledge of the country. The jury were selected so as to insure the attendance of those who knew most of the transaction. They gave a verdict from their own knowledge of the case, and not from hearing the testimony of others. Gradually, however, a change took place in this respect. At first documentary evidence, such as deeds, charters, &c., throwing light on the matter in dispute, were permitted to be laid before the jurors. The next improvement was to introduce the *vivâ voce* testimony of persons, other than the jurors, who could give any information as to the true circumstances of the case. This was certainly effected by the time of Henry VI., as appears by the treatise of Henry's Chancellor, Fortescue, "De Laudibus Legum Angliæ," in which trial by jury is boasted of as the peculiar glory of the English law, and the whole procedure is minutely described. The production of witnesses who give evidence on oath before the jury is there specially mentioned. But the jurors were still, in Fortescue's time, summoned from the neighbourhood, and were not only allowed, but required, to act upon such knowledge of the facts as they themselves possessed. The complete change in respect to the modern system, whereby jurors are summoned, not from the immediate neighbourhood, but generally from the whole county, and are bound to decide only according to the evidence laid before them, was not effected for some centuries later.*

We now return to the words of Magna Carta, which forbid a freeman to suffer "except by the lawful judgment of his peers, or the law of the land." I believe that the trial by peers here spoken of means trial by jury. The words will bear this meaning; it is certainly impossible to give them any other satisfactory meaning, and it is idle to suppose that they were thus introduced into the Great Charter without being designed to be seriously significant.

* See Forsyth, pp. 164–167.

Some writers who deny the applicability of the thirty-ninth clause of John's Charter, and the twenty-ninth of Henry III., to trial by jury, have supposed that the expression in it respecting a freeman's trial by his peers referred to the old county court and hundred criminal judicature, according to which a freeman was certainly tried *before*, if not *by*, his brother freemen. We cannot suppose (nor have I ever seen it suggested) that this clause of the Charter related to civil actions only, and merely meant those proceedings in county courts and courts baron, in which the attendant suitors, as each other's peers, adjudicated upon claims to property. The whole spirit of the clause, as well as the arrangement of its words, shows clearly that it was mainly designed as a safeguard against wrongful penal procedure, and as providing a just mode of trial in proceedings by the Government against the subject; though it was made sufficiently extensive to protect rights of property as well as rights of persons. It seems to me that the hypothesis of the trial by peers in Magna Carta meaning the criminal judicature of the county and hundred courts, is decisively contradicted by the fact, that the twenty-fourth chapter of John's Charter and the seventeenth of Henry's forbade the sheriff and other inferior officers to hold pleas of the Crown, and thus put an end, almost entirely, to the criminal authority of those tribunals. It has been explained already to how scant a relic the power of the tourn and the courts leet was thereby reduced; and it is impossible to believe that the thirty-ninth clause of John's Charter or the twenty-ninth of Henry's solemnly ordained a mode of trial, which preceding sections of those instruments had (with trifling exceptions) solemnly abolished.

The other hypothesis brought forward by those who deny that the "Judicium Parium" in Magna

Carta means trial by jury is, that the Great Charter, in speaking of trial by peers, had in view solely the great barons, who, as members and peers of the great Court of the king, had a right to be tried there by their peers. Undoubtedly this clause gives a peer of the land an indisputable right to a trial in the House of Lords; but I am led to reject the interpretation which would restrict the operation of the clause to the peerage only, by a consideration of the circumstances and documents connected with the passing of the Great Charter, and which are collected by Blackstone in the work so often referred to.

King John, about a month before the congress at Runnymede, had made a fruitless attempt to detach the great barons from the formidable national rising against him, by offering to them and their immediate followers the privileges which the thirty-ninth chapter of his Great Charter afterwards assured to every freeman of the realm. John's letters of proffered compromise are still in existence,* and in them he writes, "Be it known that we have granted to our barons who are against us, that we will neither take nor disseise them or their men, nor will we pass upon them by force or by arms, except by the law of our realm, *or by the Judgment of their Peers in our Court,*" &c.

The words "in our Court" here clearly limit the privilege of "trial by peers" to the barons, who alone were members of the king's Court, or could have their peers there to try them. Had these words been repeated in the analogous clause in the Great Charter, the interpretation which we are now considering would have appeared correct; but the phraseology of Magna Carta is widely different. Magna Carta says

* See Blackstone's "History of the Charters," and see p. 115, *supra*, and notes.

"NULLUS LIBER HOMO dissaisietur, &c., nisi per legale judicium parium suorum." It is evident that the barôns, when they rejected the insidious offer of John, and refused to make their reform a mere class intrigue instead of a great national movement, took care so to alter the terms of this important stipulation as to make it embrace all the free community. I cannot but believe that the framers of Magna Carta *did* intend to give a solemn sanction to the trial by jury, which had been for years gradually becoming prevalent, and to the merits of which I cannot suppose those illustrious statesmen to have been blind. The expression "trial by peers," as applied to trial by jury, though it may not have enough technical accuracy to satisfy a mere legal antiquary, is, and was at the time, sufficiently appropriate to justify its being so understood; and so it certainly has been generally understood for centuries, by England's jurists, judges, statesmen, and historians.*

It is but a few years since an English writer, by proffering an eulogy on trial by jury, would have laid himself open to a remark, like that of the Spartan's to the rhetorician, who volunteered a panegyric on Her-

* I have not thought it necessary to introduce in the text any formal refutation of a doctrine, which I have found in some modern law books, that although the Judicium Parium in the Great Charter means trial by jury, no peculiar sanction is thereby given to that mode of trial, because the words "vel per legem terræ" follow the words "judicium parium." Had nothing more been intended in the Great Charter than to ordain that a freeman shall not be imprisoned, &c., except by the law of the land, there would have been no need to insert the words, "per legale judicium parium" at all. But if it was designed (as I believe it was) to sanction trial by jury as the rule in our courts, though with necessary exceptions, we see the fullest reason for the Charter being worded as we find it. Of course there would be no "judicium parium" wanted, where the accused party pleaded guilty; or where the trial by battle was lawfully demanded, or where (in civil cases) there was no issue of fact taken, but merely a demurrer raised to the legal sufficiency of pleadings. Many other exceptional cases may be suggested, but they are all such exceptions as prove the rule.

cules: "Why, who ever thought of finding fault with Hercules?" But now the fashion has sprung up of sneering at the decisions of jurors; and we continually hear of schemes to transfer the duty of pronouncing on disputed acts from the jury-box to the bench. Juries are, of course, liable to error; and, when they err, their blunders are made in public, and draw at least a full share of notice; but, on the other hand, we should remember the invariable honesty, and the almost invariable patience, with which juries address themselves to their duty. No spectacle is more markworthy than that which our common law courts continually offer, of the unflagging attention and resolute determination to act fairly and do their best, which is shown by jurors, though wearied by the length of trials, which are frequently rendered more and more wearisome by needless cross-examinations and unduly prolix oratory. The juries of our agricultural districts, with a good share of smock frocks in the jury-box (the constant object of the small whispered wit of pert professionals), deserve to be studied as proofs of how much worth is veiled in low estate in England, which trial by jury calls into action. The thoughtful observer of their enduring zeal in the unpaid discharge of a burdensome function, must reverence from the very depth of his heart the twelve plain, good, and lawful men before him, "the sturdy, honest, unlettered jurors, who derive no dignity but from the performance of their duties." * Such generous fulness and fairness in hearing and thinking before deciding are not found in any other tribunal. Another inestimable advantage peculiar to jury trial is, that it is not known beforehand who will be the jurors in any particular case, so that there is no time given for the work of corruption. It is hardly known,

* Livingston's Preface to the "Louisiana Code."

even at the trial, who the individual jurors are; and, when the trial is over, the members of the jury are dispersed and lost sight of amid the mass of the community. Hence they are, while acting, exempt from all bias of fear and from all selfish motive to favour. And not only are they peculiarly free from all evil influences upon their integrity, but they are free from the suspicion of being so influenced. The people have full confidence in their honesty. The same amount of confidence (whether deserved or not) would not be accorded to permanent paid officials; and there is truth in the seeming paradox of Bentham, that it is even more important that the administration of justice should be believed to be pure than that it should actually be so. Nor are the errors of judgment which juries fall into by any means so numerous as the impugners of the system assert. The jury generally know what they are about much better than their critics do. "Twelve men conversant with life, and practised in those feelings which mark the common and necessary intercourse between man and man,"* are far more likely to discriminate correctly between lying and truth-telling tongues, between bad and good memories, and to come to a sound, common-sense conclusion about disputed facts, than any single intellect is, especially if that single intellect has been "narrowed, though sharpened," by the practice of the profession of the law.

I would also gladly draw attention to another eminent merit of our system of trial by jury, as compared with the system of trial of law and fact by a single person.† Our method of trial gives peculiar guarantees that all who take part in deciding a cause, both the judge and the jury, will exercise their best

* Curran.

† I am indebted to my friend Mr. Henry Pearson, for the suggestion of this argument in favour of trial by jury.

powers of attending and of reasoning, and will not give way to hasty impressions. According to our system, the judge, at the close of a case, sums up the evidence to the jury; and, if he expresses opinions of his own on matters of fact for their consideration, he tells them not only what he thinks, but also why he thinks it. He is, therefore, obliged to take careful notes throughout the trial, and to reason out in his own mind the whole of the case. But, if he had to try the cause, and pronounce in favour of one of the parties, without the intervention of a jury, he would be under no such necessity. He might give way to laziness, and summarily make up his mind in accordance with the bias for or against one party, which is so apt to arise in our minds early in a trial, but which is also so often, as the trial proceeds, proved to be erroneous. Our system gives safeguards of a similar nature against hasty conclusions and imperfect observation on the part of the jury. Each juror knows that it is not by him alone, but by him and his eleven fellow-jurors conjointly, that the verdict is to be given. Each juror, therefore, knows that, if any of the eleven differ from him in opinion at the end of the case, they must argue the matter out among them. Each juror, therefore, watches the entire progress of the trial with his reasoning faculties intent on every part of each litigant's case, and thus prepares himself for a full and fair discussion and judgment of the whole.

It is unquestionably in criminal charges that the value of trial by jury is most apparent, but the prevalence of that mode of trial in civil causes also, so far as they involve disputes of fact, is of incalculable advantage to the community. Mr. Forsyth, in the work which I have before mentioned, refers well on this point to the opinion of one of the most profound political writers of the present age, M. de Tocqueville :—

"We must not suppose that it is trial by jury in criminal cases only that exercises a beneficial influence, or that it can safely stand alone. In his able and philosophical work, *De la Démocratie en Amérique,* M. de Tocqueville avows his conviction that the jury system, if limited solely to criminal trials, is always in peril. And the reasons he gives for this opinion are well worthy of consideration. He says that in that case the people see it in operation only at intervals, and in particular cases; they are accustomed to dispense with it in the ordinary affairs of life, and look upon it merely as one means, and not the sole means, of obtaining justice. But when it embraces civil actions, it is constantly before their eyes, and affects all their interests; it penetrates into the usages of life, and so habituates the minds of men to its forms, that they, so to speak, confound it with the very idea of justice. The jury, he continues, and especially the civil jury, serves to imbue the minds of the citizens of a country with a part of the qualities and character of a judge; and this is the best mode of preparing them for freedom. It spreads amongst all classes a respect for the decisions of the law; it teaches them the practice of equitable dealing. Each man in judging his neighbour thinks that he may be also judged in his turn. This is in an especial manner true of the civil jury; for although hardly any one fears lest he may become the object of a criminal prosecution, every body may be engaged in a lawsuit. It teaches every man not to shrink from the responsibility attaching to his own acts: and this gives a manly character, without which there is no political virtue. It clothes every citizen with a kind of magisterial office; it makes all feel that they have duties to fulfil towards society, and that they take a part in its government; it forces men to occupy themselves with something else than their own affairs, and thus combats that individual selfishness, which is, as it were, the rust of the community. Such are some of the advantages which, according to the view of this profound thinker, result from trial by jury in civil cases.

"But, moreover, it is one great instrument for the education of the people. 'C'est là, à mon avis,' says M. de Tocqueville, 'son plus grand avantage.' He calls it a school into which admission is free and always open, which each juror enters to be instructed in his legal rights, where he engages in daily communication with the most accomplished and enlightened of the upper classes, where the laws are taught him in a practical manner, and are brought down to the level of his apprehension by the efforts of the advocates, the instruction of the judge, and the very passions of the parties in the cause. Hence, says M. de Tocqueville, 'Je le regarde comme l'un des moyens les plus efficaces dont puisse se servir la société pour l'éducation du peuple.'"

I will appeal to one authority more to show that the institution of trial by jury in this country has not only given us the fairest system of trial ever known, but has also for centuries been of incalculable national advantage as an instrument of national education. I gladly quote on this point the no less true than eloquent words of the great and good Dr. Arnold:—"The effect of any particular arrangement of the judicial power is seen directly in the greater or less purity with which justice is administered; but there is a further effect, and one of the highest importance, in its furnishing to a greater or less portion of the nation one of the best means of moral and intellectual culture, the opportunity, namely, of exercising the functions of a judge. I mean, that to accustom a number of persons to the intellectual exercise of attending to, and weighing and comparing evidence, and to the moral exercise of being placed in a high and responsible situation, invested with one of God's own attributes—that of judgment; and having to determine with authority, between truth and falsehood, right and wrong—is to furnish them with very high means of moral and intellectual culture; in other words, it is providing them with one of the highest kinds of education."

The great constitutional enactments of Magna Carta have, from the very earliest times, been regarded in that light, and treated not as temporary regulations, but as the fundamental institutions of our government and laws. Their confirmation was repeatedly exacted from the reigning sovereign by our parliaments; not because the Great Charter was supposed to become invalid without such ratification, but in order to impress more solemnly on impatient princes and profligate statesmen their duty of respecting the great constitutional ordinances of the realm. The most awful rites of religion were called in aid by the English clergy (to whom, as Hallam remarks, we are much indebted for their zeal in behalf of liberty during the thirteenth century), to bind the slippery consciences of John's son, and grandson, and to awe them by the terrors of excommunication from breaking the great compact between the Crown and the people. The most earnest efforts were also employed to make the Great Charter familiarly known throughout the land by all, as the common birthright of all, and the most stringent measures of law were devised to insure the prompt punishment of any who should dare to violate it. To quote an instance or two of this:—by the *Confirmatio Chartarum*, 25 Ed. I. (part of which has already been cited), it was ordained that—

"The charters of liberties and of the forest should be kept in every parish; and that they should be sent under the king's seal as well to the justices of the forest as to others, to all sheriffs and other officers, and to all the cities in the realm, accompanied by a writ commanding them to publish the said charters, and declare to the people that the king had confirmed them in all points. All justices, sheriffs, mayors, and other ministers were directed to allow them when pleaded before them; and any judgment contrary thereto was to be null and void. The charters were to be sent under the king's seal to all cathedral churches throughout the realm, there to remain, and to be read to the people twice a year. It was ordained that all archbishops and bishops should pronounce sentence of excommunication against those who, by word, deed, or counsel, did contrary to the aforesaid charters."

By the "*Articuli super Cartas*," a statute passed in the 28th Ed. I., the charters are ordered to be read by the sheriffs four times a year, before the people of the shire in open county court. And the statute further ordains, that for the punishing of offenders against the charters—

"There shall be chosen, in every shire court, by the commonalty of the same shire, three substantial men, knights, or other lawful, wise, and well disposed persons, which should be justices sworn and assigned by the king's letters patent under the great seal, to hear and determine without any other writ, but only their commission, such plaints as shall be made upon all those that commit or offend against any point contained in the aforesaid charters, in the shires where they be assigned, as well within franchises as without, and as well for the king's officers out of their places as for others; and to hear the plaints from day to day without any delay, and to determine them, without allowing the delays which be allowed by the common law. And the same knights shall have power to punish all such as shall be attainted of any trespass done contrary to any point of the aforesaid charters where no remedy was before by the common law, as before is said, by imprisonment, or by ransom, or by amerciament, according to the trespass."

A volume, precious to Englishmen for the merits both of its subject and of its authors, might easily be collected from the panegyrists of Magna Carta. Lord Chatham has been already quoted ; we may well recall the words of one statesman more, who is selected on account of his eminence as an historian, and as a philosophical and political inquirer. His eloquent observations are also the more valuable for citation here, because they forcibly point out the existence in our constitution of that law of progress and development, the operation of which it is one of the principal objects of these pages to illustrate. Sir James Mackintosh says of Magna Carta :—

"It was a peculiar advantage that the consequences of its principles were, if we may so speak, only discovered gradually and slowly. It gave out on each occasion only as much of the spirit of liberty and reformation as the circumstances of succeeding generations required, and as their character would safely bear. For almost five centuries it was appealed to as the decisive authority on behalf of the people, though commonly so far only as the necessities of each case demanded. Its effect in these contests was not altogether unlike the grand process by which Nature employs snows and frosts to cover her delicate germs, and to hinder them from rising above the earth till the atmosphere has acquired the mild and equal temperature which insures them against blights. On the English nation, undoubtedly, the Charter has contributed to bestow the union of establishment with improvement. To all mankind it set the first example of the progress of a great people for centuries, in blending their tumultuary democracy and haughty nobility with a fluctuating and vaguely-limited monarchy, so as at length to form from these discordant materials the only form of free government which experience had shown to be reconcilable with widely-extended dominions. Whoever in any future age or yet unborn nation may admire the felicity of the expedient which converted the power of taxation into the shield of liberty, by which discretionary and secret imprisonment was rendered impracticable, and portions of the people were trained to exercise a larger share of judicial power than ever was allotted to them in any other civilized State, in such a manner as to secure, instead of endangering, public tranquillity; whoever exults at the spectacle of enlightened and independent assemblies, which, under the eye of a well-informed nation, discuss and determine the laws and policy likely to make communities great and happy; whoever is capable of comprehending all the effects of such institutions with all their possible improvements upon the mind and genius of a people, —is sacredly bound to speak with reverential gratitude of the authors of the Great Charter. To have produced it, to have preserved it, to have matured it, constitute the immortal claim of England upon the esteem of mankind. Her Bacons and Shakspeares, her Miltons and Newtons, with all the truth which they have revealed, and all the generous virtue which they have inspired, are of inferior value when compared with the subjection of men and their rulers to the principles of justice, if, indeed, it be not more true that these mighty spirits could not have been formed except under equal laws, nor roused to full activity without the influence of that spirit which the Great Charter breathed over their forefathers." *

* Mackintosh, "Hist. Eng.," vol. i. p. 221.

## CHAPTER XIV.

Progress of the Constitution during the Reigns of the ten last Plantagenet Kings.—Growing Importance of the House of Commons.—Qualifications of Members and Electors.—Prerogatives of the Crown.—State of the Population.—Jurors.—Boroughs—Number of Electors.

It has been shown in the preceding pages that the thirteenth century saw the commencement of our nationality, and that during it the great foundations of our constitution were laid. But it would be ignorant rashness to assert that the organization of our institutions was complete even at the time of the death of Edward I., A.D. 1307. What was said of the Roman Constitution by two of its greatest statesmen, and written by another, may with equal truth be averred of the English,—that no one man and no one age sufficed for its full production.* But its kindly growth went rapidly on during the reigns of the later Plantagenets; and the historian of the last centuries of the middle ages,† traces with pride and pleasure the increase and systemization of the power of the House of Commons in asserting and maintaining the

* "Tum Lælius, nunc fit illud Catonis certius, nec temporis unius, nec hominis esse constitutionem reipublicæ."—*Cicero De Republica*, lib. ii. 21.

† See throughout the 3rd part of the 8th chapter of Hallam's "Middle Ages," and the valuable supplemental notes to the last edition. The student may also examine with great advantage the seven last lectures of the 2nd part of M. Guizot's "History of Representative Government."

exclusive right of taxation; in making the grant of supplies dependent on the redress of grievances; in directing and checking the public expenditure; in establishing the necessity of the concurrence of both Houses of Parliament in all legislation; in securing the people against illegal ordinances and interpolations of the statutes; in inquiring into abuses; in controlling the royal administration; in impeaching and bringing to punishment bad ministers and other great offenders against the laws and liberties of the land; and in defining and upholding their own immunities and privileges.

The limits of this work will only permit the citation here of a few proofs of the progress of our constitution during this time. More elaborate treatises must be referred to for full information.

In the second year of Edward II.'s reign we find the Commons, when applied to for a grant of money to the Crown, making it "upon condition that the king should take advice and grant redress upon certain articles wherein they are aggrieved. They complain that they are not governed as they ought to be, especially as to the articles of the Great Charter." *

In 1322 a statute was passed, declaring that "the matters to be established for the estate of the king and of his heirs, and for the estate of the realm and of the people, should be treated, accorded, and established in parliament, by the king, and by the assent of the prelates, earls, and barons, *and the commonalty* of the realm, according as had been before accustomed." Mr. Hallam well observes that "this statute not only establishes, by a legislative declaration, the present constitution of parliament, but recognizes it as already standing upon a custom of some length of time."† During Edward III.'s long and active reign,

* Hallam, p. 40.

† "Constitutional History of England," vol. i. p. 5.

the wars in which that sovereign was almost continually engaged, kept him dependent on his parliament for supplies of money; and the power of the Commons was thereby materially augmented, notwithstanding the high abilities of Edward, and his fondness for his royal prerogatives. The king was continually attempting to raise money by arbitrary and illegal imposts; but the Commons never ceased to remonstrate against such acts, and to insist on the fundamental right of there being no taxation without consent. The complete and permanent division of parliament into two Houses, as at present, is admitted by all writers to have been established in this reign, if not earlier.

The Commons have now formed themselves into a body or estate of the realm, distinct from the estate of the prelates and abbots, or spiritual peers, distinct from the estate of the temporal peers, distinct from the Crown, but comprehending all the rest of the free human beings that live in the land. A distinct House of Parliament represents this estate of the Commons, and is now generally (and with substantial, though not literal accuracy) spoken of as being itself that which it represents, as the Commons of the realm.

The leading feature of our constitutional history is no longer a conflict between the king and the barons, wherein the Commons, as auxiliaries of the barons, play a mere secondary part. That conflict has, to a great extent, ceased. The reign of Edward III. presents to us the aspect of the baronial aristocracy grouped round the throne, while the Commons are the party of progress. Not that the nobles of England have given up their high station of protectors of the liberties of England; on great emergencies, especially in the reign of Richard II., we shall see them acting in unison with the Commons in the national cause. But, as a general rule, it is the Lower House of Parliament that now supports the struggle for constitutional rights and for the advancement of popular power. "The Commons do not, indeed, aspire to snatch the supreme power from the hands of the king and the barons ; they would not have strength enough to do so, nor do they entertain any thought of it ; but they resist every encroachment upon those rights which they are beginning to know and to appreciate ; they have acquired a consciousness of their own importance, and know that all public affairs properly fall under their cognizance. Finally, either by their petitions, or by their debates in reference to taxation, they are daily obtaining a larger share in the government, exercise control over affairs which, fifty years before, they never heard mentioned, and become, in a word, an integral and almost indispensable part of the great national council, and of the entire political machine."*

It is also observable, that the Commons, during this reign, in their opposition to the royal power, do not attack the king himself, but they lay all blame upon his ministers, and begin to "assert and popularize the principles of parliamentary responsibility." They frequently addressed Edward, complaining of his counsellors and officers ; and in 1376 we find them exercising, for the first time, the formidable constitutional weapon of impeachment. In that year the Commons accused, before the House of Lords, the Lords Latimer and Nevil, and four commoners, Lyons, Ellis, Peachey, and Bury, who had been employed by the king in revenue matters, for various acts of ministerial misconduct.† The Lords tried and convicted them, except Bury, who did not appear to take his

* Guizot's "History of Representative Government," part ii. lect. 22.

† See 3 Rot. Parl., 323. An erroneous reference to Rymer is given in Hallam.

trial. The records of these proceedings well deserve attention, especially of the trials of Latimer and Nevil.

The right of impeachment most strikingly illustrates the great principle that the ministers and servants of the Crown are responsible for acts of misconduct in which they take part, notwithstanding that they may have acted under the order of the sovereign. But the exercise of this principle is not limited to parliamentary impeachment. It is far more ample and useful.

The supremacy of law over regal power has been made a rule of universal and constant practical application in England, by our courts early recognizing the right of every subject, who has been injured by any illegal stretch of power, to sue the officer who has been the minister of injury to him, and to recover, by the verdict of a jury, compensation in damages for the trespass that has been committed against him. Closely connected with this is the recognized right of every individual to resist the execution of an illegal act against his person or property, although it is an officer of the regular executive power of the State who seeks to commit the act, and who seeks to do it in his official character. It is no excuse for the officer that he acts by the order of regular superior authority.* Professor Lieber has well observed that this principle of ministerial responsibility is so natural to the English and their descendants in the United

* A rational exception to this rule was made in George II.'s reign by a statute (24 Geo. II. c. 44), indemnifying constables, who act, *bonâ fide*, under a justice's warrant. The same statute requires that notice of action be given to a justice, before he is sued for anything done in execution of his office, and enables him to make a legal tender of amends. For other statutes of a similar nature, see Chitty's Statutes, Title "Justices of the Peace." The late Act, 11 and 12 Victoria, c. 44, has carried indulgence to magisterial incompetency to a mischievous extent.

States of America, that few of us are struck with its vital importance to civil liberty, and with the extent to which it distinguishes a thorough government of law from a government of functionaries. In other countries an officer cannot be sued for his official acts, without the injured party first obtaining from the superior powers permission to bring his action, and obedience to the acts of regularly-constituted officials is in all cases required.*

* Lieber on "Civil Liberty and Self Government," p. 91. The whole passage is so instructive that I shall lay it before the reader; who, however, cannot do better than make Professor Lieber's volume the subject of attentive study, if he wishes to store his mind with sound leading principles in statesmanship and jurisprudence:—

"The guarantee of the supremacy of the law leads to a principle which, so far as I know, it has never been attempted to transplant from the soil inhabited by Anglican people, and which, nevertheless, has been, in our system of liberty, the natural production of a thorough government of law, as contra-distinguished to a government of functionaries. It is so natural to the Anglican tribe that few think of it as essentially important to civil liberty, and it is of such vital importance that none who have studied the acts of government elsewhere, can help recognising it as an indispensable element of civil liberty.

"It is simply this, that, on the one hand, every officer, however high or low, remains personally answerable to the affected person for the legality of the act he executes, no matter whether his lawful superior has ordered it or not, and even, whether the executive officer had it in his power to judge of the legality of the act he is ordered to do or not; and that, on the other hand, every individual is authorised to resist an unlawful act, whether executed by an otherwise lawfully-appointed officer or not. The resistance is made at the resister's peril. In all other countries, obedience to the officer is demanded in all cases, and redress can only take place after previous obedience. Occasionally this principle acts harshly upon the officer; but we prefer this inconvenience to the inroad which its abandonment would make in the government of law. We will not submit to individual men, but only to men who are, and when they are the organs of the law. A *coup-d'état*, such as we have lately seen in France, would not be feasible in a nation accustomed to this principle. All the answer which the police officers gave to men like General Cavaignac, who asked them whether they were aware they committed a high crime in arresting a representative of the people, was that they had orders from their superior, and had nothing to do with the question of legality.

"Take as an instance of the opposite to the French principle of that huge institution called *gens-d'armerie*, the following simple case.

"A sheriff, provided with the proper warrant, has the right, after request and denial to open the house-door, forcibly to open it, if a third

Edward frequently asked the advice of his parliament on questions of war and peace. Some have thought that this was done by the king through artifice, with a view to throw the responsibility of warfare on the Commons, and prevent their murmuring, when asked for subsidies, but that the Commons avoided the responsibility. But M. Guizot contends, I think correctly, that the Commons of the 14th century frequently sought and exercised the power of thus interfering in the administration of the public affairs of the kingdom. "They accepted the attendant responsibility, and they gained greatly by it. In 1328, during the minority of Edward, and while Mortimer reigned in his name, the treaty of peace with Scotland, which fully liberated that kingdom from all feudal subordination to England, was con-

party has taken refuge in it, or sent his goods there. "Every man's house is his castle," will not protect any one but the *bonâ fide* dweller in it. Nevertheless the sheriff, provided with his legal warrant, does it at his own peril; for if he break open the house, however well his suspicion may be grounded, and neither the party nor the goods sought for be there, the sheriff is a trespasser, and as such answerable to the inhabitant of the house before the courts of the land. This may be inconvenient in single cases. It may be that the maxim which has been quoted has 'been carried as far as the true principles of political practice will warrant—perhaps beyond what, in the scale of sound reason and good policy, they will warrant.' I doubt it, whatever the inconvenience in single cases may be. All law is inconvenient in some cases; but even if this opinion were well founded, how august, on the other hand, appears the law—I do not mean a single statute, but the whole self-evolving system of a common law of the land—that errs on the side of individual liberty against the public power and the united weight of Government! Another proof of the uniform acknowledgment of this principle and essential pillar of civil liberty, is this, that when a British minister obtains an act of indemnity, which is an act of impunity for certain illegal acts, which, nevertheless, necessity demanded, the act of indemnity is never for him alone, but it expresses that the act shall also cover what the inferior officers have done by the direction of the minister in the premises.

"In conclusion I would remark, that it is wholly indifferent who gives the order. If it be illegal, the person who executes it remains responsible for the act, although the president or the king should have ordered it, or the offending person should be a soldier obeying his commander. It is a stern law, but it is a sacred principle, and it has worked well."

cluded with the consent of the parliament. The Commons are expressly mentioned; and we may suppose that Mortimer was anxious thereby to cover his own responsibility for a disgraceful treaty. In 1331, Edward consulted the parliament on the question of peace or war with France, on account of his continental possessions, and also upon his projected journey to Ireland. The parliament gave its opinion in favour of peace, and of the king's departure for Ireland. In 1336, it urged the king to declare war against Scotland, saying: 'That the king could no longer, with honour, put up with the wrongs and injuries daily done to him and his subjects by the Scots.'* In 1341, after Edward's first victories in France, the parliament pressed him to continue the war, and furnished him with large subsidies; and all classes of society bestirred themselves to support the king in a conflict which had become national. In 1343, the parliament was convoked to examine and advise what had best be done in the existing state of affairs, especially in regard to the treaty recently concluded by the king with his enemy the king of France. Sir Bartholomew Burghersh told the parliament that 'as the war was begun by the common advice of the prelates, great men, and Commons, the king could not treat of, or make peace, without the like assent.'† The two Houses deliberated separately, and gave their opinion that the king ought to make peace if he could obtain a truce that would be honourable and advantageous to himself and his friends; but if not, the Commons declared that they would aid and maintain his quarrel with all their power. In 1344, when the truce with the king of France had been broken off by him, the parliament, on being consulted, manifested a desire for peace, but thought it could only be

* "Parliamentary History," vol. i. p. 93. † Ibid., p. 106.

obtained by carrying on the war with energy, and voted large subsidies for the purpose. In 1348, the war had become increasingly burdensome; all the subsidies proved insufficient; and the king again consulted the parliament 'concerning the war undertaken with its consent.' The Commons, perceiving that they had gone rather too far in their language, now showed greater reserve, and answered 'that they were not able to advise anything concerning the war, and therefore desired to be excused as to that point; and that the king will be advised by his nobles and Council, and what shall be by them determined, they would consent unto, confirm, and establish.'* In 1354, the Lord Chamberlain, by the king's command, informed the parliament: 'That there was great hopes of bringing about a peace between England and France, yet the king would not conclude anything without the consent of his Lords and Commons. Wherefore he demanded of them, in the king's name, whether they would assent and agree to a peace, if it might be had by treaty.' To this the Commons replied at first, 'that what should be agreeable to the king and his Council in making of this treaty, would be so to them;' but on being asked again, 'If they consented to a perpetual peace, if it might be had,' they all unanimously cried out, Yea! Yea! † Finally on the 25th of January, 1361, peace having been concluded by the treaty of Bretigny, the parliament was convoked, the treaty was submitted to its inspection and received its approval, and on the 31st a solemn ceremony took place in the cathedral church at Westminster, when all the members of parliament, both Lords and Commons, individually swore upon the altar to observe the peace.

* "Parliamentary History," vol. i. p. 115.
† Ibid., p. 122.

"In 1368, the negotiations with Scotland were submitted to the consideration of the parliament; the king of Scotland, David Bruce, offered peace on condition of being relieved from all homage of his crown to the king of England. The Lords and Commons replied, 'That they could not assent to any such peace, upon any account, without a disherison of the king, his heirs and crown, which they themselves were sworn to preserve, and therefore must advise him not to hearken to any such propositions;'* and they voted large subsidies to continue the war.

"In 1369, the king consulted the parliament as to whether he should recommence the war with France, because the conditions of the last treaty had not been observed; the parliament advised him to do so, and voted subsidies.

"These facts prove the most direct and constant intervention of the Commons in matters of peace and war. Nor did they seek to elude this responsibility, so long as the war was successful and national. When the subsidies became excessive, they manifested greater reserve in giving their opinion beforehand. When fortune turned "decidedly against Edward III., at the close of his reign, the Commons, as we have seen, took advantage of the right of intervention which they had acquired, to possess themselves also of the right of impeaching the ministers, to whom they attributed the misfortunes of the time. All this follows in the natural course of things, and clearly demonstrates the continually-increasing influence of the Commons in political matters."

The acknowledged right of the Commons to participate in legislation is proved (as M. Guizot well observes) by the very phraseology of the statute book. "When we open a collection of the statutes of this

* "Parliamentary History," p. 131.

reign, we find at the head of each statute one of the two following formulas: '*A la requeste de la commune de son roïalme par lor pétitions mises devant lui et son conseil, par assent des prélats, comtes, barons, et autres grantz, au dit parlement assemblés,*' &c.* Or: '*Par assent des prélats, comtes, et barons, et de tote la commune du roïalme, au dit parlement assemblés,*' &c.† Sometimes the statute begins with these words: '*Ce sont les choses que notre seigneur le roi, les prélats, seignours, et la commune ont ordiné en ce presént parlement.*'" ‡ §

Another important fact characterising the reign of Edward III., is "the regularity with which the parliament was convoked. A measure was adopted for this purpose in 1312, during the reign of Edward II., by the Lords Ordainers. Subsequently we meet with two statutes relative to the convocation of this assembly, one of which was passed in 1331, and the other in 1362. Finally, in 1377, the last year of the reign of Edward III., the Commons themselves demanded by petition that the sessions of parliament should take place regularly every year. During the reign of Edward III., we may enumerate forty-eight sessions of parliament, which make nearly one session in each year.

"Nor did the parliament merely provide for the regularity of its convocation; it took measures, at the same time, to ensure the security of its deliberations. In 1332, a royal proclamation forbade all persons to wear coats of mail, or to carry any other offensive or

* "At the request of the Commons of his realm, by their petitions laid before him and his council, and by the assent of the prelates, earls, barons, and other nobles, in the said parliament assembled."

† "By the assent of the prelates, earls, and barons, and of all the Commons of the realm, in the said parliament assembled."

‡ "These are the things which our lord the king, the prelates, Lords, and Commons have ordained in this present parliament."

§ Guizot.

defensive arms, in those towns in which the parliament was sitting: it also prohibited all games and diversions which might disturb the deliberations of the assembly. The frequent recurrence of proclamations of this kind announces the formation of a regular assembly." *

During the twenty-two years of the reign of Richard II., the power of the Commons made rapid progress, and at the accession of Henry IV. "of the three capital points in contest while Edward III. reigned, 1st, that money could not be levied; 2nd, or laws enacted without the Commons' consent; and 3rd, that the administration of Government was subject to their inspection and control, the first was absolutely decided in their favour, the second was at least perfectly admitted in principle, and the last was confirmed by frequent exercise." † They also claimed and maintained a right to appropriate to special purposes the supplies which they granted to the king; and by the impeachment of the Earl of Suffolk, Richard's favourite minister in 1386, they confirmed their right of wielding that formidable but necessary weapon against the ministers of the royal will. The attempt made by the king in 1398, to obtain a packed House of Commons deserves notice, as a royal confession that it was necessary to rule the nation through a parliament. The temporary triumph which the king obtained by this device, was soon followed by his overthrow and deposition; and thenceforth a free parliament became the popular cry when the common liberties were supposed to be in danger. ‡

The princes of the House of Lancaster, conscious that they reigned rather by the people's choice than by any lineal title to the Crown, did not venture on

* Guizot. † Hallam's "Middle Ages," vol. iii. p. 124.
‡ "Penny Cyclopædia," art. "Borough."

any open resistance to the powers which the Lower House of parliament had obtained, and they regularly held a parliament in almost every year. Some arbitrary acts on the part of the Crown may be found during their reigns, but they are far less numerous than had formerly been the case, and are clearly exceptional to the regular course of government. Even Henry V., in the zenith of his glory and popularity, never ventured to slight the authority of parliament in granting supplies in general legislation, and in participating in the administration of affairs. As the noble and learned historian of "England and France under the House of Lancaster" observes,* "Whatever money was raised by taxes, Henry owed entirely to their votes; and, as the intoxication into which his victories threw them along with the country, never tempted him to encroach upon their functions, so he showed his sense of their power by letting their chagrin at his only disaster pass away before he asked for any aid to re-establish his fortunes. An important change in the financial system was introduced in his time, and it showed in a striking manner the ascendancy of the parliament, for it was entirely of parliamentary creation,—I mean the practice of pledging, as a security for loans made to the Crown, duties already granted."

Our parliaments under the House of Lancaster, besides maintaining the rights which had been acquired by their predecessors, established others of great importance. At least it is in the records of that period that we first obtain definite proof of them. Hallam cites at length † a remarkable passage from the Rolls of Parliament of 9th Henry IV., which

* P. 236.

† 3 "Middle Ages," p. 102; see, also, Guizot's "History of Representative Government," part ii. lect. 25.

shows the recognition of two important constitutional principles; namely, 1st, that all money bills must originate in the House of Commons; and 2ndly, the right of the Houses that the king should take no cognizance of the subject of their deliberations until they had come to a decision upon it, and brought that decision regularly before him.

With respect to the first of these two points it may be further remarked, that, in the earliest parliaments, the regular course was for all statutes to originate in the proceedings of the House of Commons.

The Commons used to petition the Crown, and the king, on their petition, and by the advice of the Lords, used to enact. By ancient custom the king used to reply to all the petitions of the Commons at the end of the session; and statutes founded on petitions that were sanctioned by the Lords and granted by the Crown, were afterwards drawn up by the king's officers. Frequent frauds were committed by those functionaries, who did not faithfully reproduce in the statutes the petitions out of which they had originated. The Commons continually complained of this trickery; but at last, in Henry VI.'s time, they began to guard effectually against it, by preparing bills in their own House in the form of complete statutes, which they sent up to the House of Lords, that they might be discussed in that assembly, and, if adopted there, be presented to the king, who then had nothing more to do than to give or refuse his sanction. No precise date can be named when the House of Lords began to originate bills in their own House, which were sent thence to the Commons. But the custom soon grew up; and it became the rule of parliament that bills may commence in either House, except money bills, which, as we have seen, must come from the Commons.

The essential right of freedom of debate is to

some extent involved in the second principle of parliamentary law, which has been mentioned as solemnly recognized in the ninth year of Henry IV. There is, however, no point of parliamentary privilege which the Crown conceded to the Commons more unwillingly than full liberty of speech; but the Commons felt its full importance, and struggled manfully and perseveringly to secure it. An attack which Richard II., in the last year of his reign, made upon Thomas Haxey, a member of the Lower House, for words spoken in debate, was no slight cause of the popular indignation by which that misguided prince was driven from the throne. One of the first acts of Henry IV.'s first parliament was to annul the proceedings against Haxey. During this reign we find the Speaker of the House of Commons demanding liberty of speech of the king at the opening of every session. Every circumstance proves that under Henry IV. the Commons used greater liberty of speech than they had previously enjoyed. It was, indeed, made a subject of special praise to Sir John Tibetot, Speaker in the parliament of 1406. The king soon manifested great distrust of the extension given to this right, which was probably exercised with some of the rudeness which often marked the manners of that time. In 1410, he told the Commons that he hoped that they would no longer use unbecoming language, but act with moderation. In 1411, the Speaker, Sir Thomas Chaucer, having made the usual demand at the opening of the session, the king replied that he would allow the Commons to speak as others before had done, but that "he would have no novelties introduced, and would enjoy his prerogative." The Speaker requested three days to give a written answer to this observation, and then replied "that he desired no other protestation than what other Speakers had made; and that if he should speak anything to the king's displeasure, it might be imputed to his own ignorance only, and not to the body of the Commons," which the king granted.

We hear of no infringement upon the liberty of speech enjoyed by the Commons until the parliament of 1455, at which time a deputy from Bristol, Thomas Young, complained that he had been arrested and imprisoned in the Tower, six years before, on account of a motion which he had brought forward in the House. The object of this motion had been, to declare, that as the king then had no children, the Duke of York was the legitimate heir to the throne. The Commons transmitted this petition to the Lords, and the king commanded his Council to do whatever might be judged fitting on behalf of the petitioner.*

Other points of parliamentary privilege, such as the freedom of members from arrest, first attract attention in the records of the Lancastrian reigns; but with regard to one very important matter, the right to investigate and determine contested elections, the Commons were as yet unarmed. The judgment of election disputes was exercised by the king and his Council. And it was at this epoch that it was solemnly declared that the Commons had no share in the general judicial functions of parliament. This declaration was made in 1399, at the suggestion of the Commons themselves, and by the mouth of the Archbishop of Canterbury, who said: "That the Commons were only petitioners, and that all judgment belonged to the king and Lords; unless it was in statutes, grants of subsidies, and such like." Since this period the Commons, when they desired to interfere in judgments otherwise than by impeachment, were obliged to employ the means of bills of attainder. They

* Guizot's "History of Representative Government," part ii. lect. 25.

adopted this plan in the case of the Duke of Suffolk in 1450, and very frequently afterwards.*

The Lancastrian period of our parliamentary history is peculiarly remarkable for the statutes which were then passed respecting elections. Besides the immediate subjects which they deal with, they bear strong evidence of the increasing importance of the House of Commons, and of the anxiety of the Crown to influence the popular assembly, which it could not with safety neglect or openly control. An ancient statute of Edward I. ordains that elections ought to be free, and forbids the disturbance of their freedom.† And in the fifth year of Richard II.'s reign, an Act

* See Guizot, *ut supra*, lect. 25. The following observations of Mr. May, on bills of attainder, deserve attention:—"The proceedings of parliament in passing bills of attainder, and of pains and penalties, do not vary from those adopted in regard to other bills. They may be introduced into either House; they pass through the same stages; and, when agreed to by both Houses, they receive the royal assent in the usual form; but the parties who are subjected to these proceedings are admitted to defend themselves by counsel and witnesses before both Houses; and the solemnity of the proceedings would cause measures to be taken to enforce the attendance of members upon their service in parliament. In evil times, this summary power of parliament to punish criminals by statute has been perverted and abused; and in the best of times it should be regarded with jealousy; and whenever a fitting occasion arises for its exercise, it is undoubtedly the highest form of parliamentary judicature. In impeachments, the Commons are but accusers and advocates; while the Lords alone are judges of the crime. On the other hand, in passing bills of attainder the Commons commit themselves by no accusations, nor are their powers directed against the offender; but they are judges of equal jurisdiction and with the same responsibility as the Lords; and the accused can only be condemned by the unanimous judgment of the Crown, the Lords and the Commons." The principle which Mr. Raikes lays down in the 2nd volume of his work the "Constitution," seems to me a just one. "There can be little doubt of the competence of any community to punish great offences against itself by a retrospective national act. Such a right would seem to flow from the principle of national independence, but should not be extended to capital punishments. A community may exercise the right of separating from itself any peccant member, but such right does not extend to separate such member from the whole human race, save for such conduct as would be universally punished."—P. 73.

† Statute of Westminster the First, c. v.; see Reeve, "Hist. Law" c. iv.

was passed to punish sheriffs who were negligent in making returns of parliamentary writs, or who left out of the returns any cities or boroughs which were bound, and formerly were wont, to send members to parliament. With these exceptions, and some few other unimportant ones, it is in the reigns of the Fourth, Fifth, and Sixth Henrys that we first find the important subject of the election and return of members become an object of earnest legislative attention.

It is to be remembered, that the great instruments of the Crown, in packing a House of Commons, were the sheriffs, who were nominated by the king. When a parliament was convened, it was to these officers that the royal precept was addressed for the election of knights, citizens, and burgesses. The king's writ required that two knights should be elected for the county, and that the sheriff should cause to be elected two citizens for each city, and two burgesses for each borough in his bailiwick. As no particular cities and boroughs were specified, the sheriffs assumed a discretionary power as to what places they would consider fit cities and boroughs to return members to parliament; and this power was often grossly abused by those functionaries, who omitted or included boroughs most fraudulently and irregularly. This wholesale garbling of parliamentary representation was checked by the statute of Richard II., which has been referred to; but the sheriffs still had the power of influencing the elections and falsifying the returns of individual members, especially of knights of the shire, as these were elected in the county court, at which the sheriff himself presided.* This power was frequently used by

* A practice was attempted at one time to have the burgesses elected at the county court by delegates from the boroughs. See Hallam, p. 116, and note to p. 117; and see "Penny Cyclopædia," Boroughs, p. 188.

them at the instigation of the Crown, or of great noblemen, or for private ends of their own. Richard II. had largely availed himself of this dishonest engine in packing the House of Commons which he brought together two years before his deposition. The parliaments of his successor strove vigilantly to prevent such malpractices for the future. The statute of the 7th Henry IV. was passed "on the grievous complaints of the Commons against undue elections for shires." It contained regulations for the time and manner of the election of knights; and, among other things, ordained that all those who should be present at the county court, as well suitors duly summoned for that cause as others, should enter upon the election of knights; and then in full court they were to proceed freely and indifferently, notwithstanding any request or command to the contrary. The importance of this clause, with respect to the question of how far the elective franchise extended, will be hereafter considered. The statute also contained several clauses to secure a true return by the sheriff of the result of the election; and by an Act passed four years afterwards, severe penalties were imposed for any breach of its provisions.

Notwithstanding these enactments, the king's ministers, especially during the early part of Henry VI.'s reign, continued their attempts to influence elections; and used for this purpose not only the agency of the sheriffs, but that also of the mayors and other officers of the cities and boroughs. It was during this period that a change in the character of our municipal institutions was commenced, which will be presently described; a change that made them more open than before to the influence of corruption and intimidation. The parliament sought to check these practices in the twenty-third year of Henry VI., when it was enacted that, under peril of severe penalties, every sheriff should deliver a proper precept to the mayor or bailiff of each city or borough in the shire to elect citizens or burgesses for parliament; that the mayors and bailiffs should make true return of those which be chosen by the citizens and burgesses of the cities or boroughs where such elections be made.

The constitutional history of the reign of the Lancastrian kings is also very important, by reason of the attempts then made by the Legislature to determine the qualifications both of electors and of persons to be elected. It has been seen, that the statute 7 Hen. IV. c. 15,* while guarding against the malpractices of sheriffs in county elections, recognized or established the right of all persons who were present at the county court to vote for knights of the shire. But in the eighth year of Henry VI. was passed an Act that was framed in a very different spirit. This remarkable statute, the first disfranchising one upon record, reciting the grievous uproar and disorder at elections, chiefly occasioned by the "outrageous and excessive number of people of small substance or no value," enacted, "that for the future knights of the shire shall be chosen by people dwelling and resident in the counties, whereof every one of them shall have free land or tenement to the value of forty shillings by the year at least, above all charges." This was, indeed, a most stringent enactment, operating as a sweeping disfranchisement; for forty shillings then were equal to at least twenty pounds of the present day. This statute, coupled with one passed two years afterwards (which required the voter's freehold to be situate in the county for which he votes), contains the basis of the right of voting for counties ever since, regulated from time to time by various statutes prescribing the requisite length of

* *Supra*, p. 247.

possession, or receipt of rents and profits. The right was "*freehold, free land, or tenement,*" requiring both the tenure and the interest to be freehold, consequently excluding copyholders and leaseholders for lives.*

It will be observed, that this statute, besides fixing a property qualification for voters in county elections, had also the object of limiting the right of voting to those who were residents in the county. And another part of the same statute required, "that they which shall be so chosen, shall be dwelling and resident within the same counties." It had been endeavoured, in the preceding reign, to make residence a necessary qualification for both electors and elected, in counties and in boroughs. The first statute of Henry V. expressly ordained this. Few who bear in mind the origin of the House of Commons, will hesitate in believing with Mr. Hallam, that the old custom was, "that each county, city, or borough should elect deputies out of its own body, resident among themselves, and consequently acquainted with their necessities and grievances." Mr. Hallam thinks it likely that the practice of electing non-residents had begun in the reign of Edward III. He remarks on this statute of Henry V., that it "apparently indicates a point of time when the deviation from the line of law was frequent enough to attract notice, and yet so established as to pass for an unavoidable irregularity. There cannot be a more apposite proof of the inefficacy of human institutions to struggle against the steady course of events, than this unlucky statute of Henry V., which is almost a solitary instance in the law of England wherein the principle of desuetude

* This account of the statute 8 Hen. VI. is almost entirely taken from Mr. Warren's excellent historical introduction to his "Manual of Parliamentary Law."

has been avowedly set up against an unrespected enactment."*

The provisions of the 1 Hen. V. c. 1, the 8 Hen. VI. c. 7, 10 Hen. VI. c. 2, and 23 Hen. VI. c. 14, which required electors to be residents in the county or borough for which they voted, were almost equally inoperative in practice; and the statute of 14 George III. c. 58, which at last formally repealed the restriction of residence as to members, repealed the clauses also of the old Acts which demanded the residence of voters. The modern statute significantly recites, that certain provisions in the old Acts had been found by long usage to be unnecessary and had become obsolete; and it repeals them so far as they relate to the residence both of candidates and voters. It is, however, probable that in early times the number of non-resident voters, both in counties and in boroughs, could not have been large. With respect to the county voters, the requirement of the 10 Hen. VI. c. 2, that the land which gave the vote should be situate within the county, was always obeyed; and it is not likely that any great number of persons, in the time of the Plantagenets, were owners of freehold property

* Mr. Hallam refers to a note (Note D) at p. 53 of Peckwell's Reports of Contested Elections." The whole subject is there very learnedly and fully investigated. The restrictions of the statute seem to have been generally evaded as early as Edward IV.'s reign. An unsuccessful attempt was made in the thirteenth year of Elizabeth's reign formally to repeal the Act, as regarded boroughs. But though this failed, non-residents seem to have been continually returned both for counties and boroughs; and at last, in the case of Onslow *v.* Ripley, 1781, the Court of King's Bench resolved that "little regard was to be had to that ancient statute, 1 Hen. V., *because the common practice of the kingdom had been ever since to the contrary*." Some legal authorities try to get rid of the difficulty of treating the neglect of a statute as equivalent to the repeal of it, by drawing a distinction between such statutory provisions as are imperative, and such as are *directory* only and may be disregarded. See Dwarris on Statutes, 606, *et seq.* Our jndges of late years have shown a commendable unwillingness to exercise this dangerous discretion in dealing with the Acts of the Legislature.

in counties in which they did not reside. With respect to boroughs,* there is little doubt but that originally a man must have been a resident, and must have been a member of the court leet of the borough, in order to be recognized as a burgess. Afterwards the practice grew up in many boroughs of admitting non-residents as burgesses. This does not date earlier than Henry VI.'s reign, when boroughs were first incorporated.† In after times (down to the passing of the Reform Bill of 1832), the question whether non-residents could vote in borough elections was decided by the words of the incorporating charter, or by proof of the custom of each place.

Another point of considerable interest is suggested by a persual of the old Act, 23 Hen. VI c. 14, with respect to elections, independently of the question of residence. This is, whether any qualification of birth or estate was necessary for a member of parliament in those early times. With regard to boroughs, this does not seem to have been the case before the celebrated statute of the ninth year of Queen Anne's reign; except that it may be safely assumed that a villein would not have been eligible; and, indeed, the 1 Hen. V. c. 11, requires that the chosen burgesses shall be free. With respect to representatives of counties, the case is different. They were (as we have seen) originally the representatives of the mass of the immediate military tenants of the Crown; they were always (and still are) described in the parliamentary writs as knights; and there can be no question but that originally knights only were chosen. By degrees the practice of the voters and the sheriffs in this respect became less strict; and, at least as early as Edward III.'s reign, many persons who were not

* See Merewether and Stephens on Boroughs. † See Ibid.

knights, sat in the House of Commons as knights of shires.*

The statute of Henry VI.'s reign, to which we are referring (23. c. 14. 3. ), though it sanctioned the return of representatives of counties who were not actually knights, endeavoured to impose a twofold qualification of birth and estate. It required that knights of the shires for parliament shall be notable knights of the same counties for which they shall be chosen, or otherwise such notable esquires, *gentlemen born*, of the same counties, as shall be able to be knights, and no man to be such knight as standeth in the degree of a yeoman or under.† A knight's fee, that is to say, the amount of land which made its owner eligible for knighthood, was worth, in Edward II.'s reign, £20 a year, which is equivalent to at least £300 a year of the present time. The property qualification, therefore, which it was thus sought to establish, was considerable; but the attempt to found a qualification of gentle birth was more important still; for, if successful, it would have gone far to make a distinction of caste among the commonalty of England, and to impair that equality in the eye of the law, which has so beneficially prevailed in this nation.‡ One instance is recorded in which this very aristocratic provision of the statute was appealed to. This was six years after it was passed. Some of the electors of Huntingdonshire, in the twenty-ninth year of Henry VI., petitioned the king against the election of one Henry Gimber, because (among other reasons)

* 3 Hall. "Mid. Ag.," p. 176; 1 Douglas "Election Cases," p. 451, note D; 3 Prynne "Reg. Brev.," 167.

† Issint, que lez chivalers des counteez pour le parlement soien notablez chivalers des mezmez lez counteez ou autrement tielx notablez Esquiers *gentils homez del Nativite* dez mezmez lez counteez come soient ablez destre Chivalers: et null home destre tiel Chivaler que estoise en la degree de vadlet et desouth.—*Statutes of the Realm*, vol. ii. p. 342.

‡ See 178, *supra*.

he was not of gentle birth.* But this part of the statute appears to have been so generally disregarded, as not even to have attracted notice enough in after times to obtain a repeal.

The natural influence of ancient lineage and landed property must generally have caused the representatives of each county to be chosen from among its principal gentry, but no impassable barrier of pedigree excluded others; nor, until the reign of Anne, was any property qualification indispensable.

There is no surer proof of the growing importance of the House of Commons during the latter half of the fifteenth century, than the anxiety which was then beginning to be shown to obtain a seat in parliament. Formerly that post had been looked on as a burden, and it had been found requisite to impose a fine by statute on members who absented themselves from their duty. The electors also looked on their franchise as a grievance, inasmuch as it imposed on them the necessity of paying wages to their representatives. The excuse that a borough was too poor to raise the money to pay their burgesses in parliament was often set up, and often allowed by the sheriffs. Both county and borough members seem regularly to have received their wages to the end of Henry VIII.'s reign, and a few later instances have been found.† But there is good evidence that, during the reigns of the last Plantagenets, country gentlemen and others had begun to make eager canvass for places in parliament. Mr. Hallam cites from the Paston Collection a curious letter on this subject, which also, as he states, throws light on the creation or revival of boroughs. The writer tells Sir John Paston, "If ye miss to be burgess of Malden, and my lord chamber-

* See the proceedings in Prynne's 3rd Register, p. 157.

† See Hall. 3 "Mid. Ag.," p. 171, note; and Prynne's 4th Register, as there cited.

lain will, ye may be in another place; there be a dozen towns in England that choose no burgess, which ought to do it; ye may be set in for one of those towns an ye be friended." The date of this letter is 1472, in the reign of Edward IV. It may be observed, that one effect of the wars of the Roses, which had raged between this date and that of the statute of Henry VI., which we last referred to, had been to raise, in some respects, the importance of the House of Commons; as each of the contending parties eagerly sought the sanction of parliament to its title, and still more eagerly used the machinery of parliamentary attainders against its adversaries.

Notwithstanding the strong and steady growth of parliamentary authority, which may be traced during the fourteenth and fifteenth centuries, a king of England still possessed many and splendid attributes, that were strictly constitutional; and even the best of our monarchs frequently committed acts of arbitrary power beyond the limits of the constitution, under the colour of royal prerogative. But, without trespassing on the supremacy of the law, the royal power was ample for all purposes that could truly benefit either prince or people. The king convened, and the king dissolved the parliament. The king could add at his will new members to its Upper House, by creating peers. The king could grant his royal charter to any place he pleased to select, and thereby constitute that place a borough, with the right of sending representatives to the House of Commons. This mode of influencing parliament was indeed little used during these centuries, comparatively with the extent to which it was put in force by the Tudors; and the agency of the sheriffs, in omitting or adding boroughs, was generally employed; but, as parliament succeeded in controlling this abuse, we find the Crown reviving or creating parliamentary boroughs by its charters. The king's concurrence with the Houses was essential for all legislation, and his power of refusing assent to their petitions or bills was then frequently exercised. Our sovereigns, also, during this period, used to issue ordinances, which were acknowledged to be binding, and the boundaries between which and regular statutes it is not easy to define; though it may be generally stated that an ordinance dealt rather with an individual case than a general subject, and that an ordinance was designed to declare and enforce the law as it already existed, whereas the introduction of a new law required a statute.* Sometimes ordinances were issued by the sovereign, on petition from parliament; but they were also frequently made by the king in Council, without any parliamentary authority. This was the king's "Concilium Ordinarium," or Privy Council, consisting of the chancellor, the treasurer, the lord steward, lord marshal, lord admiral, of the judges, and of other high officers of State, all nominated by the king, and all removable at his pleasure. This Council claimed also and exercised an anomalous judicial authority, which was the constant subject of parliamentary remonstrance, but which the frequent turbulence of the times, and the insufficiency of the ordinary tribunals to deal with powerful offenders, must have rendered to some extent necessary. Another important power which was admitted in those days to belong to the crown, was that of dispensing with the observance of particular statutes by particular individuals in special cases. This, probably, was regarded as springing from the clear royal right of pardoning offenders. For it must have seemed natural that if the king, when a statute had been broken, could pardon the offence, he might, by a kind of anticipatory pardon, dispense with its

* See Reve, vol. iii. p. 358. 3 Hall. "Mid. Ag.," p. 138, *et seq.*

observance in a special instance. As has been stated in speaking of the Council, the king appointed and changed as he thought fit, the chancellor, the judges of the supreme common law courts, and the judges who tried causes and prisoners on the circuit, who were not always the same as the judges of Westminster Hall. He appointed the sheriffs, and he appointed also and dismissed as he thought fit the holders of the very important office of justice of the peace in the several counties. There had anciently been in each shire conservators of the peace, elected by the freeholders; but in Edward III.'s reign these were superseded by justices of the peace, receiving their appointment and commission from the Crown.

The king, as supreme head of the State, represented the State; or rather the king was the State in all dealings with other nations. He proclaimed war, he made treaties; he alone sent or received ambassadors; he was supreme chief of the military and naval forces of the kingdom; he had the absolute government of all foreign towns or territories that were obtained by conquest; he had the government of all forts and castles within the realm; nor could any subject embattle his house or make a place of strength without the royal licence. Many other prerogatives of minor importance, such as that of coining money, of conferring all titular ranks and honours, of appointing ports and havens for the lawful transit of merchandise, and passengers into and out of the realm; and several of a fiscal nature, such as the right to deodands, and to waifs, and wrecks of the sea, might be mentioned. But the principal powers of royalty have been enumerated, and they prove abundantly the splendour and the strength of the constitutional sceptre of our Plantagenet kings.

The constitutional privileges of the peers have been sufficiently pointed out in the preceding pages.

When we come to consider the share of political power possessed by the various classes of the mass of the nation, who collectively constitute the commonalty of the realm, the point that first fixes our attention is the elective franchise. We have already, in some degree, investigated this; and there is no need to recapitulate the old statutory provisions that have been quoted, with reference to the qualifications of electors, and also of members. But it is interesting to ascertain, if possible, the relative proportion of the whole electoral body to the whole nation, and to gain some insight into the practical working of the representative system in those ages.

We shall find nothing approaching to universal suffrage. The labouring part of the agricultural population was, certainly, during the fourteenth and fifteenth centuries, generally raised from a state of villeinage to a state of personal freedom. The process of emancipation went on rapidly during Edward III.'s reign, though the fearful insurrection in that of his successor shows how many unhappy beings were then still in a state of bondage. After that period we hear, by degrees, less and less of villeinage in England; and it was generally extinct when the Tudor dynasty came to our throne, though a few instances of it may be traced later. But the lot of the freed labourers in England was long one of severe oppression. The statute book, from Edward III.'s reign to the commencement of our modern poor-laws, in Elizabeth's time, abounds in enactments to regulate the wages, dress, and conduct of the inferior labourers, "which seem to have been framed with the same view, namely, to curb the aspiring exertions of industry and independency."* Mr. Pashley,† in his

* Eden's "State of the Poor," vol. i. p. 42.
† Pashley on "Pauperism and Poor Laws," p. 163.

excellent sketch of "Pauper Legislation before the Reign of Elizabeth," truly says :—

"Wearisome and painful would be the task of examining the oppression exercised over the whole class of labourers from the early part of the fourteenth century till the end of the fifteenth. The legislation on the subject of these poor helots seems throughout to be selfish and unjust. The labourer was never to better his condition. Imprisonment and branding on the forehead with a hot iron was the lot of the fugitive servant, although he had never *consented* to enter into the service of his lord, and had been compelled to do so for wages less than he was justly entitled to receive. Even 'artificers, and people of mysteries,' were liable to be *pressed* by the lord to get in his harvest,* and if a poor labourer's unmarried daughter of eighteen or twenty years of age, had been 'required to serve' any master, she must, under the statutory provisions, either have gone into the service, or have been committed to gaol for refusing. No child could be apprenticed to any useful craft, unless its parents were owners of land yielding a certain amount of yearly rent, and the compulsory service, such as has been described, paid for by a rate of wages below the just level, would be a perpetual cause why servants should have endeavoured to free themselves from their bondage, and why the 'valiant beggars,' of whom we read, should have so greatly increased throughout the country."

The agricultural population of the country was many times more numerous than the town population, and the agricultural labourers, such as we have seen them described, were probably a majority of the whole nation ; a wretched majority—among whom it would be idle to look for either holders of franchise or bearers

* 13 Rich. II., c. 3.

of office. When we come to the rural classes above them, to the possessors of some property, small or great, there is reason to believe that before Henry VI.'s time the right of voting for knights of the shire was very generally exercised. For by far the greater proportion of those who then had any landed property at all, held it as freeholders,* and even after the 8th Hen. VI. restricted the county franchise to 40*s.* freeholders, the number still qualified to vote was greater than we might suppose, did we not know from Fortescue † and other authorities how large was the number of men worth at least 40*s.* a year in every English county.

The same property qualification was required for jurors as for county voters in Fortescue's time. His writings, especially his treatise on the laws of England, present a most interesting and valuable picture of the political and social state of England towards the latter half of the fifteenth century. He was Lord Chancellor to Henry VI., and was the companion in exile of the young prince Edward of Lancaster, Henry's son and heir apparent, during the wars of the Roses. His treatise on the laws of England was written for the instruction of that prince; and in it he described trial by jury as the prevailing mode of trial in England, and as the peculiar glory of our institutions, compared with those of other nations. There is also a curious record of Edward the Fourth's reign, which proves how completely trial by jury was then, and long had been, regarded as an Englishman's constitutional privilege. "The rolls of parliament

* Leases for years, though not unknown, were comparatively rare to what they are at present; nor was the stable customary possession by freemen of land held of lords by base service (*i. e.* of copyholders) fully recognised till Edw. IVth's reign, if so early.

† Fortescue de Laudibus, pp. 86, 104, Amos's edition.

for the reign of Edward the Fourth,* contain a petition from two persons, Henry Bodrugan and Richard Bonethon, praying that their conviction may be annulled.† An Act had been passed in the 14th year of that reign, which authorized the justices of the King's Bench to examine Bodrugan and Bonethon on a charge of felony, and provided that if the said Henry and Richard were by their examination found guilty, they then should have such judgment and execution as they should have had if they were of the same attaint by the trial of twelve men, and like forfeiture to be in that behalf. The accused parties refused to appear, and were convicted by default. They therefore petitioned the Crown that the judgment might be annulled, on the ground that a trial by justices in this mode was unknown to the laws of England, and was a novel and dangerous innovation."‡ The very words of the petition are—'For so much as by the same Acte was ordeyned that the triall of the said offences should rest and be by examination, and not by the verdict of twelve men, after the common course of the laws of the land.' The king granted their prayer, and thus affirmed the principle of the indefeasible right of the subjects of this realm to be tried, as they have heretofore been accustomed, by a jury of their peers."§

When we direct our attention to the trading part of the community, to the dwellers in towns in those ages, we find reason to believe, that, at least in all the cities and more considerable boroughs, by far the greater number of the inhabitants had, as burgesses, the right of voting for the parliamentary representatives of the borough, the right of acting as jurors in the borough courts of justice, and generally the right

* Fortescue de Laudibus, pp. 86, 104, Amos's edition.

† Rot. Parl., 133. ‡ Forsyth, p. 426. § Forsyth, p. 426.

of taking active part in matters of local self-government. There are many conflicting theories respecting the early municipal constitutions of our boroughs, and as to the class of persons by whom the electoral franchise in boroughs was originally exercised. The four principal conflicting theories on the subject are stated at length, and their respective claims to our adoption are fairly summed up by Hallam.* Sir James Mackintosh thought that from the earliest times to which borough voters can be traced, they were of the same variety of classes as in later times before the Reform Bill. "In some places the freemen; in others, the officers of a corporation; elsewhere, freeholders, burgage tenants, inhabitants contributing to public expense, or other inhabitants with scarcely sufficient qualification of property to afford a presumption of fixed residency; these, and combinations of various sorts of them, were the principal classes among whom the elective franchise was in the earliest times shared."

But the learned researches of Serjeant Merewether and Mr. Stephens into our municipal archæology, seem to have established that, at least before Henry VI.'s reign, every freeman, who became a resident householder in a borough, capable of paying scot (*i. e.* his share of local taxation), and of bearing lot (*i. e.* of discharging in turn the local offices), was sworn and enrolled at the burough leet, and became a burgess. The boroughs were not then incorporated; the earliest instance of incorporation being in the eighteenth year of Henry VI.'s reign, when a charter of incorporation was given to Hull. This was followed by other instances; and our courts of law adopted the doctrine, that where no early charter of incorporation could be proved, an early, but lost one would be presumed; in other words, they set up the doctrine

* "Constitutional History."

of incorporation by prescription. The mayor and leading men of the corporations, acting by the corporate seal, and as the whole aggregate body, soon began to monopolize authority, and to exercise the power of selecting the burgesses, frequently among non-residents. The Crown also began to grant charters of incorporation, with clauses which gave exclusive powers to certain officers of the corporation, or to certain select bodies. By these means, and by the capricious growth, and establishment of an infinite variety of local usages, the electoral as well as the municipal system of our boroughs became widely changed from its primitive character; and that mass of abuses and anomalies grew up, which was only eradicated by the Reform Bill and Municipal Corporation Bill of the last reign.

But, while the boroughs were untampered with, and while all freeholders in counties had a right to take part in the elections (that is to say, during the far greater part of the two centuries which we have been examining), the electoral franchise must have been in the hands, or within the reach, of almost all whom we can term the middle classes in England. M. Guizot's observations on this deserve attention; though, while we concur with their truth, it is impossible not to protest in spirit against the atrocious character of the legislation against the labourers, which has been previously referred to, the effect of which was to keep them in the dependence and ignorance which M. Guizot speaks of, and whence, in a great degree, originated that incapacity for political rights, on which he founds his opinions. His words are: "The true, the sole general principle which is manifested in the distribution of electoral rights as it then existed in England, is this, that right is derived from, and belongs to, capacity. This requires some explanation.

"It is beyond doubt, that at this period, setting aside the chief barons, whose personal importance was such that it was necessary to treat with each of them individually, the freeholders, the clergy, and the burgesses of certain towns, could alone act as citizens. Those not comprised in one or other of these classes were chiefly poor husbandmen, labouring on subordinate and precarious means. They included all men invested with real independence, free to dispose of their person and wealth, and in a position to rise to some ideas of social interest. This it is which constitutes political capacity. This capacity varies according to time and place; the same degree of fortune and enlightenment is not everywhere and always sufficient to confer it, but its elements are constantly the same. It exists wherever we meet with the conditions, whether material or moral, of that degree of independence and intellectual development which enables a man freely and reasonably to accomplish the political act he is required to perform. Assuredly, considering the masses, as they should be considered in such a matter, these conditions are not met with in England in the fourteenth century, elsewhere than among the freeholders, the clergy, and the burgesses of the chief towns. Beyond these classes, nothing is found but almost servile dependence and brutal ignorance. In summoning these classes, then, to join in the election, the electoral system summoned every capable citizen. It was derived, therefore, from the principle that capacity confers right; and among citizens whose capacity was recognized, no inequality was established.

"Thus neither the sovereignty of the majority nor universal suffrage were originally the basis of the British electoral system. Where capacity ceased, limitation of right was established."

## CHAPTER XV.

State of the Constitution under the Tudors.—Revival of Spirit in the House of Commons.—Weak but arbitrary Character of the first two Stuart Kings.—Charles I. sincere, but an Aggressor on the Constitution.—The Petition of Right.

THE gradual progress of the free principles of our constitution is no longer to be traced under the Tudors, with the same regularity which is observable under the Plantagenets, from John's reign downwards. There seems at first sight to be a reaction towards despotism ; but this appearance of degeneracy is only on the surface. Slavish things were said and done in high places, and there was a dearth of measures of improvement, not because the nation had grown false-hearted to itself, or feeble-hearted, but because the order of its former leaders in struggles for liberty now no longer supplied it with chieftains, and the ranks of society whence the new reformers were to spring, had not yet acquired full importance and self-reliance. The dreadful civil wars of York and Lancaster had hewn the barons of England down to a scanty and scared remnant, which the subtle policy of Henry VII. and the resolute ferocity of Henry VIII. tended more and more to weaken. But deep thought and bold inquiry were active throughout the nation, under the mighty impulses given to the mind by the general diffusion of the art of printing, by the revival of the study of the classics, by the exciting interest of the great geographical discoveries effected about this period, and, above all, by the Reformation. Our parliaments were, indeed, disgracefully submissive under the two last Henrys.* Such was the shameful facility with which verdicts of guilty were then obtained from juries in State prosecutions, principally through the iniquitous system of fining and imprisoning any juror who dared to return a verdict against the wish of the Crown; the judges, in their application and exposition of the criminal law, were such servile tools of the sovereign; and human life was lavished on the scaffold with such savage prodigality, that we cannot be surprised that, while the peerage ceased to furnish hereditary tribunes of the people, men of inferior position shrank at first from coming forward as State martyrs :—

"Nec civis erat qui libera posset
Verba animi proferre et vitam impendere vero."

Thus it was that the Court of Star-Chamber (as the old court of the king's Concilium Ordinarium was now called) exercised an extensive and anomalous jurisdiction, by means of which men were arbitrarily fined and imprisoned, and often sentenced to cruel mutilations, for any alleged misconduct, which the lords and prelates of the Council, or any minister of the Crown, might think fit to impute to them. Thus, too, the subjects' money was frequently ex-

* The following observations of Lord Bolingbroke on Henry VIII.'s reign are important. "Henry VIII., by applying to his parliaments for the extraordinary powers which he exercised, and by taking these powers for such terms, and under such restrictions as the parliament imposed, owned indeed sufficiently that they did not belong of right to the Crown. He owned likewise in effect, more than any prince who went before him, how absolutely the disposition of the crown of England belongs to the people of England, by procuring so many different and opposite settlements of it to be made in parliament."—*Bol.*, vol. i. p. 375.

torted without parliamentary assent, under the name of benevolences or loans. These things, and other violences, were endured to an extent, which, under the Plantagenets, would have met with firm remonstrance, if not with armed resistance. But the independent power of the gentry and of the wealthier portions of the middle classes was steadily, though silently increasing; and under the last three Tudors we find the House of Commons gradually resuming the firm free tone and bearing, and the resolution to maintain and work out the rights of the people, which the great barons had formerly displayed at Runnymede and Lewes.* Under Elizabeth, the popular party in the House of Commons was organized and active; and more than once successful in its efforts at State reform. Much, indeed, in her reign was endured for her sake, and not for want of a knowledge of its unconstitutional character, or of spirit to resist it. Many a haughty speech and many a harsh act of Elizabeth's were forgiven and forgotten by Englishmen, when they thought of the true English heart and daring of the Queen, whom they had seen cheering her troops at Tilbury, and defying the spiritual thunders of the Vatican, and the more perilous thunders of the Armada; who had sent out Drake, Raleigh, Cavendish, Hawkins, and Frobisher, to beard England's foes and spread England's fame beyond the southern and western waves. But when the imbecile, though insolent, Stuarts came to our throne, and made our national honour a by-word abroad, while at home they paraded each most offensive claim to arbitrary power in the most offensive manner, no such patriotic forbearance could be expected. For-

* The pains taken by the Crown during these reigns to extend the royal influence in the House of Commons by creating new boroughs and interfering with elections, prove the importance of the parliament. See Hallam's "Const. Hist.," vol. i. p. 60.

tunate for England, indeed, it was that two such weak princes as the first James and Charles, reigned next after Elizabeth; that we had not a succession of active and prosperous sovereigns, under whom overgrown prerogative might have been allowed to take too deep root, while the national liberties perished amidst the blaze of the national glory.*

The memory of Charles I. is entitled to all possible benefit of the excuse, that he believed himself to be fully entitled to the arbitrary power, which he attempted to exercise. Bolingbroke correctly observes of the first Stuart, that "The doctrines which established the unbounded and ineffable prerogative of the king; which reduced the privileges of parliament to be no longer an ancient and undoubted right and inheritance, but derived them from the permission and toleration of the Crown, and declared them liable to be retrenched at the will of the prince; and which by necessary consequence changed at once the nature of the English constitution, from that of a free to that of an arbitrary government; all these doctrines, we say, or the principles on which they were established, had been already publicly and frequently asserted by King James. They were the language of the Court; and a party had been formed in the nation who made profession of them. They were maintained in conversation. They were pleaded for in print; and they became soon afterwards the disgrace and profanation of the pulpit."† And he afterwards, with equal truth, observes of Charles himself, that "King Charles came a party man to the throne, and that he continued an

* The first session of James's first parliament deserves notice, as it was then that the right of the House of Commons to determine all matters concerning the election of its own members was established. See "Lord John Russell on the Constitution," p. 57, and Hallam's "Const. History," vol. i.

† Bol., vol. i. pp. 487, 488.

invasion on the people's rights, whilst he imagined himself only concerned in the defence of his own. We avow it as an opinion we have formed on reading the relations published on all sides, and to which, it seems to us, that all the authentic anecdotes of those times may be reconciled. This prince had sucked in with his milk those absurd principles of government which his father was so industrious, and, unhappily for king and people, so successful in propagating. He found them espoused, as true principles both of religion and policy, by a whole party in the nation, whom he esteemed friends to the constitution in Church and State. He found them opposed by a party, whom he looked on indiscriminately as enemies to the church and to monarchy. Can we wonder that he grew zealous in a cause which he understood to concern him so nearly, and in which he saw so many men who had not the same interest, and might therefore be supposed to act on a principle of conscience equally zealous? Let any one, who hath been deeply and long engaged in the contests of party, ask himself on cool reflection, whether prejudices concerning men and things have not grown up and strengthened with him, and obtained an uncontrollable influence over his conduct. We dare appeal to the inward sentiments of every such person. With this habitual bias upon him, King Charles came to the throne; and to complete the misfortune, he had given all his confidence to a madman. An honest minister might have shown him how wrong his measures were; a wise one how ill-timed. Buckingham was incapable of either. The violence and haughtiness of his temper confirmed his master in the pursuit of these measures; and the character of the first minister became that of the administration." *

* Bol., vol. i. pp. 516, 517.

But the circumstance that the king acted conscientiously, though mistakenly, in his aggressions on the constitution, did not alter the fact of his being an aggressor,* nor did it diminish the necessity of opposing his aggressions, as was done in the parliament to which we owe the Petition of Right.

The first two parliaments of Charles I. had been hastily dismissed by him in petulant discontent, because they adhered to the old constitutional plan of making the grant of supplies depend upon the redress of grievances. Those grievances were actively continued by the Crown and its ministers; some of them being the arbitrary billeting of soldiers, the forcing of loans to the king, under the title of benevolences, the imprisoning those who refused to lend, several of whom, on suing out their writ of Habeas Corpus, were, in defiance of it, remanded to prison.

Still, with whatever rigour unparliamentary methods of getting money were resorted to, Charles found, as the early Anglo-Norman kings had found, that no tyranny could extort so much from the nation, as could be gained from it, if its consent to the levy was first obtained. His third parliament was therefore summoned, which met in March, 1628, and continued with one prorogation till March 1629. "The prime intellectual manhood of England" now

* "In England the royal power was the aggressor. Charles I., full of haughty pretensions, though devoid of elevated ambition, and moved rather by the desire of not derogating in the eyes of the kings, his peers, than by that of ruling with a strong hand over his people, twice attempted to introduce into the country the maxims and the practice of absolute monarchy: the first time, in presence of parliament, at the instigation of a vain and frivolous favourite, whose presumptuous incapacity shocked the good sense and wounded the self-respect of the humblest citizen: the second time, by dispensing with parliament altogether, and ruling alone by the hand of a minister, able and energetic, ambitious and imperious, though not without greatness of mind, devoted to his master, by whom he was imperfectly understood and ill supported, and aware too late that kings are not to be saved solely by incurring ruin, however nobly, in their service."—*Guizot's English Revolution*, pp. 5, 6.

came forward to the rescue of the constitution. Wentworth (who had not yet gone over to the Court), Selden, Pym, Holles, Coke, Eliot, and Hampden were of this parliament, and other men of energy and ability, intent "on vindicating our ancient vital liberties, by reinforcing our ancient laws made by our ancestors; by setting forth such a character of them as no licentious spirit should dare to enter upon them." *

The debates of the House of Commons, and their conferences with the House of Lords on this momentous subject (as they are collected in the second volume of the Parliamentary History), are full of interest and instruction for the student of our constitution. "The liberty of the subject in person and estate" was the great theme of these discussions; and an amount of learning, spirit, sense, and eloquence (though not unmingled with quaintness and pedantry) was brought to bear on it, which we could scarcely parallel in any subsequent part of the records of our Parliamentary Oratory. Besides passing resolutions, which asserted the right of every Freeman not to be imprisoned or restrained, except for lawful cause expressed in a lawful warrant, and also his "ancient and undoubted right to have full and absolute property in his goods and estate, and not to be taxed without assent of parliament," the Commons applied to the Lords to join them in declaring and ascertaining the rights and liberties of the subject. This led to several conferences between the two Houses, in which, among the managers in behalf of the Commons, appeared, Selden, Coke, Glanville, Noye, and other lawyers of such eminence, that the Peers considered it fair that the Attorney-General, and other Counsel for the

* Speech of Wentworth.

Crown, should be heard before them in support of the Royal Prerogative.

The principal argument of the Crown lawyers, in defence of the assumed Royal right of arbitrary imprisonment, was drawn from the words "*Vel per legem terræ*," in the clause of Magna Carta, which was relied on in behalf of the subject.* The Attorney-General admitted that the Great Charter was binding on the Crown, but he maintained "that it did not restrain the king from imprisoning a subject, but with this clause, *nisi per legale judicium parium suorum, vel per legem terræ*," and he said "how far *lex terræ* extends, is, and ever was, the question." He further maintained that "the law hath ever allowed this latitude to the king or his privy council, which are his representative body, in extraordinary cases to restrain the persons of such freemen, as, for reasons of state, they find necessary for a time, without the present expressing the causes thereof: which, if it should be expressed, might discover the secret of the state in that point, and might easily prevent the service by that discovery." Selden, and the other managers of the Commons, denied the truth of this interpretation of the great clause of the Great Charter (which, if admitted, would authorize the king to kill as well as to imprison), and argued that the words "*per legem terræ*" meant "process of the law."

Many references were made on both sides to old law-books and reports, but the managers in behalf of the Commons had a clear superiority in this part of the argument. They referred, in particular, to a case in the sixteenth year of Henry VI.'s reign, in order to show that the mere command of the king to imprison a man was no justification for the imprisonment, even though the king ordered it in his royal presence. One

* See p. 134, *supra*.

of the counsel for the Crown, Serjeant Ashley, who had gone far beyond his leader the Attorney-General in arguing for the Royal Prerogative, was rebuked by the Lord President, and ordered into custody by the House of Lords, for the unconstitutional doctrines which he had advanced. Ashley in his argument,* had boldly appealed to the right divine of kings. He explicitly "left fencing," and justified the actual case of a loan of money "required and refused, and thereupon a commitment," and he concluded, "that for offences against the State, in cases of State government, the king or his council hath lawful power to punish by imprisonment without showing particular cause, where it may tend to the disclosing of the secrets of State government."

The House of Lords showed their repudiation of such tenets of royal arbitrary power, by their own somewhat arbitrary punishment of the advocate who enounced them. But the zeal of the Lower House was not fully communicated to the Upper one, and several delays took place, during which the king endeavoured to soothe the Commons with vague promises; but Sir Edward Coke warned them that general words were no sufficient satisfaction for particular grievances. "Did ever Parliament rely on messages? The king must speak by a record, and in particulars, and not in generals. Let us put up a Petition of Right; not that I distrust the king, but that we cannot take his trust save in a parliamentary way."

The Petition of Right was accordingly drawn up by the Commons. The Lords proposed in a conference to add the following clause:—"We humbly present this petition to your Majesty, not only with a care of preserving our own liberties, but with due regard to leave entire that *sovereign power* with

* Parliamentary History, vol. ii. p. 315.

which your Majesty is entrusted for the protection, safety, and happiness of your people." The Commons saw clearly the dangerous effect of this stipulation in favour of the royal prerogative, and peremptorily refused to concur in the amendment. The expressions used on this occasion, by some of the vigilant guardians of our liberties, are remarkable.* On the return of the Commons to their own House from the conference, when this addition had been proposed, the addition was debated. The first speaker was Mr. *Alford*, who said, "Let us look into the Records and see what they are; what is 'sovereign power?' Bodin saith, that it is free from any conditions. By this we shall acknowledge a regal, as well as a legal power. Let us give that to the king the law gives him, and no more."

Mr. *Pym.*—"I am not able to speak to this question, for I know not what it is. All our Petition is for the laws of England, and this power seems to be another distinct power from the power of the law. I know how to add sovereign to the king's person, but not to his power; and we cannot 'leave' to him a 'sovereign power;' for we never were possessed of it."

Mr. *Hackwell.*—"We cannot admit of these words with safety; they are applicable to all the parts of our Petition: it is in the nature of a saving, and by it we shall imply as if we had incroached on his prerogative. All the laws we cite are without a saving; and yet, now, after the violation of them, must we add a saving? I have seen divers petitions where the subject claimed a right, yet there I never saw a saving of this nature."

Sir *Edw. Coke.*—"This is magnum in parvo. This is propounded to be a conclusion of our Petition. It is a matter of great weight; and, to speak plainly,

* Parl. Hist., vol. ii.

it will overthrow all our Petitions; it trenches to all parts of it; it flies at loans, at the oath, at imprisonment, and at billeting of soldiers; this turns all about again. Look into all petitions of former times; they never petitioned wherein there was a saving of the king's sovereignty. I know that prerogative is part of the law, but 'sovereign power' is no parliamentary word. In my opinion it weakens Magna Charta, and all the statutes; for they are absolute, without any saving of 'sovereign power;' and should we now add to it, we shall weaken the foundations of law, and then the building must needs fall. Take we heed what we yield unto; Magna Charta is such a fellow, that he will have no 'sovereign.' I wonder this 'sovereign' was not in Magna Charta, or in the confirmations of it. If we grant this, by implication we give a 'sovereign power' above all law. Power, in law, is taken for a power with force; the sheriff shall take the power of the county; what it means here, God only knows. It is repugnant to our Petition; that is, a Petition of Right, grounded on acts of parliament."

Mr. Selden well referred to the attempt made by Edward I. to render illusory his confirmation of the Great Charter by inserting the words, "*Salvo jure coronæ nostræ.*" Selden reminded his hearers of the resistance which was made to that dangerous interpolation, and how the king gave way, and the obnoxious words were given up.* The House of Lords, on being informed of the objections made by the Commons to their addition, sought to fortify it by reasons which were reported to the Lower House by the Lord Keeper. He said (among other things) that "they meant to give the king nothing now but what was his before; and, as to the words 'sovereign power,' as he

* See p. 158 *supra*.

is a king, he is a sovereign, and must have power; and the words were easier than 'prerogative.'" Mr. Mason then combated the reason of the Lord Keeper in a long and able speech, in which he pointed out that if the Lords' addition to the Petition of Right were adopted, the Judges would infallibly construe the Petition as a solemn parliamentary acknowledgment of the king's having, beyond his ordinary prerogative (by which he could not impose taxes, or imprison,) an extraordinary and transcendent 'sovereign power,' for the protection of the people, for which purpose he might tax, imprison, or billet soldiers as he pleased. He warned the House that all such acts of sovereign power would be said to be for the protection of the people, and that the king alone would determine whether they were so or not. He pointed out the impossibility of such questions being dealt with by a parliament "which is a body made up of several writs, and may be dissolved by one commission," and if the matter were to be brought before the courts of law "why then the judges and the judgments may be easily conjectured."—Mr. Glanville in a subsequent conference with the Lords, urged these and other arguments against the addition with full force and skill; and Sir Henry Martyn justly appealed to the conduct and demeanour of the Commons as entitling them to the absolute conjunction of the Upper House.

"The moderate and temperate carriage of the House of Commons in this parliament," said Sir Henry, "be it spoken without vanity, and yet in much modesty, may seem to deserve your Lordships' assistance in this petition *ex congruo et condigno:* especially if you would be pleased to consider the discontents, pressures, and grievances, under which themselves in great number, and the parts for which they serve, lamentably groaned, when they first arrived here;

and which was daily represented unto them by frequent packets and advertisements out of their several counties, all which, notwithstanding, have not been able to prevail upon our moderation, or to cause our passion to overrule our discretions ; and the same yet continueth in our hearts, in our hands, and in our tongues ; as appeareth in the mould of this Petition, wherein we pray no more but that we may be better treated hereafter. My lords, we are not ignorant in what language our predecessors were wont to express themselves upon much lighter provocation ; and in what style they framed their petitions ; no less amends could serve their turn than severe commissions to inquire upon the violators of their liberties ; banishment of some, execution of other offenders ; more liberties, new oaths of magistrates, judges, and officers, with many other provisions written in blood. Yet from us there hath been heard no angry word in this Petition. No man's person is named. We say no more than what a worm trodden on would say (if he could speak), 'I pray, tread on me no more.'"

At length, after considerable discussion, the peers gave way, and the bill having passed both Houses as the bill, the whole bill, and nothing but the bill, awaited only the royal assent to become law, and "to form a memorable era in the English Government." *

On the 2nd of June, A. D. 1628, the peers were assembled, the Commons summoned, and the king appeared in the House of Lords to give his answer in parliament to the bill. But, to the surprise of all men, Charles, instead of using the well-known ancient form of words by which such a bill receives the royal assent, addressed the parliament and told them, "The king willeth that right be done according to the laws and customs of the realm, and that the statutes be

* Hume.

put in due execution, that his subjects may have no cause to complain of any wrong or oppression contrary to their just rights and liberties; to the preservation whereof he holds himself in conscience as well obliged, as of his prerogative."

The Commons returned highly incensed with this evasive circumlocution. They forthwith began to assail the favourites of the Crown, and impeached a Dr. Manwaring who had preached a sermon, which had afterwards been printed by the king's command, in which discourse the right divine of kings to deal as they pleased with their subjects' property on emergencies, whether parliament consented or not, and the duty of passive obedience in the subject, were openly and unreservedly maintained. The Commons procured the trial and condemnation of this satellite of arbitrary power, and were proceeding to assail others higher in Charles's councils, when the king's obstinacy at length gave way, and the Petition of Right received the royal assent in the customary form of Norman French, and this second great solemn declaration of the liberties of Englishmen was declared to be the law of the land, amidst the general rejoicings of the nation.

---

## PETITION OF RIGHT.

3 Car. I. c. 1.

The Petition exhibited to his Majesty by the Lords Spiritual and Temporal, and Commons, in this present Parliament assembled, concerning divers Rights and Liberties of the Subjects, with the King's Majesty's royal answer thereunto in full Parliament.

To the King's Most Excellent Majesty.

Humbly shew unto our Sovereign Lord the King, the Lords spiritual and temporal, and Commons in Parliament assembled, that whereas it is declared and enacted by a statute made in the time of the reign of King Edward I., commonly called *Statutum de tallagio non concedendo*,* that no tallage or aid shall be laid or levied by the King or his heirs in this realm, without the good will, and assent of the archbishops, bishops, earls, barons, knights, burgesses, and other the freemen of the commonalty of this realm; and by authority of Parliament holden in the five-and-twentieth year of the reign of King Edward III., it is declared and enacted, that from thenceforth no person should be compelled to make any loans to the King against his will, because such loans were against reason and the franchise of the land; and by other laws of this realm it is provided, that none should be charged by any charge or imposition called a benevolence, nor by such like charge; by which statutes before mentioned and other the good laws and statutes of this realm, your subjects have inherited this freedom, that they should not be compelled to contribute to any tax, tallage, aid, or other like charge not set by common consent, in Parliament.

II. Yet nevertheless, of late divers commissions directed to sundry commissioners in several counties, with instructions, have issued; by means whereof your people have been in divers places assembled, and required to lend certain sums of money unto your Majesty, and many of them, upon their refusal so to do, have had an oath administered unto them not warrantable by the laws or statutes of this realm, and have been constrained to become bound to make appearance and give utterance before your Privy Council and in other places, and others of them have been therefore imprisoned, confined, and sundry other ways molested and disquieted; and divers other charges have been laid and levied upon your people in several counties by lord lieutenants, deputy lieuten-

* This supposed statute found a place among our records very early, and its recognition by the Petition of Right gave it *thenceforth* the authority of a statute. But Blackstone, in his work on the Charters, has shown that it was originally nothing more than an intended compendium of the Confirmatio Chartarum. See too, Guizot, "Essais," p. 311, n.; and Hallam's "Supplemental Notes," p. 306.

ants, commissioners for musters, justices of peace and others, by command or direction of your Majesty, or your Privy Council, against the laws and free customs of the realm.

III. And whereas also by the statute called "The Great Charter of the Liberties of England," it is declared and enacted, That no freeman may be taken or imprisoned, or be disseised of his freehold or liberties, or his free customs, or be outlawed or exiled, or in any manner destroyed, but by the lawful judgment of his peers, or by the law of the land

IV. And in the eight-and-twentieth year of the reign of King Edward III., it was declared and enacted by authority of Parliament, that no man, of what estate or condition that he be, should be put out of his land or tenements, nor taken, nor imprisoned, nor disherited, nor put to death without being brought to answer by due process of law.

V. Nevertheless, against the tenor of the said statutes, and other the good laws and statutes of your realm to that end provided, divers of your subjects have of late been imprisoned without any cause shewed; and when for their deliverance they were brought before justices by your Majesty's writs of *habeas corpus*, there to undergo and receive as the court should order, and their keepers commanded to certify the causes of their detainer, no cause was certified, but that they were detained by your Majesty's special command, signified by the lords of your Privy Council, and yet were returned back to several prisons, without being charged with anything to which they might make answer according to the law.

VI. And whereas of late great companies of soldiers and mariners have been dispersed into divers counties of the realm, and the inhabitants against their wills have been compelled to receive them into their houses, and there to suffer them to sojourn, against the laws and customs of this realm, and to the great grievance and vexation of the people.

VII. And whereas also by authority of Parliament, in the five-and-twentieth year of the reign of King Edward III., it is declared and enacted, that no man should be forejudged of life or limb against the form of the Great Charter and the law of the land; and by the said Great Charter and other the laws and statutes of this your realm, no man ought to be adjudged to death but by the laws established in this your realm, either by the customs of the same realm, or by Acts of Parliament: and whereas no offender of what kind soever is exempted from the proceedings to be used, and punishments to be inflicted by the laws and statutes of this your realm; nevertheless of late time divers commissions under your Majesty's great seal have issued forth, by which certain persons have been assigned and appointed commissioners with power and authority to proceed within the land, according to the justice of martial law, against such soldiers or mariners, or other dissolute persons joining with them, as should commit any murder, robbery, felony, mutiny, or other outrage or misdemeanor whatsoever, and by such summary course and order as is agreeable to martial law, and as is used in armies in time of war, to proceed to the trial and condemnation of such offenders, and them to cause to be executed and put to death according to the law martial.

VIII. By pretext whereof some of your Majesty's subjects have been by some of the said commissioners put to death, when and where, if by the laws and statutes of the land they had deserved death, by the same laws and statutes also they might, and by no other ought to have been judged and executed.

IX. And also sundry grievous offenders, by colour thereof claiming an exemption, have escaped the punishments due to them by the laws and statutes of this your realm, by reason that divers of your officers and ministers of justice have unjustly refused or forborne to proceed against such offenders according to the same laws and statutes, upon pretence that the said offenders were punishable only by martial law, and by authority of such commissions as aforesaid; which commissions, and all other of like nature, are wholly and directly contrary to the said laws and statutes of this your realm.

X. They do therefore humbly pray your most excellent Majesty, that no man hereafter be compelled to make or yield any gift, loan, benevolence, tax, or such like charge, without common consent by Act of Parliament; and that none be called to make answer, or to take such oath, or to give attendance, or be confined, or otherwise molested or disquieted concerning the same or for refusal thereof; and that no freeman, in any such manner as is before mentioned, be imprisoned or detained; and that your Majesty would be pleased to remove the said soldiers and mariners, and that your people may not be so burthened in time to come; and that the aforesaid commissions, for proceeding by martial law, may be revoked and annulled; and that hereafter no commissions of like nature may issue forth to any person or persons whatsoever to be executed as aforesaid, lest by colour of them any of your Majesty's subjects be destroyed or put to death contrary to the laws and franchise of the land.

XI. All which they most humbly pray of your most excellent Majesty as their rights and liberties, according to the laws and statutes of this realm; and that your Majesty would also vouchsafe to declare that the awards, doings, and proceedings, to the prejudice of your people in any of the premises, shall not be drawn hereafter into consequence or example; and that your Majesty would be also graciously pleased, for the further comfort and safety of your people, to declare your royal will and pleasure, that in the things aforesaid all your officers and ministers shall serve you according to the laws and statutes of this realm, as they tender the honour of your Majesty, and the prosperity of this kingdom.

*Quâ quidem petitione lectâ et plenius intellectâ per dictum dominum regem taliter est responsum in pleno parliamento, viz. Soit droit fait comme est desiré.*

---

There has been no necessity for us to enter into the acrimonious controversies, which are connected with the name and fate of Charles I., while our attention has been directed to the conduct of his earlier parliament, especially to that to which we are indebted for the Petition of Right.

We are not obliged to base our approbation of the proceedings of these assemblies on the testimony of writers hostile to the Crown. The authority of the royalist Clarendon is unexceptionable on this subject, and it is unmistakable. Clarendon says, of Charles's first three parliaments,* "I do not know any formed

* "History of the Rebellion," vol. i. p. 8.

act of either House that was not agreeable to the wisdom and justice of great courts upon those extraordinary occasions. And whoever considers the acts of power and injustice of some of the ministers in the intervals of parliament, will not be much scandalized at the warmth and vivacity of those meetings.

"In the second parliament there was a mention, and intention declared, of granting five subsidies, a proportion (how contemptible soever in respect of the pressures now every day imposed) scarce ever before heard of in parliament. And that meeting being upon very unpopular and unplausible reasons immediately dissolved, those five subsidies were enacted throughout the whole kingdom with the same rigour, as if, in truth, an Act had passed to that purpose. Divers gentlemen of prime quality, in several counties of England, were, for refusing to pay the same, committed to prison, with great rigour and extraordinary circumstances. And could it be imagined, that those men would meet again in a free convention of parliament without a sharp and severe expostulation, and inquisition into their own right, and the power that had imposed upon that right? And yet all these provocations, and many other, almost of as large an extent, produced no other resentment than the Petition of Right (of no prejudice to the Crown), which was likewise purchased at the price of five subsidies more, and in a very short time after that supply granted, that parliament was likewise, with strange circumstances of passion on all sides, dissolved."

So far, therefore, as the passing of the Petition of Right, it is impossible to proceed in the reign of Charles I. without entering, "the ground debateable," though even here I feel that after every possible caution—

"Incedo per ignes
Suppositos cineri doloso."

But it would be hopeless to go further, and to seek coldly to deal with "that momentous period of our history which no Englishman ever regards without interest, and few without prejudice—the period from which the factions of modern times trace their divergence, which after the lapse of two centuries still calls forth the warm emotions of party spirit, and affords a test of political principles." So Hallam has correctly styled the period commencing with the struggle between Charles I. and the Long Parliament, that met in 1640. The same remarks might with equal truth be applied to the ten preceding years, during which "the king had in a manner renounced the constitution, and instead of governing with the assistance and concurrence of a parliament, governed by illegal acts of power." * They apply, indeed, to the whole time between the dissolution of the parliament that passed the Petition of Right in 1629, and the restoration of Charles II. in 1660. In a work which is designed to be kept as clear as possible from party doctrines, I shall necessarily pass over these thirty years—years of unparalleled interest in history; but which are rather years of abnormal and revolutionary struggles, than of English constitutional government.

* Bolingbroke.

## CHAPTER XVI.

The Restoration.—Affection of the English Nation for their old Institutions.—Effects of the Period of Revolution.—Military Tenures abolished.—Habeas Corpus Act.—Custom of Fining Jurors for their Verdicts pronounced Illegal.—Revolution of 1688.—The Bill of Rights.—The Act of Settlement.—Kingship in England since the Revolution.—Its Limitations.—Its enduring Value.—House of Lords.—Attempt to check Creation of Peers.—Benefits of the House of Peers to the Country.—House of Commons.—Borough Members.—Rotten Boroughs.—Reform Bill.

THE restoration of monarchy in 1660, with the enthusiastic consent and joy of the whole nation, except a few disappointed military adventurers, and a few high-minded but fanatic zealots for aristocratic republicanism, is a great fact in our history. It proves how deeply the affection for our ancient institutions is rooted in the heart of the English people. It proves that the genius of our nation is incapable of reconciling itself either to the tumultuary vehemence of a single dominant popular assembly, however high may be the intellectual eminence of many of its members, or to the stern regimen of a military autocrat, whatever lustre it may derive from the successes of his foreign administration. But still the nation had not passed through these thirty eventful years between 1629 and 1660, without experiencing some permanent results on the national character. "From the time of the great revolutionary crisis, the English people had the good fortune to profit by experience, and the good sense not to give themselves up to extreme parties. It is from the reign of Charles II. that this good sense, which is the political intelligence of a free people, has presided over the destinies of England. The revolution through which the English nation had just passed had terminated in three great results.

"In the first place, the king could never again separate himself from the parliament. The cause of monarchy was gained, but that of absolute monarchy was lost forever. Theologians and philosophers, like Filmer or Hobbs, might preach the dogma or maintain the principle of absolute power, and their ideas might excite the indignation or the favour of speculative thinkers or vehement partisans. In the opinion of the nation, however, the question was practically decided: royalists and revolutionists regarded the close union and the mutual control of the Crown and parliament as the right of the country, and as necessary to its interests.

"In the second place, the House of Commons was in effect the preponderant branch of the parliament. Its direct or formal sovereignty was a revolutionary principle which was now generally decried and execrated; and the Crown and the House of Lords had recovered their rights and their dignity. But their overthrow had been so violent and complete, that, even after the fall of their enemies, they were unable to re-establish themselves in their ancient ascendancy; and neither the faults nor the reverses of the House of Commons could obliterate the effect of its terrible victories. The royalist party were now masters in that assembly, and, in its relations to the Crown and the administration of the country, inherited the conquests of the Long Parliament. In spite of some appearances of an opposite tendency, the preponderant influence of the House of Commons over the affairs of the country was, from the reign of Charles II., daily more obvious and decisive.

"These two political facts were accompanied by one of still higher importance, relating to the religious condition of the country: the complete and definitive ascendancy of Protestantism in England was the other great result of the Revolution." *

No attempt was made after the Restoration to revive some of the instruments of royal misgovernment, which the Long Parliament had overthrown. The Court of Star Chamber had been abolished, nor was it ever revived. The vexatious profits of the military tenures had been laid aside, and the 12 Car. II., c. 24, abolished military tenures altogether, converting them into common freeholds, and thus swept away those feudal rights of the Crown to wardships, primer seisins, aids, homages, &c., which had long been so burdensome to the nobility and gentry, who held lands by military tenure. There are some other statutes of this reign which deserve mention on account of their constitutional importance.

The first regular parliament of Charles passed an important Act to prevent the Legislature being overawed, and their votes coerced in future by riotous and seditious mobs under the guise of petitioners. That statute (13 Car. II. st. 1, c. 5) is still in force, and enacts that "no person or persons whatsoever shall repair to his Majesty or both or either of the Houses of Parliament, upon pretence of presenting or delivering any petition, complaint, remonstrance, declaration, or other addresses, accompanied with excessive numbers of people, nor at any one time with above the number of ten persons."

The Habeas Corpus Act, also, which was passed in this reign (31 Car. II., c. 2), is of great constitutional value, though it by no means introduced any new principle into our system, or formed any such epoch in the acquisition of the national liberties, as some writers represent. But it made the remedies

* Guizot on the English Revolution.

against arbitrary imprisonment short, certain, and obtainable at all times and in all cases. The statute itself enacts—

"1. That on complaint and request in writing by or on behalf of any person committed and charged with any crime (unless committed for treason or felony expressed in the warrant; or as accessory or on suspicion of being accessory before the fact to any petit treason or felony; or upon suspicion of such petit treason or felony plainly expressed in the warrant; or unless he is convicted or charged in execution by legal process), the Lord Chancellor or any of the judges in vacation, upon viewing a copy of the warrant, or affidavit that a copy is denied, shall (unless the party has neglected for two terms to apply to any court for his enlargement) award a *habeas corpus* for such prisoner, returnable immediately before himself or any other of the judges; and upon the return made shall discharge the party, if bailable, upon giving security to appear and answer to the accusation in the proper court of judicature. 2. That such writs shall be indorsed as granted in pursuance of this Act, and signed by the person awarding them. 3. That the writ shall be returned, and the prisoner brought up within a limited time according to the distance, not exceeding in any case twenty days. 4. That officers and keepers neglecting to make due returns, or not delivering to the prisoner or his agent within six hours after demand a copy of the warrant of commitment, or shifting the custody of the prisoner from one to another without sufficient reason or authority (specified in the Act), shall for the first offence forfeit £100, and for the second offence £200 to the party grieved, and be disabled to hold his office. 5. That no person once delivered by *habeas corpus* shall be re-committed for the same offence, on penalty of £500. 6. That every person committed for treason or felony, shall, if he requires it, the first week of the next term, or the first day of the next session of *oyer* and *terminer*, be indicted in that term or session, or else admitted to bail, unless the queen's witnesses cannot be produced at that time; and if acquitted, or not indicted and tried in the second term or session, he shall be discharged from his imprisonment for such imputed offence; but that no person, after the assizes shall be open for the county in which he is detained, shall be removed by *habeas corpus* till after the assizes are ended, but shall be left to the justice of the judges of assize. 7. That any such prisoner may move for and obtain his *habeas corpus* as well out of the Chancery or Exchequer, as out of the King's Bench or Common Pleas, and the Lord Chancellor or judges denying the same on sight of the warrant or oath that the same is refused, forfeits severally to the patry grieved the sum of £500. 8. That this writ of *habeas corpus* shall run into the counties palatine, cinque ports, and other privileged places, and the Islands of Jersey and Guernsey. 9. That no inhabitant of England (except persons contracting or convicts praying to be transported, or having committed some capital offence in the place to which they are sent) shall be sent prisoner to Scotland, Ireland, Jersey, Guernsey, or any places beyond the seas within or without the queen's dominions, on pain that the party committing, his advisers, aiders, and assistants, shall forfeit to the party aggrieved a sum not less than £500, to be recovered with treble costs; shall be disabled to bear any office of trust or profit; shall incur the penalties of *præmunire;* and shall be incapable of the queen's pardon."—3 *Black. Com.* 137.*

* Such is the substance of that great and important statute. But as the Act is confined to imprisonments on *criminal*, or supposed *criminal* charges, the 56 Geo. III., c. 100, was passed, extending the power of issuing a writ of *habeas corpus* to other cases. By this statute it is enacted,

These enactments, and especially the Habeas Corpus Act, make the name of Charles II. figure creditably in our statute-book, and there is one judicial decision of this reign, which established a constitutional principle of the highest value, or rather which put an end to a long-continued abuse of the most perilous character.

Under the Tudor princes the Court of Star Chamber assumed the power of punishing jurors by fine and imprisonment for returning verdicts contrary to the evidence. Such was the pretext on which the court pretended to act; but the real cause of their dangerous and oppressive interference generally was, that the jury had acquitted the prisoner in a State trial, contrary to the wishes of the Crown and its ministers.

Attempts were made to exercise, through the Courts of Common Law, the same violent means of perverting justice. It is to be recollected that, under all our kings, prior to the Act of Settlement, the judges were not merely appointed by the king, but held their commissions only during his pleasure, and it will readily be understood how, in State prosecutions, a trial before a jury, who knew that they would be themselves ruinously fined and cruelly imprisoned, if they acquitted the prisoner, must have become "a mockery, a delusion, and a snare." But in 1670, on a trial of the celebrated Quaker Penn and Mead at the Old Bailey for an unlawful assembly, a juryman named Bushel (who deserves the imperishable grati-

that where any person shall be confined or restrained of his liberty (otherwise than for some criminal or supposed criminal matter, and except persons imprisoned for debt or by process in any civil suit), it shall and may be lawful for any judge or baron, upon complaint made to him by or on behalf of the party so confined or restrained, if it shall appear by affidavit or affirmation that there is probable and reasonable ground for such complaint, to award in vacation time a writ of *habeas corpus ad subjiciendum* returnable immediately.

tude of Englishmen*) was firm, and encouraged his fellow jurors to be firm, against all the threats of the court, and acquitted the prisoners. The recorder (who tried the case) set a fine of forty marks on each of the jurors for perverseness and contumacy. Bushel refused to pay the fine, and the recorder thereon committed him to prison. He sued out a writ of Habeas Corpus from the Court of Common Pleas, and on a return being made to it that he had as a juror acquitted Penn and Mead "*contra plenam et manifestam evidentiam*," the subject was elaborately discussed; and Chief Justice Vaughan, "in a judgment replete with masculine sense, luminous argument, and profound historical research," pronounced the return insufficient, and the fine and imprisonment illegal. From that time forth the invaluable doctrine, that a jury in the discharge of their duty are responsible only to God and their consciences, has never been shaken or impeached.†

Chief Justice Vaughan's conduct in Bushel's case is, however, an almost solitary exception to the infamous character of the State Trials and other judicial proceedings in Charles II.'s reign. There are, indeed, few periods in our history more discreditable and more unpleasing to dwell on, than the twenty-eight years between the Restoration and the Revolution. They

* See an excellent epitome of this trial, and the subsequent proceedings in the Common Pleas, in Mr. Phillimore's "History of the Law of Evidence," p. 250; see also Mr. Hepworth Dixon's "Life of Penn."

† In very early times, when the jurors were themselves witnesses, and gave a verdict from their own personal knowledge of the transaction (see p. 189, *supra*), they were punishable for a wilfully-false verdict (that is, for wilfully-false evidence) by a writ of attaint. For this purpose twenty-four other jurors were summoned, who reinvestigated the case, and according to whose decision of it, the first jury were either freed from blame or severely punished. As jurors ceased to be witnesses, and heard and acted upon the testimony of others, the process of attaint fell into disuse. Sir T. Smith, in Elizabeth's reign, speaks of it as then obsolete. It was formally abolished only in George IV.'s reign.

must certainly be studied in order fully to perceive the necessity and rightly to appreciate the benefits of that last-mentioned great event. But the limits of the present volume are unsuited for the purpose; and, indeed, the great historical work, with which Mr. Macaulay is enriching our literature, has made the leading scenes of 1688 and the immediately preceding years, familiar to every educated Englishman. I can but sketch their outlines here; and there is no need of long comments. Differences of opinion as to many points in the characters of the first three Stuart king's will be found in writers of eminence, but there is no discrepancy as to the last. Even Hume, the artful and unscrupulous partisan of the House of Stuart, confesses of James II. that "almost the whole of this short reign consists of attempts always imprudent, often illegal, sometimes both, against whatever was most loved and revered by the nation." Some of the grievances whereof the English of those days complained most bitterly—those, namely, which arose from the king's open encouragement of Roman Catholics, in defiance of the laws respecting members of that church, and from his evident zeal for making that creed the established religion of the land, in lieu of the Protestant—may not press with the proper amount of importance on the minds of some modern readers, unless they bear in mind the condition of Europe at that time, and consider how completely the bigotry and the ambition of Louis XIV. had identified the progress of Roman Catholicism with the progress of despotic principles. James was the hireling of Louis, and was animated by the same feelings. He strove to gain a simultaneous triumph over Church and State in England, and to lay the national faith beneath the pope's feet, while he cast down the national liberties beneath his own.

The natural consequence of this was, that a spirit

of ultra-Protestantism mingled with and became an animating principle of the opposition which was raised against his assaults upon the constitution. The political struggle became necessarily for the time a religious one. And in that age the successful maintenance of Protestant ascendancy involved the rescue and the advancement of constitutional freedom.

James II. came to the throne in 1685, and found, in the circumstances of that period, peculiar facilities for the advancement of arbitrary power. During the last year of his predecessor's reign, the Crown had succeeded in humbling the popular party, and in destroying many of its chiefs. The attempts which Charles the II.'s last parliament had made to assert the power of the House of Commons, had been successfully punished by dissolution ; and much had been done to render any future House of Commons as subservient to the Crown, as had been the case in the worst years of Henry VIII. This had been effected by a daring, but crafty, attack on the charters of the corporate boroughs, which were the strongholds of the popular party. The Crown-lawyers, in 1683, filed an information against the corporation of the city of London, alleging that its Charter had been forfeited for certain imputed misdemeanors ; and the packed judges of the Court of King's Bench gave, as a matter of course, judgment in favour of the Crown. The corporation of the capital was then re-modelled, so as to make it subservient to the royal will. The same course was taken against other corporate places ; and very many more were intimidated into surrendering their charters to the Crown, and receiving new ones, which were framed on a far more oligarchical plan, and which gave to the Crown the right of appointing the first members.* This course was steadily pursued

* See Hallam, 2 "Const. Hist.," p. 614.

during the last years of Charles II.'s reign, and the first of that of James; and its effect was to place in the hands of the Crown the nomination of a large proportion of the members of the House of Commons, and also to give its adherents the power of domineering in all the daily details of local municipal politics over their Whig fellow-townsmen. The great mass of the nation, weary of the turbulent struggles of recent years, was now almost blindly zealous in its devotion to the royal will. Abroad, James could reckon on the ready support of Louis XIV., the most powerful monarch of the age. James defeated easily, in the beginning of his reign, two insurrections, which, under Argyle in Scotland and Monmouth in England, were attempted against him by the violent part of the enemies of his House; and the truth of the adage, that an unsuccessful revolt strengthens the force against which it is directed, was seemingly exemplified in the passive submission of the nation to the cruelties with which those revolts were visited by the military and the judicial ministers of the royal will. King James established and maintained a disciplined army of 20,000 men, though in profound peace, and though, so far from having any transmarine possessions of his Crown to coerce or protect, he had in Ireland an apparently inexhaustible supply of fanatic and devoted followers, to repress any possible movements that England might attempt in defence of Protestantism and constitutional law.

Providentially for this country, James was too violent to be crafty or even prudent, in the execution of his schemes. He was as ostentatious in the premature display of his designs against the people's Church and State, as he was pusillanimous when those designs called forth resistance, though at an earlier period of his life, when admiral of our fleets in battle, he had exhibited courage of the highest order. He commenced his reign by a violation of the cardinal principle of the constitution, which forbids the taking of the subjects' money by the Crown, save by consent of parliament. James showed of how little value the safeguards of the Great Charter, or the Petition of Right, and of the numerous other statutes in confirmation of them, would be to the people who endured his reign, by arbitrarily levying, at his accession, the Customs' and Excise duties, the parliamentary grant of which to the Crown had been limited to the life of the late king. James, however, was not averse to parliaments, provided they would appoint his revenue as he desired, and would register his edicts with the same submissive facility which his royal brother of France found in the parliaments of Paris.* He called a parliament, which met May 19th, 1685. Not content with relying on the effect of the royal war against the corporations, which has already been alluded to, the Court put in force every artifice; and used injustice and violence of the grossest kind throughout England, to manage the elections. An eminently servile House of Commons was the result, which granted to James, for his life, a revenue of two millions a-year. This was an ampler income than any former king of England had enjoyed; and, aided by the subsidies which James received from Louis XIV., made him independent of parliament for the rest of his reign, so far as regarded the important point of pecuniary supplies. But James dismissed even this compliant assembly, because they hesitated at carrying into effect his projects in favour of the Roman Catholic against the Protestant church. James now "showed plainly that, with a bench of judges to pronounce his commands, and an army to

* See his speech to his parliament, and the comments on it, in Mr. Wingrove Cooke's "History of Party," vol. i. p. 391.

enforce them, he would not suffer the mockery of constitutional limitations to stand any longer in his way."* He openly carried into execution his assumed right to dispense, by royal prerogative, with the observance of the laws of the land; and eleven out of the twelve judges pronounced a judgment in favour of that right, in a case which the king caused to be brought before them, having first carefully weeded the bench of those members who retained any scruples of conscience, and having appointed new judges in their stead.†

Under the same claim of possessing a kingly prerogative superior to all law, James, in 1686, set up a high court of ecclesiastical commission, in direct defiance of the Act of Parliament passed in Charles I.'s reign, which put down the High Commission Court then existing, and provided that no new court should be erected with the like power, jurisdiction, and authority. Among other acts of flagrant tyranny committed by this infatuated prince, are his expulsion of the fellows of Magdalen College, Oxford, for refusing to elect as their president, in obedience to royal mandate, and in violation of the law of the land and their oaths, a Roman Catholic nominee of the Crown; his command to all clergymen to read publicly in their churches the royal declaration of indulgence, by which the king abrogated a large number of statutes; and his prosecution of the seven bishops as seditious libellers, for presenting to him a petition, wherein they respectfully stated their unwillingness to put into execution an illegal order.

There was for a time an apparent submissiveness in England to this royal overthrow of the constitution.

* Hallam, vol. iii. p. 83.

† See Hale's case, "State Trials," xi. 1166; and see the comments on it of Hallam, 3 "Const. Hist." 86; Mackintosh's "View of Reign of James II.," p. 59.

But the heart of the nation was sound and true; and, as men became gradually aware of the real nature of the crisis which the rashness of the king had hurried on, all parties laid aside their animosities against each other, and a public feeling was created for the rescue of the national faith and the public liberty. It was evident that such a government, as James was setting up, was a despotism, unmitigated by any effectual check; and the savage cruelty of Jeffries, and of the other judicial wretches, whom James delighted to honour, had taught the people that such a despotism would be as oppressive in practice as it was degrading in theory. Nor could Englishmen of that age, when they looked to the foreign policy of England, feel that consolation for the loss of domestic freedom, which the subjects of an absolute monarch sometimes derive from the increased power and glory of the State. James was the paid vassal of Louis XIV.; and England, under James, was forced to stand tamely by, whilst the king of France wrought his ambitious schemes against the independence of the rest of Europe.

I have already alluded to the important influence which the general abhorrence and dread of Popish ascendancy exercised in extending and animating the national resistance to King James. Many were roused into action by that feeling, who might have regarded with apathy any amount of royal encroachment upon merely civil rights. And both by the well-known character of James himself, and by the character of the fanatic priests and confessors who were his favourite councillors, it was made manifest that the declarations of general toleration, which James put forward, were mere pretences. Even the Dissenters from the Anglican Church saw clearly that the king's ultimate object was to restore the compulsory domination of Roman Catholicism in England; and that he would not scruple, when he thought that a convenient time had arrived, to employ for that purpose means as savage and unsparing, as those by which his patron and model King Louis XIV. was striving to extirpate Protestantism and all liberty of conscience in France.

A good and brave man, in the beginning of 1688, might have felt all this, and yet might have shrunk from that tremendous remedy of armed opposition to established government, which can never be rightly attempted, while there is any rational hope of deliverance by other means. Before that memorable year was half over, no such hope remained. There was no longer any prospect that, if the nation were patient for a few years under James, it might recover its liberties without strife or peril under a wiser and more temperate successor to the throne. This idea might have been entertained during the first years of James's reign, while the Protestant Princess Mary, the wife of William of Orange, was immediate heir to the English Crown. But the birth (June 10th, 1688) of James's son by his second Queen, Mary of Modena, put an end to all such hopes; and deprived even the most timid conspirators among the patriotic party of all pretexts for delay.*

William, Prince of Orange, Stadt-Holder and Captain-General of the Dutch Commonwealth, was naturally the chief to whom the leading men of the English popular party looked in their need. To attempt a rising without the aid of some regular troops and a competent commander would have been to expose themselves and their untrained followers to certain destruction by the disciplined army of the king. An auxiliary force was needed, not large enough to conquer a great country like England against the country's will, but sufficient to form a

* See Hallam's remarks, "Const. Hist.," vol. i. p. 112.

neuclus, round which the national levies might be raised, and organized in the country's cause. It was also all-important that the commander of that force should be a man trustworthy, not only in respect of military and political ability, but also in respect of personal integrity, and of deep devotion to the general cause of civil and religious freedom. Such a man had William proved himself from his youth up. His own close relationship with the Royal Family of England, and his marriage with the Princess Mary, gave him a natural interest in the political well-being of England, and diminished the repugnance which must be always felt at calling in the sword of the stranger to turn the scale in civil disputes. Moreover, the inferior strength of Holland relatively to this country, and the deep need which the Dutch nation had that England should be free and great, in order to aid them in opposing effectively the grasping ambition of Louis XIV., were safeguards, in 1688, against the peril, which a wronged people too often incurs, when it employs foreign aid against its home oppressors;—the peril of becoming the slaves of their allies, and of purchasing a party-triumph by the sacrifice of their country's independence.*

On the last day of June, 1688, the celebrated invitation signed by Lords Danby, Devonshire, Shrewsbury, and Lumley, Admiral Russel, Henry Sidney and the Bishop of London, was sent to William, on which he determined to commence the great enterprise of his life. The chief of the English Whigs

* The tenth chapter of Sir James Mackintosh's "View of the Reign of James II.," contains a masterly examination of the causes and circumstances by which alone a people can be justified in taking up arms against established government. Though written with immediate reference to the Revolution of 1688, it is also a lucid and argumentative statement of general principles on this all-important point, which the historical student and modern politician will find invaluable, especially with reference to the events of the "Annus Mirabilis," 1848.

had, for some time previously, been in communication with him, and now the English Tories and High Churchmen also had gradually been goaded by the aggressions of James to treat the then present crisis of Church and State as an exceptional case to their favourite maxims of passive obedience and unlimited non-resistance. On the other hand, the Whigs throughout the great national movement that ensued, abated the violence with which they had previously sought to carry out the opposite doctrines. Men of all ranks and of all party denominations coalesced, not to introduce new forms of government, but to restore the English constitutional monarchy, on sure foundations, and with new safeguards for its old principles. William landed at Torbay in Devonshire on the 5th of November. There were soon risings in his favour throughout England, and after an almost bloodless march, he on the 18th of December entered London, amid the rejoicings of the population. Nearly all James's followers had deserted him, many under circumstances of disgraceful perfidy and meanness; James himself fled in despair from Whitehall to Feversham on the 10th of December; he was accidentally discovered there and brought back; but on the 18th he again left Whitehall, and lingered for a few days at Rochester. But on the 23rd, he finally left England, and fled to France, where he landed on the last day of the year.

On taking possession of the capital, William assembled the Lords Spiritual and Temporal then in London, and also all gentlemen who had been members of any parliament in Charles the II.'s reign, together with the municipal authorities of London. By their advice and at their request, he assumed the Provisional Government of the country, and issued letters summoning a Convention of the estates of the realm.

Under these writs the House of Lords, consisting of about ninety peers and bishops, and a House of Commons regularly elected by the various counties and boroughs, assembled on the 22nd of January, 1689. On the 28th, the House of Commons passed their great vote, that King James had abdicated, and that the throne was thereby vacant. The House of Lords at first were less resolute, and many of that body were in favour of appointing a regent, but continuing the title of James as nominal king. After long and interesting discussions on this and several other important points, the House of Commons prevailed, and their vote was assented to by the Lords. The Upper House forthwith passed a resolution that the Prince and Princess of Orange should be declared King and Queen of England, and all the dominions thereunto belonging. The Commons wisely interposed a solemn declaration of the people's rights, which was subsequently embodied in the Bill of Rights.

William, on taking the throne by virtue of the final resolution in his favour, to which both Houses came on the 13th of February, 1689, summoned a regular parliament; and one of the first acts of that parliament was to pass the great statute which has just been named, and which is the third great bulwark of English liberty. The preamble of the Bill of Rights narrates clearly, forcibly, and fully, the violations of the known laws and free institutions of the realm, which the late king had committed, and establishes guarantees against similar wrongs. I will at once transcribe this most important of modern statutes, adding a few brief explanatory notes to some of its provisions.

## An Act for Declaring the Rights and Liberties of the Subject, and Settling the Succession of the Crown.

Whereas the Lords Spiritual and Temporal, and Commons, assembled at Westminster, lawfully, fully, and freely representing all the estates of the people of this realm, did, upon the thirteenth day of February, in the year of our Lord one thousand six hundred eighty-eight, present unto their Majesties, then called and known by the names and style of William and Mary, Prince and Princess of Orange, being present in their proper persons, a certain declaration in writing, made by the said Lords and Commons, in the words following; viz.—

Whereas the late King James II., by the assistance of divers evil counsellors, judges, and ministers employed by him, did endeavour to subvert and extirpate the Protestant religion, and the laws and liberties of this kingdom:—

1. By assuming and exercising a power of dispensing with and suspending of laws, and the execution of laws, without consent of Parliament.

2. By committing and prosecuting divers worthy prelates, for humbly petitioning to be excused from concurring to the said assumed power.

3. By issuing and causing to be executed a commission under the Great Seal for erecting a court, called The Court of Commissioners for Ecclesiastical Causes.

4. By levying money for and to the use of the Crown, by pretence of prerogative, for other time, and in other manner than the same was granted by Parliament.

5. By raising and keeping a standing army within this kingdom in time of peace, without consent of Parliament, and quartering soldiers contrary to law.

6. By causing several good subjects, being Protestants,

* See *supra*, p. 259, as to the dispensing power exercised by our early kings. James assuming the power of dispensing generally with the observance of a whole class of statutes by a whole class of people. See authorities as to the dispensing power in Amos's "Fortescue," p. 31. Lord Coke, while admitting the legality of it in special cases and within particular limits, had reprobated in the most forcible manner the notion that the Crown had a general power of abrogating or changing laws.

to be disarmed, at the same time when Papists were both armed and employed, contrary to law.

7. By violating the freedom of election of members to serve in Parliament.

8. By prosecutions in the Court of King's Bench, for matters and causes cognisable only in Parliament; and by divers other arbitrary and illegal courses.

9. And whereas of late years, partial, corrupt, and unqualified persons have been returned and served on juries in trials, and particularly divers jurors in trials for high treason, which were not freeholders.

10. And excessive bail hath been required of persons committed in criminal cases, to elude the benefit of the laws made for the liberty of the subjects.

11. And excessive fines have been imposed; and illegal and cruel punishments inflicted.

12. And several grants and promises made of fines and forfeitures, before any conviction or judgment against the persons upon whom the same were to be levied.

All which are utterly and directly contrary to the known laws and statutes, and the freedom of this realm.

And whereas the said late King James II. having abdicated the government, and the throne being thereby vacant, his Highness the Prince of Orange (whom it hath pleased Almighty God to make the glorious instrument of delivering this kingdom from popery and arbitrary power) did (by the advice of the Lords Spiritual and Temporal, and divers principal persons of the Commons) cause letters to be written to the Lords Spiritual and Temporal, being Protestants, and other letters to the several counties, cities, universities, boroughs and cinque-ports, for the choosing of such persons to represent them, as were of right to be sent to Parliament, to meet and sit at Westminster upon the two-and-twentieth day of January, in this year one thousand six hundred eighty and eight, in order to such an establishment, as that their religion, laws and liberties might not again be in danger of being subverted; upon which letters, elections have been accordingly made.

And thereupon the said Lords Spiritual and Temporal, and Commons, pursuant to their respective letters and elections, being now assembled in a full and free representation of this nation, taking into their most serious consideration the best means for attaining the ends aforesaid, do in the first place (as their ancestors in like case have usually done) for the vindicating and asserting their ancient rights and liberties, declare :—

1. That the pretended power of suspending of laws, or the execution of laws, by regal authority, without consent of Parliament, is illegal.

2. That the pretended power of dispensing with laws, or the execution of laws by regal authority, as it hath been assumed, and exercised of late, is illegal.

3. That the commission for erecting the late Court of Commissioners for Ecclesiastical Causes, and all other commissions and courts of like nature, are illegal and pernicious.

4. That levying money for or to the use of the Crown, by pretence and prerogative, without grant of Parliament, for longer time or in other manner than the same is or shall be granted, is illegal.

5. That it is the right of the subjects to petition the King, and all commitments and prosecutions for such petitioning are illegal.*

6. That the raising or keeping a standing army within the kingdom in time of peace, unless it be with the consent of Parliament, is against law.†

7. That the subjects which are Protestants, may have arms for their defence suitable to their conditions, and as allowed by law.‡

8. That elections of members of Parliament ought to be free.

* This does not repeal the statute of Charles II. against *tumultuous* petitioning.—See R. *v.* Gordon, Doug. Rep. 592.

† See Comment on this, *infra;* and see Lieber, p. 95.

‡ "In connection with the rights of personal liberty and security, is the right of the subject to carry arms for his defence, suitable to his condition and degree, and such as are allowed by law. There is an ancient enactment, however [2 Edw. III. c. 3], against going armed under such circumstances as may tend to terrify the people, or indicate an intention of disturbing the public peace; and by a modern statute [60 Geo. III. c. 1] the training persons without lawful authority to the use of arms is prohibited, and any justice is authorized to disperse such assemblies of persons as he may find engaged in that occupation, and to arrest any of the persons present."—*Stephens' New Commentaries*, vol. i. p. 140.

9. That the freedom of speech, and debates or proceedings in Parliament, ought not to be impeached or questioned in any court or place out of Parliament.

10. That excessive bail ought not to be required, nor excessive fines imposed; nor cruel and unusual punishments inflicted.

11. That jurors ought to be duly impanelled and returned, and jurors which pass upon men in trials for high treason ought to be freeholders.

12. That all grants and promises of fines and forfeitures of particular persons before conviction, are illegal and void.

13. And that for redress of all grievances, and for the amending, strengthening, and preserving of the laws, Parliaments ought to be held frequently.

And they do claim, demand, and insist upon all and singular the premises, as their undoubted rights and liberties; and that no declarations, judgments, doings or proceedings, to the prejudice of the people in any of the said premises, ought in any wise to be drawn hereafter into consequence or example.

To which demand of their rights, they are particularly encouraged by the declaration of his Highness the Prince of Orange, as being the only means for obtaining a full redress and remedy therein.

Having therefore an entire confidence that his said Highness the Prince of Orange will perfect the deliverance so far advanced by him, and will still preserve them from the violation of their rights, which they have here asserted, and from all other attempts upon their religion, rights, and liberties:

II. The said Lords Spiritual and Temporal, and Commons, assembled at Westminster, do resolve that William and Mary, Prince and Princess of Orange, be, and be declared, King and Queen of England, France and Ireland, and the dominions thereunto belonging, to hold the Crown and royal dignity of the said kingdoms and dominions to them the said Prince and Princess during their lives, and the life of the survivor of them; and that the sole and full exercise of the regal power be only in, and executed by, the said Prince of Orange, in the names of the said Prince and Princess, during their joint lives; and after their deceases, the said Crown and royal dignity of the said kingdoms and dominions to be to the heirs of the body of the said Princess; and for default of such issue to the Princess Anne of Denmark, and the heirs of her body; and for default of such issue to the heirs of the body of the said Prince of Orange. And the Lords Spiritual and Temporal, and Commons, do pray the said Prince and Princess to accept the same accordingly.

III. And that the oaths hereafter mentioned be taken by all persons of whom the oaths of allegiance and supremacy might be required by law, instead of them; and that the said oaths of allegiance and supremacy be abrogated.

I, A. B., do sincerely promise and swear, That I will be faithful and bear true allegiance to their Majesties King William and Queen Mary: So help me God.

I, A. B., do swear, That I do from my heart abhor, detest, and abjure as impious and heretical, that damnable doctrine and position, that Princes excommunicated or deprived by the Pope, or any authority of the See of Rome, may be deposed or murdered by their subjects, or any other whatsoever. And I do declare, that no foreign prince, person, prelate, state, or potentate hath, or ought to have, any jurisdiction, power, superiority, pre-eminence, or authority ecclesiastical or spiritual, within this realm:

So help me God.

IV. Upon which their said Majesties did accept the crown and royal dignity of the kingdoms of England, France, and Ireland, and the dominions thereunto belonging, according to the resolution and desire of the said Lords and Commons contained in the said declaration.

V. And thereupon their Majesties were pleased, that the said Lords Spiritual and Temporal, and Commons, being the two Houses of Parliament, should continue to sit, and with their Majesties' royal concurrence make effectual provision for the settlement of the religion, laws and liberties of this kingdom, so that the same for the future might not be in danger again of being subverted; to which the said Lords Spiritual and Temporal, and Commons, did agree and proceed to act accordingly.

VI. Now in pursuance of the premises, the said Lords Spiritual and Temporal, and Commons, in Parliament assembled, for the ratifying, confirming and establishing the said declaration, and the articles, clauses, matters, and things therein contained, by the force of a law made in due form by authority of Parliament, do pray that it may be declared and enacted, That all and singular the rights and liberties asserted and claimed in the said declaration, are the true, ancient, and indubitable rights and liberties of the people of this kingdom, and so shall be esteemed, allowed, adjudged, deemed, and taken to be, and that all and every the particulars aforesaid shall be firmly and strictly holden and observed, as they are expressed in the said declaration; and all officers and ministers whatsoever shall serve their Majesties and their successors according to the same in all times to come.

VII. And the said Lords Spiritual and Temporal, and Commons, seriously considering how it hath pleased Almighty God, in his marvellous providence, and merciful goodness to this nation, to provide and preserve their said Majesties' royal persons most happily to reign over us upon the throne of their ancestors, for which they render unto Him from the bottom of their hearts their humblest thanks and praises, do truly, firmly, assuredly, and in the sincerity of their hearts, think, and do hereby recognize, acknowledge and declare, that King James II. having abdicated the government, and their Majesties having accepted the Crown and royal dignity as aforesaid, their said Majesties did become, were, are, and of sovereign right ought to be, by the laws of this realm, our sovereign liege lord and lady, King and Queen of England, France, and Ireland, and the dominions thereunto belonging, in and to whose princely persons the royal State, Crown, and dignity of the said realms, with all honours, styles, titles, regalities, prerogatives, powers, jurisdictions and authorities to the same belonging and appertaining, are most fully, rightfully, and entirely invested and incorporated, united and annexed.

VIII. And for preventing all questions and divisions in this realm, by reason of any pretended titles to the Crown, and for preserving a certainty in the succession thereof, in and upon which the unity, peace, and tranquillity, and safety of this nation doth, under God, wholly consist and depend, the said Lords Spiritual and Temporal, and Commons, do beseech their Majesties that it may be enacted, established and declared, that the Crown and legal government of the said kingdoms and dominions, with all and singular the premises thereunto belonging and appertaining, shall be and continued to their said Majesties, and the survivor of them, during their lives, and the life of the survivor of them. And that the entire, perfect, and full exercise of the regal power and government be only in, and executed by, his Majesty, in the names of both their Majesties during their joint lives; and after their deceases the said Crown and premises shall be and remain to the heirs of the body of her Majesty; and for default of such issue, to her Royal Highness the Princess Anne of Denmark, and the heirs of her body; and for default of such issue, to the heirs of the body of his said Majesty: And thereunto the said Lords Spiritual and Temporal, and Commons do, in the name of all the people aforesaid, most humbly and faithfully submit themseles, their heirs and posterities for ever; and do faithfully promise, That they will stand to, maintain, and defend their said Majesties, and also the limitation and succession of the Crown herein specified and contained, to the utmost of their powers, with their lives and estates, against all persons whatsoever that shall attempt anything to the contrary.

IX. And whereas it hath been found by experience, that it is inconsistent with the safety and welfare of this Protestant kingdom, to be governed by a Popish Prince, or by any King or Queen marrying a Papist, the said Lords Spiritual and Temporal, and Commons, do further pray that it may be enacted, That all and every person and persons that is, are, or shall be reconciled to, or shall hold communion with, the See or Church of Rome, or shall profess the Popish religion, or shall marry a Papist, shall be excluded, and be for ever incapable to inherit, possess, or enjoy the Crown and government of this realm, and Ireland, and the dominions thereunto belonging, or any part of the same, or to have, use, or exercise any regal power, authority, or jurisdiction within the same; and in all and every such case or cases the people of these realms shall be and are hereby absolved of their allegiance; and the said Crown and government shall from time to time descend to, and be enjoyed by, such person or persons, being Protestants, as should have inherited and enjoyed the same, in case the said person or persons so reconciled, holding communion, or professing, or marrying as aforesaid, were naturally dead.

X. And that every King and Queen of this realm, who at any time hereafter shall come to and succeed in the Imperial Crown of this kingdom, shall, on the first day of the meeting of the first Parliament, next after his or her coming to the Crown, sitting in his or her throne in the House of Peers, in the presence of the Lords and Commons therein assembled, or at his or her coronation, before such person or persons who shall administer the coronation oath to him or her, at the time of his or her taking the said oath (which shall first happen), make, subscribe, and audibly repeat the declaration mentioned in the statute made in the thirteenth year of the reign of King Charles II., intituled "An act for the more effectual preserving the King's person and government, by disabling Papists from sitting in either House of Parliament." But if it shall happen, that such King or Queen, upon his or her succession to the Crown of this realm, shall be under the age of twelve years, then every such King or Queen shall make, subscribe, and audibly repeat the said declaration at his or her coronation, or the first day of meeting of the first Parliament as aforesaid, which shall first happen after such King or Queen shall have attained the said age of twelve years.

XI. All which their Majesties are contented and pleased shall be declared, enacted, and established by authority of this present Parliament, and shall stand, remain, and be the law of this realm for ever; and the same are by their said Majesties, by and with the advice and consent of the Lords Spiritual and Temporal, and Commons, in Parliament assembled, and by the authority of the same, declared, enacted, or established accordingly.

XII. And be it further declared and enacted by the authority aforesaid, That from and after this present session of Parliament, no dispensation by *non obstante* of or to any statute, or any part thereof, shall be allowed, but that the same shall be held void and of no effect, except a dispensation be allowed of in such statute, and except in such cases as shall be specially provided for by one or more bill or bills to be passed during this present session of Parliament.

XIII. Provided that no charter, or grant, or pardon granted before the three-and-twentieth day of October, in the year of our Lord One thousand six hundred eighty-nine, shall be any ways impeached or invalidated by this Act, but that the same shall be and remain of the same force and effect in law, and no other than as if this Act had never been made *

* The ultra-radical as well as the ultra-monarchical disparagers of "the Glorious Revolution" describe it as a mere oligarchical movement. It is well on this subject to have the judgment of that sagacious investigator and dispassionate critic of our institutions and history, M. Guizot. "It has often been said in France, and even in England, that the Revolution of 1688 was exclusively aristocratic; that it was planned and achieved by the higher classes for their own advantage, and was not accomplished by the impulse or for the good of the people.

"This is a remarkable example, among many others, of the confusion of ideas and the ignorance of facts which so often characterize the judgments passed on great events.

"The two political changes effected by the Revolution of 1688 are the most popular to be found in history; it proclaimed and guaranteed, on the one hand, the essential rights common to all citizens, and, on the other, the active and effectual participation of the country in its own government. A people so ignorant of its highest interests as not to know that this is all which it needs, or ought to demand, will never be able to found a government or to maintain its liberties.

"Considered from a moral point of view, the Revolution of 1688 had a still more popular character; since it was made in the name and by the force of the religious convictions of the nation, and was designed principally to give them security and ascendancy. In no country, and at no time, were the form and destiny of the Government more powerfully influenced by the prevalent faith of the governed.

"The Revolution of 1688 was popular in its principles and results, and was aristocratic only in the mode of its execution; the men of weight and mark in the country by whom it was conceived, prepared, and carried through, being the faithful representatives of the general interests and sentiments. It is the rare felicity of England, that powerful and intimate ties were early formed, and have been perpetuated, among the different classes of society. The aristocracy and the people living amicably, and deriving prosperity from their union, have sustained and controlled each other. The natural leaders of the country have not held themselves aloof from the people, and the people have never wanted leaders. It was more especially in 1688 that England experienced the benefit of this happy peculiarity in her social order. To save her faith, her laws, and her liberties, she was reduced to the fearful necessity of a revolution; but she accomplished it by the hands of men disciplined in

The provisions in the Bill of Rights, which declare that it is illegal to raise or keep a standing army within the kingdom in time of peace, unless with consent of parliament, deserve particular attention; not only because they take away the ordinary instrument of despotism against freedom, but because they insure the observance of the great constitutional rule which the statute afterwards ordains—the rule that parliaments ought to be held frequently. The maintenance of a regularly-disciplined force has long been indispensable for the defence of the transmarine possessions of England, and of England herself from the hostility of foreigners, and also to enable her to maintain her due degree of power and importance in the commonwealth of nations. The consequence has been, that ever since the Bill of Rights, an annual Act of Parliament has been passed authorising the keeping on foot a defined number of troops, and giving the Crown the power of exercising martial law over them. This annual Act is called the Mutiny Act. It endures only for a single year; so that there must be a session of parliament every year, and a new Mutiny Act passed, or the army would be disbanded.* In addition to this important guarantee for the regular meeting of parliament, a system of settling the royal revenue was established in William's reign, which necessitated the observance of the same constitutional principle. The House of Commons then determined no longer to vote to the Crown certain general large sums of revenue, to be applied to

habits of order and experienced in government, and not by those of revolutionists. The very men who were the authors of the change contained it within just limits, and established and consolidated the institutions to which it gave birth. The cause of the English people triumphed by the hands of the English aristocracy: this indeed was the great characteristic of the Revolution, and the pledge of its enduring success."

* For information on the laws respecting the marines, the navy, the militia, the yeomanry, &c., see Stephens' "Blackstone," vol. ii. p. 566.

particular purposes according to the Royal discretion, but they appropiated specific parts of the revenue to specific purposes of government. This principle had been previously attempted, but it is only since 1688 that it has been steadily enforced. As Mr. Hallam states, " The Lords of the Treasury, by a clause annually repeated in the Appropriation Act of every session, are forbidden, under severe penalties, to order by their warrant any monies in the Exchequer so appropriated to be issued for any other purpose, and the officer of the Exchequer to obey any such warrant. This has given the House of Commons so effectual a control over the executive power,—or, more truly speaking, has rendered it so much a participation in that power, that no administration can possibly subsist without its concurrence; nor can the session of parliament be intermitted for an entire year, without leaving both the naval and military force of the kingdom unprovided for." *

In order to obviate the confusion that was likely to arise as to the right to the Crown, in the event (which actually occurred) of there being no surviving issue of William and Mary, of the Princess Anne, or of William, it was found necessary, in 1700, to fix more definitely the succession of the Crown, and it was now further limited to the Princess Sophia, Electress of Hanover, and her heirs, she being granddaughter of James I., and the next in succession who held the Protestant faith. In the statute by which this was done, called the Act of Settlement, several very important constitutional provisions were introduced. Eight articles were inserted in the Act, which were to take effect from the accession of the House of Hanover.

1. That whosoever shall hereafter come to the possession

* "Const. Hist.," vol. iii. p. 159.

of this Crown, shall join in communion with the Church of England, as by law established.

2. That in case the Crown and imperial dignity of this realm shall hereafter come to any person, not being a native of this kingdom of England, this nation be not obliged to engage in any war for the defence of any dominions or territories which do not belong to the Crown of England, without the consent of Parliament.

3. That no person who shall hereafter come to the possession of this Crown, shall go out of the dominions of England, Scotland, or Ireland, without consent of Parliament.

4. That from and after the time that the further limitation by this Act shall take effect, all matters and things relating to the well governing of this kingdom, which are properly cognisable in the Privy Council by the laws and customs of this realm, shall be transacted there, and all resolutions taken thereupon shall be signed by such of the Privy Council as shall advise and consent to the same.

5. That, after the said limitations shall take effect as aforesaid, no person born out of the Kingdom of England, Scotland, or Ireland, or the dominons thereunto belonging (although to be naturalized or made a denizen—except such as are born of English parents), shall be capable to be of the Privy Council, or a member of either House of Parliament, or to enjoy any office or place of trust, either civil or military, or to have any grants of land, tenements, or hereditaments, from the Crown, to himself, or to any other or others in trust for him.

6. That no person who has an office or place of profit under the King, or receives a pension from the Crown, shall be capable of serving as a member of the House of Commons.

7. That, after the said limitation shall take effect as aforesaid, judges' commissions be made *quamdiu se bene gesserint*, and their salaries ascertained and established; but upon the address of both Houses of Parliament, it may be lawful to remove them.

8. That no pardon under the Great Seal of England be pleadable to an impeachment by the Commons in Parliament.

Some of these provisions require a little comment and explanation.

The second, third, and fifth were obviously caused by the jealousy that was felt of a new and foreign dynasty. The third, which sought to impose so marked a restraint on the personal freedom of the sovereign, was repealed in the very first year after George I. became king. The fourth was designed to be a far more important constitutional regulation, and it draws our attention again to the subject of the king's *Consilium Ordinarium*, or Privy Council, which has been spoken of at an earlier part of this work.*

It has there been pointed out that our sovereigns had their regular Council, consisting of the chief officers of State, and of such persons as the king thought fit to summon. They took an oath of fidelity and secrecy, and these were the king's privy councillors. The obnoxious judicial power which was practised first by the Council, and afterwards by a portion of it organized as the Court of Star Chamber, has also been referred to. The abolition of this tribunal did not interfere with the existence of the Privy Council in its natural and legitimate capacity.

The number of the privy councillors was gradually found inconvenient for practical government, and the custom grew up of a few members of it, who really were the active and confidential ministers of the Crown, deliberating apart. This select body acquired the name of the "Cabinet Council," with which we are all practically familiar, though the term "Cabinet Minister" is unknown in constitutional forms. For some time it appears to have been usual for the Cabinet Council, when they had resolved upon a measure, to lay it before the Privy Council for their assent and adoption, but no further discussion took

* See p. 238, *supra*.

place, and the ratification was a mere formality. Out of a desire to ascertain more easily the main individual promoters and advisers of State measures, it was endeavoured in the Act of Settlement to revive the old system, to compel the discussion of all State affairs in full Privy Council, and to discriminate between those who promoted and those who dissuaded each resolution, by making all who voted for it sign their names to it. It was, however, soon perceived that this system would cause infinite delay and embarrassment in governing the kingdom, and the clause was repealed by a statute in Queen Anne's reign, before the time when its provisions were to have come into operation.*

The practice above referred to, of summoning all the Privy Council to adopt and ratify the previously-arranged measures of the Cabinet, has also long become obsolete. And it is correctly stated † that "the office of privy councillor, as distinct from cabinet minister, is now little more than a titular distinction, conferring the title of right honourable on the bearer of it." Royal proclamations and orders still emanate, as the law requires, from the Privy Council, but by long-established usage no privy councillor attends, unless especially summoned. Each, however, though he be not a cabinet minister, and though he be in actual opposition to the ministry of the day, has the right of attending, and that right was exercised in a very memorable and important crisis in our constitutional history, when Queen Anne was on her deathbed, and when the Dukes of Argyll and Somerset suddenly appeared in the council-chamber at Kensington Palace, and disconcerted all the measures of Bolingbroke

* See Hallam's "Constitutional History," vol. iii. p. 249.

† "Pictorial History of England," vol. iv. p. 672.

and his coadjutors, for bringing in the Pretender after the queen's decease.*

The sixth article in the Act of Settlement was designed to put a stop to the rapidly-increasing influence which the Crown was acquiring over the House of Commons, by being able to confer places and pensions on its members. This power had been made an engine of extensive and grievous corruption during the last bad reigns, and had excited just popular indignation. But the framers of the Act of Settlement, though laudably anxious to check this abuse, went into the opposite extreme, which Mr. Hallam truly calls "the preposterous extremity of banishing all servants of the Crown from the House of Commons."

This sweeping clause of the Act of Settlement

* For the present practical power of the Privy Council, their jurisdiction in inquiring into State offences and committing for trial, and the important functions that several modern statutes have vested in a portion of the Council, called the "Judicial Committee of the Privy Council," see Bowyer's "Commentaries on the Constitution," p. 126. It has been mentioned in the text that the queen's orders and proclamations are issued in Privy Council. This is in several cases required and authorized by statute; but the sovereign has also a general constitutional prerogative of issuing proclamations, which is vested in the sovereign alone, though exercised by the sovereign in and by the advice of her Council. Mr. Bowyer observes as to this part of the prerogative, "These proclamations have then a binding force, when (as Sir Edward Coke observes) they are grounded upon and enforce the laws of the realm. For though the making of laws is entirely the work of a distinct part—the legislative branch of the sovereign power—yet the manner, time, and circumstances of putting those laws into execution must frequently be left to the discretion of the executive magistrate; and therefore his constitutions or edicts concerning these points, which we call proclamations, are binding upon the subject, while they do not either contradict the old laws or tend to establish new ones, but only enforce the execution of such laws as are already in being, in such manner as the queen shall judge necessary. Thus the established law is that the queen may prohibit any of her subjects from leaving the realm; a proclamation, therefore, forbidding this, in general for three weeks, by laying an embargo upon all shipping in the time of war, will be equally binding as an Act of Parliament, being founded on a prior law." See also Hallam's Constitutional History, vol. i. p. 457, et seq., and Coke's Reports, 12, cited by Mr. Hallam in his note at p. 453 of the same volume.

never came into operation. It was repealed in the fourth year of Anne's reign. Another Act on the subject was passed in the same reign, by which every member of the House of Commons, accepting an office under the Crown, except a higher commission in the army, must vacate his seat, but may be re-elected; and by which, also, persons holding offices created since the 25th of October, 1705, were incapacitated from being elected or re-elected members of parliament. The statute excluded at the same time all such as held pensions during the pleasure of the Crown; and, to check the multiplication of placemen, it was enacted, that no greater number of commissioners should be appointed to execute any office, than had been employed in its execution at some time before that parliament.

The seventh article of the Act of Settlement, that which provides for the independence of the judges, is the most important of all. The Stuart kings had been in the habit of systematically packing the bench, in order to secure decisions favourable to the Crown, on all points of law; and in order also that unscrupulous partizans of the Court should preside at all State trials, and work out the royal partialities and hatreds. Men who showed any independence in such matters, or who were known to be opposed to the views of the Court, were summarily dismissed from the bench, and more obsequious tools of the Government were appointed on the eve of any important judicial proceeding. While this could be done, the liberties of the subject were never safe. There was not one that might not be brought in some form before a court of law, to be upheld or nullified; and the sovereign who could garble at his will the administration of the laws, needed care little who made them. Without open violence, it was always in his power, "constitutionally to ruin the constitution." * The Act of Settlement gave the remaining necessary bulwark to our national freedom, when it made the judges irremovable, except on the joint requirement of both Houses of Parliament; and when also, by requiring their salaries to be fixed and ascertained, instead of depending on the caprice of the Crown, it freed them from all influence, and from all suspicion of being under the influence of corruption or intimidation.

It is to be observed that the Act of Settlement, while it gave a new dynasty the right to reign in England, solemnly acknowledged on that solemn occasion the existence and authority of all the subjects' rights. The conclusion of the Act of Settlement is as follows:—

"IV. And whereas the laws of England are the birthright of the people thereof, and all the kings and queens who shall ascend the throne of this realm ought to administer the government of the same according to the said laws, and all their officers and ministers ought to serve them respectively according to the same; the said Lords Spiritual and Temporal, and Commons, do therefore further humbly pray, That all the laws and statutes of this realm for securing the established religion, and the rights and liberties of the people thereof, and all other laws and statutes of the same now in force, may be ratified and confirmed, and the same are by his Majesty, by and with the advice and consent of the said Lords Spiritual and Temporal, and Commons, and by authority of the same, ratified and confirmed accordingly."

It would be superfluous to point out categorically how completely this Act, the Petition of Right, and the Bill of Rights, recognize and confirm the primary great constitutional principles which the Great Char-

* The phrase is Vergniaud's.

ter first established. But, before proceeding to the Reform Bill of 1832 (which seems next in constitutional importance), it may be useful to consider shortly the actual state of the English Government and nation soon after the Revolution of 1688, and during the early part of the last century.

With the expulsion of the Stuarts, the long struggle between the king and the people ended: and the substitution on the English throne of a line of princes, who derived their title confessedly through the nation's will, extinguished all those absurd dogmas as to the right divine of kings, the patriarchal principle of government, the duty of the subject to submit to all royal orders, and the like, which had previously been never-failing pretexts for sanctioning or excusing violations of constitutional right, and graspings after absolute power. Indeed, since the reign of William, the royal heads of our limited monarchy have exercised comparatively little personal interference in State affairs. Our kings and queens have carried on the government of the country through ministers, who have been, and necessarily must be, dependent on parliament for their tenure of office. Not that the personal opinions or character of the sovereign of this country ever can be unimportant. "His habits and tastes are always matters of notoriety, and often of imitation. Access to his society is always coveted. He may give that access in a manner useful, or mischievous, or absolutely indifferent. He may call to his Court those who are most distinguished by genius or by knowledge; or those whose only merit is their birth or their station; or parasites, buffoons, or profligates. Even in the appointment of ministers, he may sometimes exercise a sort of selection. He is sometimes able to delay, for a short period, the fall of those whom he likes, and the accession of those whom he dislikes; and he can sometimes permanently exclude an individual." *

He can, indeed, do more than this, provided parties are nearly balanced in the country. In such a state of things the personal adherents of the sovereign (and a band more or less numerous of such there will always be) can turn the scale, and determine the adoption or rejection of measures of the greatest moment both in foreign and domestic policy. The influence exercised by George III., in very critical times, by means of "the king's friends" is notorious. The power of dissolving parliament is also a strong engine in the sovereign's hands, whereby he may protect himself from ministers personally distasteful to him, and gain at least the chance of seeing a House of Commons returned, whose feelings may harmonise with his own. But if the national will, as expressed by the two legislative assemblies, is decided and strong on one side of a question, and if a dissolution of parliament only causes a solemn popular ratification of the expression of that will in the house of Commons, the sovereign is powerless to oppose it. Unless parliament passes the customary annual Mutiny Bill, and unless it gives the customary annual votes for pecuniary supplies, the armed forces of the State must be disbanded, and the whole machinery of government must be stopped.

The principle that our monarchy is hereditary, has been maintained in practice ever since the accession of the House of Hanover, and there is every cause to hope and believe that it long will be so. We all feel (as Cromwell was warned that our ancestors felt) that our old limited hereditary monarchy is a blessing to the country, if it be only on account of the quiet and good order which its principle of succession insures,

* Edinburgh Review of Lord Brougham's "Political Philosophy."

compared with the mischief which would follow, if the post of chief magistrate among us were to be intrigued for by the ringleaders of clubs, or fought for by ambitious soldiers. It is, of course, impossible to secure a succession of good and wise princes; nor can human foresight calculate when a Marcus Aurelius will be followed by a Commodus. Hence, our constitution is rightly cautious and restrictive. It is framed not for a single generation, or with reference to the personal qualities of a particular ruler, but it is the fruit of the experience of many ages, and is designed for duration and permanence. It therefore provides checks and securities against the ambition, and passions, and weaknesses of human nature; and it fixes limitations sufficient to secure a large amount of good government, and to protect liberty, even under a bad prince.* But it leaves open a large field for the exercise of the virtues of a good one. The constitutional sovereigns of England who understand and act up to their true political duties, without seeking to overstep them; who also employ the high influence of their station and example for the encouragement of social and domestic virtue, for the advancement of learning and the well-judged patronage of art, earn nobly the gratitude of the people: and that debt would be paid honestly, if requisite, in act as well as in feeling. No one who did duty on the ever-memorable 10th of April, 1848, will forget how far personal enthusiasm for our thoroughly English-hearted queen was combined on that day with zeal for constitutional order, in producing the majestic manifestation of true public opinion, and in putting down the mischievous schemes

* See Bolingbroke, vol. i. p. 60, and some very beautiful remarks of the American statesman Webster, on the jealous spirit of Constitutional Liberty, in Lieber, on "Civil Liberty and Self-Government," p. 124. Professor Lieber's own comments well deserve perusal.

to imitate foreign revolution, which some misguided men then attempted.

Our House of Lords, at the revolution of 1688, consisted of about 150 temporal Peers, and 26 bishops. I have before indicated the causes that originally made the English an hereditary peerage: and gradually it became a fixed maxim that the individual whom the sovereign summoned by his royal writ to the House of Lords, acquired thereby not only the right to sit in the particular parliament during which the writ issued, but a right for himself and heirs to become and be thenceforth a peer of the realm. Thenceforth every peer of full age has been held entitled to his writ of summons at the commencement of every parliament. But although it is not in the power of the Crown to sway the deliberations of the House of Lords by excluding old peers, the prerogative of creating new temporal peers at discretion has been retained by the Crown, both before and after the Revolution, though a strong effort was made in George I.'s reign to cut down this important constitutional prerogative. A bill limiting the House of Lords after a very small increase should have been made to its then actual members, was brought in by Lord Sunderland's ministry, and carried easily through the Upper House, but lost in the Commons, fortunately for the interest of all orders in the State, but especially for the permanent interest and existence of that very body, which the bill was designed with short-sighted policy to strengthen.

The House of Lords would then have been free from all constitutional check; whereas, now the prerogative of the Crown in making new peers is an effective controlling power. When this is borne in mind, and when it is remembered also to how large an extent the Upper House is continually recruited from the commonalty; how a peerage is the stimulus for energy and the valued prize of eminence; there are few or none but will rejoice in the permanence and desire the stability of our House of Lords. Men of Conservative principles will naturally cling to "the peers of England, pillars of the State." And even the most vehement Reformer must, on reflection, feel their value. The necessity of a second legislative chamber is almost universally admitted;* nor could a speculator frame one that would work better than our present peerage. Such a second chamber, in order to be of the least use, must not be a mere duplicate of the House of Commons; but must, if elective, be, like the American Senate, chosen by a more limited and opulent body of voters than that which elects the House of Commons. But it is self-evident that in this country an Upper House, elected solely by the wealthy class of the community, would be infinitely more oligarchical and obstructive to reform, than the House of Lords has ever been.

The House of Commons continued to consist of knights of the shires, and representatives of the cities and boroughs. The introduction of members for the Universities of Oxford and Cambridge can hardly be considered material in point of number, though it may furnish an important precedent for the application of the principle of educational representation. The mode in which particular boroughs acquired, lost, or regained the right of sending representatives, has become a topic of comparatively little practical interest since the Reform Bill. It seems probable that under the Plantagenets every town of any consequence received a writ directing it to return burgesses to parliament; but it is clear that, from the commencement of our representative system, some very inconsiderable places returned members. Sometimes the negligence

* See note at p. 178 for the valuable observations of Professor Lieber on this necessity for a second chamber.

or partiality of the sheriffs omitted towns that had formerly received writs; and frequently new boroughs, as they grew into importance, or from some private motive, acquired the right of representation. Gradually it became a recognised principle, that the right of a borough to return members, having once existed, can never be lost: and the 111 cities and towns which returned members at the accession of Henry VIII. continued to exercise their privilege down to 1832.

We have, in a previous chapter, examined the subject of who were the electors in the boroughs in early times; and it has been pointed out that, as the power of the House of Commons increased, the composition of the electoral bodies became an object of growing attention to the Crown; and especially under the last Tudors and the Stuarts, sedulous efforts were made to mould and influence the municipal composition of those parliamentary boroughs which were also corporate cities and towns. By machinations of this kind, by the silent effect of "the great innovator, Time," in reducing many places which had once been populous into wretched hamlets, and by many boroughs having (as has before been mentioned) been originally selected by the Crown to return members on account of their liability to Crown influence,* a large number of the parliamentary boroughs became the mere instruments of powerful individuals, who owned the few houses in them which gave a right of voting, or who purchased the suffrages of a little clique of self-elected electors. These close, or rotten boroughs as they were familiarly termed, gave great

* The latest instance of the Crown creating a borough with a right to send members, was in Charles II.'s reign. This caused some little debate in the Commons, but was ratified by them. The Commons, in subsequent reigns, would, unquestionably, have resisted any further exercise of this power, "on the broad maxim of having exclusive privilege in matters relating to their own body, which the House was become powerful enough to assert against the Crown."—See Hallam.

facilities for the increase of the indirect influence of the Crown, but they also favoured the ambition of wealthy subjects; and it is to be borne in mind that they peculiarly aided the efforts of the commercial classes to raise themselves into an equality with the territorial aristocracy.* This last, the landed interest, made, in the ninth year of Queen Anne, a great struggle to secure its ascendancy, by excluding the rest of the community from parliament. With this view the landed gentry obtained the passing of an Act by which every member of the Commons, except those for the universities, was required to possess, if a knight of the shire, a freehold or copyhold estate of clear 600*l.* per annum, and, if representative of a borough, a like landed qualification to the amount of 300*l.* per annum. It has been shown that the old statute of Henry VI., requiring county representatives to be chosen from "notable knights, or such as shall be able to be knights," had fallen into desuetude; and the new law went far beyond it, and would, if effectually carried out, have converted our House of Commons into an odious deputation of landed oligarchs. This law, however, has been systematically evaded, nor are the provisions of the modern statute,† which has made personal as well as real property qualify its owner for parliament, much more efficacious in attaining the only proper object of such restrictions, that, namely, of preventing needy adventurers from obtaining seats in the House. Neither of these Acts having required a member to possess the stipulated qualification during all the time that he continues to be member, it always has been and is enough to procure for the occasion a colourable transfer from some person who really holds the requisite property, which transfer

* See Hallam's "Constitutional History," vol. iii. p. 402.
† 1 & 2 Vict. c. 48.

is cancelled or reversed directly the member has taken his seat. This practice may be almost said to have received the sanction of the Legislature by what took place when the 33 Geo. II. c. 30, was passed. That statute, which first made it necessary for the newly-elected member to swear to his qualification on taking his seat, contained, when it was first brought forward, a clause requiring every member who should at any time during the continuance of the parliament to which he was elected, sell, dispose of, alien, or in any wise encumber the estate which made his qualification, to deliver in on oath a statement for a new or further qualification before he should again presume to sit or vote as a member of the House of Commons. But the Legislature rejected this clause; and thus deliberately sanctioned the system by which men of no property, but who can find wealthy friends with confidence in their honour, obtain seats as English members.†

The laws which regulate the duration of parliament, belong also to the period between the Revolution and the accession of George III.; and are not only of great constitutional importance, but have given rise to one of the practical political questions of the present time. There is an ancient statute of Edward II.'s reign (5 Edw. II. c. 29*), which is principally a confirmation of Magna Carta, but which contains at its close the following additional provisions:—"Forasmuch as many people be aggrieved by the king's ministers against right, in respect to which grievances no one can recover without a common parliament; we do ordain that the king shall *hold* a parliament once in the year, or twice if need be." And a statute of the next reign (4 Edw. III. c. 14)

* See Smollett's History of England, book iii. c. 13, sect. 56. Statutes of the Realm, i. 165.

ordains that "a parliament shall be holden every year once, and more often if need be." These Acts are generally supposed to have only provided that there should be an annual meeting of parliament, and not that there should be a new parliament every year. Certainly these statutes had been in either sense little heeded in practice, and there was no explicit enactment as to how often there should be a new parliament until the Triennial Bill of 1642 was passed by the Long Parliament. After the Restoration this salutary statute was repealed at the king's special request; and one of Charles II.'s parliaments, which was found eminently loyal and corruptible, was prolonged in mischievous existence for the enormous period of seventeen years. In the year after the Great Revolution a bill was brought in and passed both Houses to limit the duration of parliament to three years. King William refused his assent to it; but the Commons renewed their exertions; the repeated exercise of the royal veto* would have been perilous to its possessor, and a Triennial Bill became law in 1694. But in 1717 it was deemed unsafe by the ministers of the newly-arrived Hanoverian king to risk a general election, and the celebrated Septennial Act was passed, which has hitherto stood firm against the repeated attempts that have been made to obtain a return to triennial parliaments.

Not wishing to complicate this work by the discussion of Scotch or Irish topics, I purposely pass over the Act of Union with Scotland, passed A.D. 1707, as I shall presently pass over the similar Act with regard to Ireland, passed A.D. 1800.

The influence of the middle classes, which had

* See Lieber, p. 163, and Tremenheere on the American and English Constitutions, p. 168, for some instructive remarks on the disuse of the royal veto in England since William III.'s reign, compared with its frequent exercise by the American Presidents.

been greatly developed and augmented during the period between the Great Revolution and the accession of George III., increased in a rapidly-accelerated ratio during the long and eventful reign of the last-mentioned sovereign.

"The extension of commerce and manufactures, after the treaty of Paris, in 1763, was rapid and unprecedented. Large manufacturing and commercial towns arose in all parts of the country, the inhabitants of which were but little influenced by those powerful ties which generally connect an agricultural population with the superior land-owners. With the increase of opulence and population consequent upon the increase of manufactures and trade, education and the desire of political information became more generally diffused. The press acquired great influence. Political journals were established in every considerable town, in which the conduct of public men and the policy of all the measures of Government were freely canvassed. The improved facilities of internal communication afforded the means of conveying intelligence with astonishing rapidity from one part of the country to another; so that most persons began to take an interest, not only in what was going on around them, but in public affairs, and in the concerns of the remotest part of the empire. Prejudices and established opinions of all sorts were openly attacked. The structure of the political fabric, and the rights and privileges of the different ranks and orders of society, were subjected to a searching investigation, and their claim to respect began to be tried by reference to their usefulness rather than their antiquity. Public opinion, expressed through the medium of a thousand different channels, became a check on the executive scarcely inferior in efficacy to the existence of a popular assembly. Under such circumstances we need not wonder that the enterprising citizens of great manufacturing and commercial towns, as Manchester, Birmingham, Sheffield, &c., felt daily more dissatisfied at being denied the privilege possessed by so many inferior boroughs, of sending representatives to the House of Commons. They began, during the American war, publicly to manifest their impatience at such exclusion; and, deriving confidence from their numbers, their wealth, and their intelligence, they prosecuted their claims to participate directly in the privileges of the constitution with a boldness which would probably have been long ago successful, if the progress of peaceful reformation had not been arrested by the violence of the French Revolution. The alarms occasioned by that event, and the war that grew out of it, suspended for a while the demand for a remodelling of the representative system. But after the peace of 1815, these solicitations were renewed; and the reasonableness of the claim, united with the great accession of popular influence and the excitement occasioned by the movements on the Continent in 1830, made it imprudent any longer to disregard it."

I have been quoting the words of a well-known liberal statesman, Macculloch; but the opinions which they express are now universally admitted. And Mr. Warren, an eminent champion of Conservatism, fairly says, at the commencement of his able description* of the great changes of 1832,—"It may be stated at the outset, and no intelligent, candid, and considerate person can avoid the conclusion, that important changes were called for in order to adapt our ancient and free institutions to the altered circumstances of the times."

The passing of the Reform Bill in 1832 is an event too recent to make any detailed narrative of it neces-

* Warren's "Parliamentary Law," p. 5.

sary or proper here. By that statute, the number of county members for England and Wales, was increased from 95 to 159; the number of members for the metropolis and its adjacent districts was augmented to 18; 56 parliamentary boroughs were wholly, and 31 partially disfranchised; and 43 new boroughs were created, 22 of which return two members, and 21 one member each. With respect to the county franchise, the old forty-shilling freeholders were retained; except freeholders for life in certain cases, where the amount of yearly value required is 10*l*. But three other great classes of voters were introduced. These were:— First, copyholders of 10*l*. a year. Secondly, leaseholders, if lessees, or assignees, of a term of sixty years, of 10*l*. yearly value; if of a term of twenty years, of 50*l*. yearly value; and the sub-lessees or assignees of underleases, respectively, of the yearly value of 10*l*. and 50*l*., subject to conditions as to length of possession. Thirdly, occupying tenants, without reference to the length of time for which the tenancy was created, but at a yearly rent of 50*l*., and subject to a condition as to the length of time during which the occupation has continued.* No condition of residence was imposed on county voters. In cities and boroughs some ancient rights were reserved, but subject to important restrictions as to residence. But the great feature of the Reform Act was the new household franchise which it introduced, and gave to 10*l*. householders, subject, however, to conditions as to residence and payment of rates, and liable to be temporarily lost by the receipt of parish relief.

Such are substantially the provisions of the celebrated Reform Bill of 1832; the results of which have in many respects differed from those hoped and feared by its friends and its enemies; but the general

* See Warren, p. 10.

effect of which has undoubtedly been to increase the proportion of political power in the hands of the middle classes of this country. And under the term "Middle Classes," it is here meant to include all those who are below the landed aristocracy, and above such artizans and labourers as depend solely on manual labor for subsistence. Without entering into the existing political questions which spring out of the present distribution of political power in this country, we may usefully close these discussions with some examination into the details of how it is actually distributed.

## CHAPTER XVII.

Number of Population.—Distribution of Political Power.—The Crown.—Number of Parliamentary Electors.—Education.—Property.—Exercise of Political Powers in matters not Parliamentary.—Local Self-government.—Property Qualification.—Influence of Public Opinion.—Right of Free Discussion, and Liberty of the Press.

THE total number of the human beings living in England and Wales at the time of the last Census (March 31, 1851) was seventeen millions nine hundred and twenty-seven thousand six hundred and nine.* The whole of this population enjoys full and equal protection by the law of the land; but our present object is to ascertain who enjoy active political rights, and in what degrees. In this investigation women and children are first to be excluded; and, therefore, in order to obtain the number of males of full age in the total population of nearly eighteen millions, we may follow the usual statistical rule, and divide by four, which will give, in round numbers, about four millions and a half as the number of Englishmen and Welshmen of mature age, who were living in the land, when the people were last num-

* See, for these numbers and the number of electors, the two valuable volumes lately published by the Census Commissioners, and a parliamentary return ordered by the House of Commons, No. 106, 1853.

bered; and if we assume the present amount to be nearly the same (the difference being on the side of increase), our computation will be accurate enough for all practical political purposes.

In considering the various constitutional rights which are, or may be, exercised by the various members of these four millions and a half, we will follow the Aristotelian classification of the active functions of political government, which has been already cited and adopted in the first chapter of this work.*

First, we are to consider who participate directly or indirectly in legislation and deliberation for the commonweal; and we are to remember that in a State where no taxes can be levied, save by express law, the legislative function includes the taxing function. Next we must turn our attention to administrative duties; what are the offices and magistracies of the State? who are eligible to them, and how appointed? Thirdly, we must ascertain who take part in the dispensation of justice in criminal or in civil matters.

Before, however, we discuss these three classes of political functions separately, as regards the English people, we may properly observe, that in each and all of them the Crown is supreme. The Queen is an essential constituent part of the imperial legislative power. The Queen calls parliament together, and can at her pleasure prorogue or dissolve it. In all matters of civil government, in all that relates to the inner life of the State, the Queen is the chief magistrate of the nation, and all other magistrates act by her commission. In all that relates to the outer life of the State, in its dealings with other States, the Queen (to use the felicitous expression of Mr. Warren),† is "the visible representative of the majesty of the State." She

* See p. 7, *supra*.

† Warren's "Blackstone," p. 204.

has the sole prerogative of making war or peace; it is in her name that all treaties are concluded, and ali international duties are performed.

The command of all the military and naval forces of the State is hers also. In judicial matters the Queen is regarded by the Constitution as the fountain of justice, and she is "over all persons, and in all causes, as well ecclesiastical as civil, in these her dominions, supreme."

But while thus we find royalty to be "the roof and crown" of our Constitution in whatever aspect it is regarded, we know also that the formal limitations, which the ancient ordinances of the Constitution have imposed on the free will and free power of individual sovereignty, are many and strong; and (as we have already had occasion to remark *) the practical limitations are stronger still. The necessity of obtaining annual supplies of money for the enormous expenses of the State, and the necessity of the annual renewal of the Mutiny Bill, in order to keep our military forces embodied, make annual Sessions of Parliament inevitable. And, though our Sovereigns are personally irresponsible, they must rule through responsible advisers: and no minister can carry on the affairs of the State without the sanction of the constitutional representatives of the public, on whom he is really dependent for his tenure of office. During eight reigns there has not occurred (nor is it likely that there will ever again occur) any gross royal violation of the great cardinal maxims of the Constitution.

Let us resume our consideration of how political power is distributed among the people of England; and, first, as to parliamentary power.

Enough has been already said in previous chapters respecting the position, rights, and privilege of those

* See *supra*, p. 301.

who actually compose the Two Houses; of the Peers, and of the elected Representatives of the Commons. I pass at once to the consideration of the number of the people by whom the members of the House of Commons are elected; and who thus, indirectly, exercise parliamentary power.

The number of Englishmen and Welshmen who voted at the last General Election, in 1852, was three hundred and forty-one thousand eight hundred and thirty.

The disproportion between this number, and the four millions and a half which we have seen to be the aggregate of the adult male population, appears at first sight to be enormous; but there are some other calculations to be attended to, which will diminish the surprise which it excites. In the first place, though only the small number that has been mentioned, actually polled, we must ascertain how many were entitled to vote at the last election,* and we shall find that the number of registered electors then was nine hundred and eighteen thousand six hundred and eighty-three. As many of these had votes in more than one capacity, or for more than one place, and consequently were counted more than once in the aggregate of the registers, we must make some deduction from this number. Altogether we may perhaps safely estimate that rather more than one man in every five in England and Wales has a right to vote

* See Parliamentary Return, House of Commons, No. 106, 1853. It appears by this return that the number of county voters for England and Wales who polled at the last election, was 115,153; the number on the register was 507,754. These return 159 members. The number of borough electors who polled was 225,677; the number on the register was 410,929. These return 339 members. In a great number of counties and many boroughs there was no contest in 1852; so that the number of actual voters does not even give a test of those who both possessed and valued the franchise.

in the election of the representatives of the Commons Estate in the Lower House of Parliament.*

But the mere element of numbers (though of primary importance) can never be the sole one to be taken into account when the distribution of the electoral franchise is considered. Intelligence and property must have their weight. The extension of education and the extension of the suffrage are topics inseparably united for consideration in a statesman's mind; and with respect to the claims of property there may be great difference of opinion as to the amount of authority that should be given to it; but few deny that it should have some degree of influence in the electoral system.

With respect to education there are no complete statistics to show the extent to which it is diffused or deficient among the various classes that make up the great bulk of the population. But there can be no doubt as to there being a fearful amount of ignorance and consequent debasement among very large numbers of our population. Much information on this subject is collected in Mr. Pashley's valuable work on Pauperism. That careful and accurate inquirer and sound and fair thinker describes the three millions of our population who (according to his calculations) require and actually receive parish relief in the course of every year, as "ignorant, degraded, and miserable;" and he truly states that they "indicate the existence of a still larger class to which they belong, which is but little, if at all, less ignorant, degraded, and miserable than themselves." Some of the instances which he cites of the depth of the ignorance

* The proportion was calculated to be one in five in 1839, according to the returns then furnished. See Macculloch's "Stat. Account of Brit. Empire," vol. ii. p. 105.

that prevails among them show it to be, as he terms it, "appalling." *

The melancholy amount of pauperism that still exists in the country, is also a subject to be deeply considered by all, who in any degree recognize property as part of the basis of a sound electoral system. The number has been already cited from Mr. Pashley of the recipients of parish relief at some time or another during the year. The figures are fearfully emphatic—3,000,000! The number constantly chargeable and entirely supported out of the poor rates, is reckoned to be not less than a million.

* No one can read without deep interest and sympathy the following passages, which conclude Mr. Pashley's first chapter:—

"Now that 3,000,000 of our population, belonging to an ignorant, degraded, and miserable pauper class, actually receive parish relief in the course of every year, and indicate the existence of a still larger class to which they belong, and which is but little, if at all, less ignorant, degraded, and miserable than themselves, it becomes high time not merely for Christian philanthropists, but for practical statesmen, to turn their attention to effecting some elevation and improvement in the condition and instruction of the great masses of the people. The ignorance in which those masses are left may be seen in some of Mr. Clay's valuable reports on the Preston House of Correction. The appalling ignorance of criminals is a proof, if proof be needed, of the total want of education of the whole class from which the bulk of criminals is supplied. In 1850 Mr. Clay says, 'With reference to 1636 male prisoners, it is a fact that 674 were unable to read in the slightest degree; 646 were ignorant of the Saviour's name, and unable to repeat a word of intelligible prayer; and 1111 were unable to name the months of the year in their proper order; while 713 were well acquainted with the exciting adventures and villanies of Turpin and Jack Sheppard, and admired them as friends and favourers of the poor, inasmuch as if they did rob, *they robbed the rich for the poor.*'

"Sadly does the State neglect its duty when such is the intellectual, moral, and religious condition of a numerous class of its children. The Pagans of the ancient world admitted the existence of this duty: and it has been justly observed that 'the philosophers of antiquity well knew what an important part of man's work it was to educate the young to become worthy active members of their civil commonwealths. Hence education was ever a main element in their scheme of polity, whether practical or ideal.' But this duty we, who call ourselves Christians, and profess to follow the divine precept, 'Love one another,' entirely neglect to fulfil."

I abstain here from entering into a discussion as to the practical inferences to be drawn from these facts. But they are facts which must modify the strong conclusions, to which the mind might be hurried by a bare comparison of the number of voters with the number of the population. Nor, on the other hand, will I do more than advert to the circumstance that very many of the most intelligent members of the middle class are at present without votes. There is also the important fact of the change that has taken place in the lower classes of our town population as to their desire for and their capacity for political power. It is to be remembered that the aggregate town population is now one-half of the entire population of England; formerly the proportion was much smaller.

But the artizans and mechanics of the present day are not only different in number, but are wholly different in spirit from their apathetic predecessors. The packing of the population in large manufacturing towns, the progress of education (lamentably imperfect as it has been, especially for the best objects of education), the springing up of a cheap press and a cheap literature, the ferment caused in men's minds by the American War of Independence and by the French Revolutions, the growing habit of combining and acting in organized bodies,—these, and other causes, have worked the great alteration.* There may be much vice, much violence, much ignorance among these masses; but no one who has watched them will deny that they contain hundreds and thousands of honest hard-working men, who read, study, and discuss the political events of the day with growing interest and intelligence;

* There is in the second volume of Mr. Bancroft's "American War," a graphic account of England as it was in 1763, which deserves an attentive perusal for the important contrasts which it shows between that England and the England of the present day.

who support materially, though indirectly, the weight of taxation, and whose manual toil heaps up our national wealth.

There yet remains a point of view from which the present state of the franchise is to be regarded, in order to judge it correctly; that is, not merely to see in how many hands the franchise is, but to examine also within whose reach it is. And we shall find that though the borough franchise is not to be obtained unless a man takes a 10*l.* house and resides in it, the county franchise of 40*s.* freehold is easily attainable by any man who possesses or can save a very moderate sum. Since the Reform Bill, societies have been formed for the purchase of estates and multiplication of small freeholds in the counties, for the express purpose of giving votes. An attempt was made to stop this system, and to treat such acquisitions of freeholds as void, under certain statutes of the reigns of William and Anne. But the Court of Common Pleas, before which the decisions of the revising barrister were brought by appeal, confirmed the votes; and established the important principle that the sale of land, when the property is really intended to pass to the purchaser, is legal, notwithstanding it is made with a view of multiplying votes, and that the votes so created are good.*

Hitherto we have been considering the participation in the deliberative, and legislative, and taxing functions of government, solely as regards participation, either as peer, or as elected commoner, or as elector of representatives of the Commons. We have been speaking of parliamentary power only. And undoubtedly this is the noblest and most important of all political power; for, not only is our Parliament the great organ of the English Constitution, but it is

* Ses the cases collected in Mr. Warren's book, p. 367.

also the great organ of the Constitution of the British Empire; of England and her sister kingdoms of Scotland and Ireland, and also of her magnificent colonial and other transmarine dominions in North America, in India, and Australia, in almost every region of the habitable globe. To adopt not only the sagacious thoughts, but also the beautiful language of Burke, "The Parliament of Great Britain sits at the head of her extensive empire in two capacities; one, as the local legislation of this island, providing for all things at home, immediately, and by no other instrument than the executive power. The other, and, I think, her nobler capacity, is what I call her imperial character, in which, as from the throne of heaven, she superintends all the several inferior legislatures, and guides and controls them all without annihilating any." *

But though the British parliament is thus clearly the noblest scene of deliberative and legislative political functions, that the British Empire or the whole world can exhibit:—though, when we bear in mind the paramount influence which the House of Commons now influences on the Government of England,† as well as the unparalleled extent to which England's policy influences the fortunes of the world, we may safely assert that the position of a member of the English House of Commons, if honourably acquired, and well and wisely used, is the noblest that ever was opened to civilised man; insomuch, that even the haughty station of a senator of Old Rome in the

* Speech on American Taxation, 19th of April, 1774. We have now (1855) upwards of fifty colonies and minor transmarine dependencies, besides our magnificent Indian dominions with their population of a hundred and fifty millions, for whom the British Parliament was lately called on to legislate, and soon will have to legislate again.

† See M. Guizot's remarks on the preponderant influence of the House of Commons, at p. 268, *supra*.

palmiest days of her Commonwealth ppears poor in comparison with it:—though we feel, therefore, that the privilege of a voice in the selection of the members of that House is the franchise most earnestly to be sought, and most conscientiously and firmly to be exercised:—though we gladly acknowledge all these attributes of Parliamentary supremacy, we must also rejoice in the fact, that an Englishman's direct exercise of deliberative and legislative powers is not limited to Parliament (of which but very few can ever become members); nor is his acquaintance with electoral duties and the working of political machinery limited to the occasions when he votes for representatives in the House of Commons;—occasions that cannot be of very frequent recurrence. There are almost innumerable other spheres of political action, each comparatively humble and limited in itself, but collectively of infinite importance, on account of the universality of their operation, and the daily and hourly duties and interests of every man's life which they affect. Every parish has its vestry; that is to say, "an assembly, where the inhabitants of a parish meet together for the despatch of the affairs and business of the parish." * Every borough has its town council, every poor-law union has its board of guardians. Each of these (and many more might be mentioned) is a deliberative, a legislative, and a taxing body. In each of these the elections of various functionaries are conducted; and many of them are themselves representative bodies, varied and renewed by generally annual elections. We shall have occasion to speak of the principle of local self-government (which these little assemblies aid in developing) more fully, when we deal with the administrative part of governmental functions, in which that principle is

* Burn.

concerned the most. But our vestries, our borough councils, and the like, are also invaluable in qualifying our nation for taking part in, and for living under, Imperial Parliamentary Government. They are themselves local parliaments. They bring the principles and the practice of legislation and of representation home to every man's door, and they familiarize every man with them in his daily life. They diffuse, so to speak, a parliamentary atmosphere throughout the land. They habituate us with public speaking; and they accustom us to hear and to think, as well as to speak. They train us to due observance of the necessary forms and restrictions of public discussion. They mature in us that aptitude for orderly association, and that capacity for organized energy, which seem to be instinctive to men in England and in the United States, but are so very scarce and imperfect elsewhere.* They foster the principle of acquiescence by the Minority in carrying out the resolutions of the Majority, so long as those resolutions are unreversed, together with the freest action by that Minority in endeavouring to procure a legitimate reversal of those resolutions.† They aid in creating, and they mate-

* "Foreigners frequently express their surprise at the ease with which, in our country meetings, societies, bodies, communities, and even territories, self-constitute and organize themselves, and transact business without violence, and without any force in the hands of the majority to coerce the minority, or in the hands of the minority, to protect itself against the majority. One of the chief reasons of this phenomenon is the universal familiarity of our people with parliamentary practice, which may be observed on board of any steamboat where a number of persons, entire strangers to one another, proceed to pass some resolution." Professor Lieber observes this of America. It is equally true of England.

† "The obedience of a loyal free citizen is an act of self-directing compliance with a rule of action; and it becomes a triumph of reason and freedom when self-directing obedience is thus paid to laws which the obeyer considers erroneous, yet knows to be the laws of the land, rules of action legitimately prescribed by a body of which he forms a constituent part. This noble attribute of man is never politically developed except by institutions. To obey institutions of self-government has nothing galling in it on the ground of submission. We do not obey a person

rially strengthen among us that rare and difficult sentiment which Mr. Grote, in his remarks on certain of the Athenian institutions, has finely termed "a Constitutional Morality—a paramount reverence for the forms of the Constitution, enforcing obedience to the authorities acting under and within these forms, yet combined with the habit of open speech, of action subject only to definite legal control, and unrestrained censure of those very authorities as to all their public acts, combined too with a perfect confidence in the bosom of every citizen, amidst the bitterness of party contest, that the forms of the Constitution will not be less sacred in the eyes of his opponents than in his own."

Most truly also does the same great historian remark on the same subject that "The diffusion of such constitutional morality, not merely among the majority of any community, but throughout the whole, is the indispensable condition of a government at once free and peaceable; since even any powerful and obstinate minority may render the working of free institutions impracticable, without being strong enough to conquer ascendancy for themselves. Nothing less than unanimity, or so overwhelming a majority as to be tantamount to unanimity, on the cardinal point of respecting constitutional forms, even by those who do not wholly approve of them, can render the excitement of political passion bloodless, and yet expose all the authorities in the State to the full licence of pacific criticism." *

Unquestionably these local vestries and town coun-

whom, as individuals, we know to be no more than ourselves, but we obey the institutions of which we know ourselves to be as integral a part as the superiors clothed with authority. The religious duty of obeying for conscience' sake is not excluded from this obedience. On the contrary it forms an important element."—Lieber, p. 285.

* "History of Greece," vol. v.

cils, and similar meetings of which we have been speaking, do in themselves, and in the elections connected with them, too often present scenes of coarseness, turbulence, and worse faults, at which the thoughtless man may laugh, and the thoughtful man must grieve ; but, take them for all in all, they are essential elements of our free system ; and without them England would not long continue to be a constitutional or a great country.

I pass on now to the second class of constitutional functions, the Administrative. They are rightly placed by the old Greek teacher after the Deliberative, as subordinate to them. He, who bears office in a constitutional State, must execute office only according to law ; and the makers of law are, therefore, his superiors.

Our Parliament, indeed, not only makes laws, but it practically controls every measure of administration, either foreign or domestic. But though it can direct or prevent, and though it, and it alone, furnishes the means by which every measure can be executed, it, of itself, performs no executive duties. Our purpose is now to examine the chief executive and administrative offices of the State, whether of general or of merely local authority. Offices of a judicial nature will be reserved for the third head of the classification of Constitutional Functions, which we have adopted ; and it seems needless to repeat here, what has been already more than once dwelt on in this work as to the Crown's right of appointment to all military and naval commands, and as to the Crown's dependence on Parliament for the maintenance of the armed forces of the nation.*

The highest offices of State are unquestionably those which are usually held by the constitutional and responsible advisers of the Crown, who, in the name

* See p. 315, *supra*.

of their sovereign, carry on the administration of this great empire, both in matters of general interest and in all of external policy. These are generally about fifteen in number. They are called κατ' ἐξοχήν the Ministers of State. They are all privy councillors, and they alone form "the Cabinet," a term which has been adverted to in a previous chapter. The chief of them, by long usage, holds the office of First Lord of the Treasury, whence he is commonly called the Premier, and sometimes the Prime Minister. Among the other more important Cabinet offices are those of the Chancellor of the Exchequer, on whom devolve the important and anxious duties connected with the finances of the Empire, and the obtaining from Parliament the necessary taxes and grants of supply: and those of the four Secretaries of State, three of whom hold the seals for Home, for Foreign, and for Colonial affairs respectively—the fourth (whose office, as distinct from the Colonial, is of recent creation) is the Secretary for War. Another member of the Cabinet is the Lord Chancellor. It is unnecessary to specify the others here, or to give a detailed list of the numerous subordinate officials. Theoretically the Crown may choose any of its liege subjects as its ministers,* but practically the choice is very limited. Inasmuch as ministers can only carry on the government by means of parliamentary majorities, their presence in Parliament is indispensable; and it is necessary that no small proportion of them, both as to number and as to talent, shall be members of the House of Commons. This, and the heavy expense attendant on official life in this country, and the natural unwillingness of many of the ablest men, who are engaged in commerce or other active occupations, to sacrifice their business for a pre-

* There are a few remaining disabilities on religious grounds, which do not require particularizing here.

carious tenure of office, contribute materially to the operation of party cliques, of family influences, and of personal jealousies, in depriving the country of the best services of the best men. This is unquestionably one of the gravest difficulties connected with the present working of our Constitution, especially amid emergencies such as war inevitably creates. Various remedies have been proposed, which it would be improper to discuss here. But this much may be averred, that even if the causes of embarrassment which have been referred to, were far greater, it would be cowardice and folly were we on their account to renounce our Constitution, or to despair of our country. There is nothing in them which magnanimity on the part of individuals, and liberality on the part of the public, may not amply overcome.

In the Board of Trade, in the General Board of Health, and other similar bodies, and above all in the Central Poor Law Board, we find officers of State who exercise most momentous functions affecting the social economy of the realm. On the general policy of setting up such gigantic engines of centralization, some remarks will be offered presently. We pass meanwhile to the more important territorial officers whom the Crown appoints in each county. These are the lord-lieutenant, and the sheriff, and justices of the peace, who perform administrative duties of considerable importance, besides those which devolve on them in their judicial capacity. The lord-lieutenant, who is now practically the most important Crown-officer in each shire, is usually a nobleman who has property there situate. He represents the sovereign in her rights and powers as chief of the old common-law military force of each county. In case of invasion, or menaced invasion, or of rebellion, it is through the lord-lieutenant that the indisputable prerogative of the Crown to call on all its subjects to bear arms and serve against the enemy would be exercised. The lord-lieutenant is accordingly the regular chief of the county militia, which may be regarded substantially as a common-law national force, though its duties, liabilities, and powers, are in many important respects extended and regulated by statutes made in that behalf. Besides this military authority, the lord-lieutenant in practice exercises the high civil power of selecting the justices of the peace; for it is on his recommendation that the Lord Chancellor (by custom, though not invariably, or by any means necessarily) adds the name of each new justice to the commission of the peace for the county.

The lord-lieutenancy is an office of comparatively modern date, not to be distinctly traced before the times of Philip and Mary, and not definitely and continuously established until the reign of Charles II. The lord-lieutenancy has practically much diminished the importance of the ancient office of the shrievalty, though still in theory "the executive government of every county is vested in the sheriff," * who is entrusted with all the Queen's business in his bailiwick, and to whom the royal warrant, by which he is appointed, solemnly entrusts "the custody of the county." † The sheriff is the chief conservator of the Queen's peace within his shire: he may arrest and commit to prison all who break or attempt to break the peace; he has power, and it is his duty, to pursue, apprehend, and commit to gaol, all traitors, murderers, and felons; he executes the sentence and the process of the Queen's courts, both criminal and civil; and, besides the officers regularly employed by him for those duties, he may, if requisite, command the aid of any person in his county; and may even summon the whole force of the county,

* Bowyer's Commentaries, p. 374.

† Statute 3 and 4 Will. IV. c. 99, sec. 3, and Schedule.

called by our lawyers the *posse comitatus*, a summons which every able-bodied commoner must obey under penalty of fine and imprisonment. He has the like authority in case of invasion; though, as we have seen, the lord-lieutenant is practically the chief of the local military force of each shire. The sheriff is still the chief executive officer in parliamentary elections. When a new parliament is to be summoned, the clerk of the Crown (by the Lord Chancellor's warrant) issues a writ under the great seal to the sheriff of each county, requiring him to cause the election of the county representatives and also of those of each city and borough within his shire that returns members. For this latter purpose, the sheriff issues his precepts to the head of each of these municipal constituencies. They return the precepts to him with the names of the persons elected, and he returns to the clerk of the Crown the writ which he had received, with the names of all chosen either as county or borough members. We have seen that the authority of the sheriffs in parliamentary elections was formerly made the engine of much interference by the Crown, and of much fraud and oppression.* But abuses of this nature have long been obsolete; and there is little danger of their ever reviving, while election proceedings are watched keenly by the press and the public.

The sheriff was anciently elected by the inhabitants of the county, but has for some centuries past been appointed yearly by the sovereign out of a list of three recommended by the judges and other high officers of the Crown. No express law prescribes any qualification of residence or property; but by usage he is a person of condition and estate, residing in the shire for which he is to act.

The next in order of the administrative district

* See p. 221, *supra*.

officers appointed by the Crown are the justices of the peace. (We now speak of them as regards their *administrative* functions only; their *judicial* powers will be considered elsewhere.) These important officers (as observed before) were formerly called conservators of the peace, and were chosen by the freeholders in the county court; but since the beginning of the reign of Edward III., the Crown has appointed by commission "keepers of the peace," who, when judicial powers were conferred on them in a later period of the same reign, took the more dignified title of justices. As has been mentioned already, the justices for each county are now usually appointed from among the resident gentry in it on the recommendation of the lord-lieutenant. A property qualification is prescribed by statute (with certain exemptions) of £100 a year landed property in England or Wales. The office is determinable at the pleasure of the Crown. Justices have special power to keep the peace, and they have an important *preventive* authority, in being empowered to require sureties for good behaviour from evil-doers; an authority that has been suffered too much to fall into disuse. All inns and places of public assembly require the annual licence of the justices of the peace for the district. They have controlling power in many other local matters; and their joint action with the popular bodies of each parish or other local district is necessary in many appointments and in the enforcement of local taxation. When assembled in their general sessions for the county, they have (besides their judicial authority) the power of levying county rates, of introducing the new constabulary force, and many more executive functions.

In some of our principal cities stipendiary magistrates are appointed by the Home Secretary (as empowered by statute); these are usually men who have been regularly educated to the legal profession, and who have had considerable practice and experience as barristers. With this exception the high local officers whom we have been considering—the lords-lieutenant, the sheriffs, and the justices—act without pay. Generally speaking, the justices of the peace in our large towns are appointed under the provisions of the Municipal Corporations Acts, by commission from the Crown. They need not possess the qualification by estate which is required for county justices; nor need they be on the burgess roll, but they must be resident within the borough, or within seven miles of it.

The institution of justices of the peace has been justly eulogised as calling into social and political activity the unbought energies of our gentry and of the chief members of our middle classes, to perform the numerous local duties of provincial administration, which in continental Europe are discharged by paid officers under the direct control of the central government. It is indeed deeply to be wished that modern English gentlemen who aspire, like their ancestors, to be justices for their counties, would, like their ancestors, make the study of the laws of their country a regular part of their education.*

The contrast as to the centralization or localization of administrative power, which exists between England and other civilized countries (except the great Anglo-American Republic, where the old English spirit of local self-government has been preserved and even strengthened), becomes more and more remarkable, as we watch the modes in which the numerous administrative duties (each petty in itself, but aiding to form an aggregate of infinite importance) of social and civil order are discharged. From the Saxon times down-

* Formerly it was as much a matter of course for a young English country gentleman to become a student at one of the Inns at Court, as it was for him to study at Oxford or Cambridge.

wards, each local district among us has in local matters governed itself. We have never known what is called an administrative hierarchy: that is to say, a supreme central authority sending its prefects, its sub-prefects, and other salaried officials into every department, and directing and performing by them every duty of police and the like, and professing to provide through them for every local emergency. As Mr. Bowyer well observes in his Commentaries, "Our English civil polity is constructed on perfectly different principles. Its main principle is to engraft legal power upon social power, and thus make use of the means naturally produced by the social state of the people to govern them by law. Now there are two species of government into which men living in a social state fall by a kind of instinct—the first is government by patriarchal superiors or chiefs, who are respectable for their personal qualities or their rank, or powerful from their wealth, especially that which consists in land; and the second is government by magistrates elected by those who are to obey them. These are the two forms of government upon which the whole system of our local and provincial polity is constructed. They are both productive of peace and harmony, because they are agreeable to nature, and they are also (under due regulation) highly favourable to liberty."

We have maintained these free principles in our internal government, while we have matured a concentrated state government for the general interests of the realm. It has been our happiness to combine the system of local distribution of power in matters of local importance, with the system of centralization of power in matters of imperial and commonwealth policy.* We

* See De Tocqueville, De la Democratie en Amérique, vol. i. c. 5, for the distinction between *Centralisation gouvernementale* and *Centralisation administrative*.

have seen in an earlier part of this work how beneficial has been the fact that we have had *one* Parliament for all England, and not separate legislative and taxing assemblies for separate counties or separate provinces;* and the fact that the principle of local self-government has always prevailed among us, is at least equally important. The practice of our nation for centuries establishes the rule, that except for matters clearly of direct general and imperial interest, centralization is unconstitutional. I dwell on this topic, because during the last few years the principle of local self-government has been menaced, if not impaired, and because hasty and unreflecting observers can hardly have appreciated its national importance. On the contrary, we are all apt to be struck at first sight with the superior regularity, harmony, and quiet vigour of action, which centralized administration seems to secure in favourable instances abroad; while the brawls, the jobbing, and the capriciousness of our own local boards and popular officers force themselves upon every man's notice at home. But we must look deeper, and judge more comprehensively. We must not limit our attention to capital cities, and to the most frequented lines of communication with them; we must not take the temporary energy which the strong will of a single remarkable autocrat may diffuse through his officials, as a permanent and general proof of the benefits of centralization. We must ascertain the state of remote provinces and obscure towns. We must learn what has been the customary spirit and conduct of administrative functionaries under successive sovereigns. We must consider the condition of more empires than one at the present time as to good or bad government, as to venality or integrity, as to spirit or apathy in local regimen, and

* See p. 181, *supra*.

in local public works. On the other hand, let us look below the rough husk of local self-government in our own country. We shall find superior fairness in design, and superior honesty in execution. We shall find infinitely more force than centralization ever could produce; we shall find that force to be far more general in its operation; and we shall find it far more enduring and certain, because it springs, not from the accidental idiosyncracy of an individual ruler, but from the national spirit, and from the ancestral habits of a whole people. We ought to reflect also upon the pernicious indirect effects which administrative centralization produces in a State, and on the advantages which we as a nation derive from being self-trained and locally practised in the discharge of political duties. We should listen to the testimony of intelligent foreigners, of men who have lived under the plausible administrative hierarchy which we have looked at, and who speak feelingly as to its effects. The fifth chapter of the well-known masterpiece of the great French statesman, De Tocqueville, is devoted to the exposition of this truth—to the distinction between centralization in matters of imperial government, and centralization in administrative matters of local interest; to demonstrating the necessity of the first, and the pernicious effects of the second, notwithstanding its specious appearances.*

Professor Lieber, a German by birth and education, but by choice and adoption a citizen of the great

* De notre temps nous voyons une puissance, l'Angleterre, chez laquelle la centralisation gouvernementale est portée à un très-haut dégré. L'état semble s'y mouvoir comme un seul homme; il soulève à sa volonté des masses immenses, réunit et porte partout où il le veut tout l'effort de sa puissance. L'Angleterre, qui a fait de si grandes choses depuis cinquante ans, n'a pas de centralisation administrative. . . . . Je pense que la centralisation administrative n'est propre qu'à enerver les peuples qui s'y soumettent," &c. &c. The late Sir Robert Peel bore emphatic testimony to the value of De Tocqueville's work as a study for the English statesman.

Anglo-American commonwealth, in his valuable work on Civil Liberty and Self-government, after describing the principles of the American Congress and the English Parliament as free institutions, expressly states, "Yet the self-government of our country, or of England, could be considered by us little more than oil floating on the surface of the water, did it consist only in congress and the state legislatures with us, and in parliament in England. Self-government, to be of a penetrative character, requires the institutional self-government of the country or district; it requires that every thing which, without general inconvenience, can be left to the circle to which it belongs, be thus left to its own management."

The benefits of this local self-government are earnestly expounded in many other parts of the same treatise; and in another work (his Political Ethics) Professor Lieber bears personal witness to the contrary results of the centralizing system. He says there, that "it is necessary to have seen nations, who have been forced for centuries to submit to constant and minute police interference, in order to have any conception of the degree to which manly action, self-dependence, resoluteness, and inventiveness of proper means, can be eradicated from a whole community. On this account, systematic interference weakens governments, instead of strengthening them, for in times of danger, when popular energy is necessary, when 'every man must do his duty' or the State is lost, men, having forgotten how to act, look listlessly to the government, not to themselves. The victories of Napoleon over the many States east and south of France were, in a great measure, owing to this natural course of things."

I will cite only one authority more, but it shall be a high one. Perhaps no man of modern times was better fitted to judge correctly of such matters than the German historian Niebuhr. He was a man (like our own historian Grote) before whose eyes the annals and institutions of almost every State, ancient or modern, were made to shed light on the annals and institutions of the rest. He was also a man of practice and action: frequently employed by his own government in arduous duties, and personally conversant with many of the greatest men of a fearfully great epoch. Niebuhr had spent part of his early manhood in England, and knew, therefore, the working of our system of local government, as well as the working of the centralization which prevailed in Prussia; and having these means of knowledge, he at the close of the war in 1815, in order to induce, if possible, the Prussian Court to reorganize the Prussian State on better principles, edited a work on the "Internal Administration of Great Britain," in which it is maintained that "British liberty depends at least as much on the local self-appliances of local government, as it does upon Parliament." *

* See Lieber's account of this work, in note to p. 278 of "Civil Liberty and Self-government." I feel that I ought not to pass on from this part of my subject without referring to Mr. Bowyer's observations (Commentaries, p. 373), that "the self-governing spirit of our English system of internal polity explains that remarkable willingness to obey, and even assist, the law which has sometimes excited the admiration of foreigners in this country." I would also gladly draw attention to the observations of Mr. M'Gregor, in his valuable edition of De Lolme, on the extent to which our system of local self-government ensures the tranquillity of the country during the ministerial crises and interregna that occasionally occur in our parliamentary government. Mr. M'Gregor says,—"Within the last two years, when for several days after the first resignation of Lord John Russell, and when it was said, 'there was no government,' a distinguished foreigner, in conversation with the editor in the portico of the Athenæum Club, alluded to the absence of excitement in such an event, to the tranquillity and security which prevailed in the town and country; and he then remarked 'that nothing could be more instructive to legislators, statesmen, and rulers, than the condition of England at that time. In France,' he said, 'the idea of the country being without a government for a day would create consternation. Here industry is not in the least impeded; the funds and public securities are not disturbed; tranquillity prevails everywhere; everybody is attending to his par-

I would request the reader to bear also in mind on this subject the observations which have been made in some preceding pages,* as to the effect produced on the national character by the existence of our numerous local bodies as deliberative and legislative assemblies.

I have endeavoured to sketch the higher local functionaries in each shire,† but the limits of this work forbid me from entering into any detailed description of the other numerous officers in town and country, who attend to the almost infinite variety of daily political and social duties; and who are occu-

ticular pursuit; ships arrive and depart, discharge and take on board their cargoes; railway traffic is as brisk as ever; public and private carriages roll on as usual; prices are not disturbed; intercourse by your steam-packets and by post goes on as usual; and were it not for a leading article in the newspapers, it would be difficult to ascertain that the ministry had resigned, or whether a new ministry was likely to be formed.' The truth is, that in Great Britain we govern ourselves; each locality has its self-government, and every British house is, in fact, a little government within itself. This is the secret of the tranquillity and security which has so long prevailed in our streets, and in our towns, in our fields and highways, while the nations of continental Europe have been plunged in the calamities of revolution and bloodshed." While this sheet is passing through the press, a paper by the French statesman, Count Montalembert, on the "Political Future of England," has been published, in which he forcibly exposes the evils which must ensue, if there is any increase of administrative centralization, of what he terms "Bureaucratie," in this country. Especially he shows its debasing influence on a nation in a point of view which I had omitted in the text. The multiplication of salaried functionaries creates a population of place-hunters. Count Montalembert wisely warns us to reflect on this. He says with perfect truth, that "an universal thirst after salaried public employment is the worst of social maladies. It infects the whole body politic with a venal and servile humour, which in no way excludes, even among those who may be the best paid, the spirit of faction and anarchy. It creates a crowd of hungry suitors, capable of every excess to satisfy their longings, and fit instruments for every base purpose as soon as they are in place. A people of *solliciteurs* is the most despicable of all peoples. There is no ignominy of which it is not capable." Count Montalembert was partly educated in England, and knows our institutions well.

* P. 324, *supra.*

† The coroner, who was formerly a far more important officer than now, is still elected by the freeholders.

pied in preserving the peace, in attending to the watching and lighting, to sewage and drainage, to the repair of roads and bridges, to the relief of the poor, and those numerous other subjects which we are apt to disregard on account of their homely and every-day character, but which are of even more importance to our safety, comfort, and social well-being, than are the more showy and exciting privileges and duties which attach to the parliamentary elector and his representative. Full information may be gained from Mr. Archbold's books on the "Duties of a Justice of the Peace," and from those on the "Duties of a Parish Officer;" from Sir Christopher Rawlinson's edition of the Municipal Corporations Act; Lawes' work on the Public Health Acts; and from Scott's edition of the very important statute of the last session, which has regulated the local self-government of the metropolis and its vicinity; a vast district, or rather a country in itself, with a population of two millions and a half, exceeding the number of the whole inhabitants of England at the time when the Great Charter was obtained. It is to be generally observed, that with few exceptions, and those quite modern, our local authorities, both in town and country, receive no salary. The rule of our Constitution is, that it is a man's duty to "bear lot" in maintaining good order and in upholding the social economy of the district in which he resides. His fulfilment of this duty is to be freely given, and not sold to the State. Another important general observation is, that there is nothing like universal suffrage in matters of local political power. The principle of requiring some property qualification in electors, is now as firmly established with regard to the appointments to local offices, as it is with regard to the choice of parliamentary representatives. If we look both to rural and to town districts, we shall find that it is only ratepayers (that is to say, those who have some house or other fixed holding in the district, and who, in proportion to the value thereof, contribute to the local taxes) that can take part in the parish vestry,* or act as burgesses in the municipal corporations.† The same may be observed with regard to the voters for guardians in the poor-law unions,‡ for members of the local boards of health; § and it is, I believe, universally applicable to the appointment of the governing bodies in the numerous towns whose self-government is regulated by the provisions of special statutes. Indeed the principle of property qualification (of Timocracy, to take the term of the old Greeks) is often to be found in stronger action in local than in imperial politics; as in many parochial and other district matters the same individual enjoys a plurality of votes (not exceeding six) according to the amount of his property.|| With regard also to the holding of office (except in those cases where hired officers may be appointed), a property qualification is almost always ordained by our law. It is not merely by residence in a parish, but by also being rated on property worth 4*l.* a year or upwards, that a man is qualified for the office of petty constable.¶ The churchwarden must be a ratepayer and a householder.** It is "substantial householders"†† who are to be overseers. The poor-law guardian, and the member of the local board of health, must be a ratepayer for his district; and the surveyor of highways

* Stat. 58 Geo. III. c. 68, s. 3. See Archbold's "Parish Officer," p. 408.

† See 5 and 6 Will. IV. c. 76, s. 3.

‡ See 4 and 5 Will. IV. c. 76, s. 38.

§ See 11 and 12 Vict. c. 63.

|| See 7 and 8 Vict. c. 101, s. 15, election of guardians; 11 and 12 Vict. 63. s. 20, local boards of health; 58 Geo. III. c. 68, s. 3, vestries.

¶ 5 and 6 Vict. c. 108, s. 5.

** Archbold's "Parish Officer," p. 10.

†† 43 Eliz. c. 2, s. 1.

must hold rated property either in the parish for which he acts, or the adjoining one. When we come to the town populations, we shall find that every municipal councillor, or alderman, or mayor, must hold property to a considerable amount. So, in the Act for the management of the metropolis, and every town Act, the possession of a certain amount of local property is made an indispensable condition for the exercise of local political authority.*

In proceeding to the third head under which Constitutional functions have been classed, to the exercise of judicial rights and powers, it is to be premised that our House of Commons retains the formidable, though now rarely used, weapon of impeachment; that the peers are still judges in cases of impeachment; and a few words ought to be added as to the mode in which the House of Lords now exercise the superior and ultimate appellate jurisdiction which they possess (with few exceptions) in all cases of law and equity from the whole United Kingdom. It might seem perilous that a high aristocratic body, which is itself one of the branches of the legislature, should hold such judicial authority in cases where political interests are involved, and party feelings interested. But all objections of this character must have been removed by the dignified forbearance with which, for many years past, the great body of the House of Peers has acted in judicial matters. That august assembly always contains peers who fill, or have filled, the highest stations in our courts of law and equity. It is to these (commonly called the Law Lords) that the other peers leave the entire decision of the cases brought before the House. This forbearance has been signally manifested during the present reign, in a

* There seems to be an exception (probably unintentional) as to members of the Central Metropolitan Board of Works, 18 and 19 Vict. c. 120, s. 45.

memorable case* of the greatest political excitement, and in which the feelings of a great majority of the lords present would have unquestionably led them to vote against the judgment which they most honourably permitted to go forth as the judgment of the House, as it was the judgment of the majority of the law lords, who alone voted.

Passing on to the general administration of justice, and beginning with the criminal law as first in constitutional importance,† we shall find that the great constitutional principle of trial by jury is still respected so far as regards all trials for offences of a graver character, and which subject the person convicted of them to severe punishment. The judges of the superior common law courts at the assizes, and the justices of the peace of each county, and the recorders of the principal cities and boroughs, at their respective sessions, preside at the trials of prisoners against whom charges of this description are preferred;‡ it is still necessary that the grand jury should consider that the witnesses for the prosecution make out a *primâ facie* case of guilt before the accused party is put upon his trial; and the question of fact as to guilty or not guilty, is still determined by the verdict of the petty jury, the twelve good and lawful men, who have been the best guardians of English liberty from the earliest times of the English nation. But for upwards of a century, the practice of exposing persons charged with minor offences, to trial and "summary conviction" by one or two justices of the peace has been growing more and more prevalent.

It is deeply to be regretted that so little heed has been paid to the sage and humane warnings of Black-

* O'Connell's case.

† See note at p. 183, *supra*.

‡ The most serious cases are tried at the assizes exclusively.

stone against the increase of this system of withdrawing criminal charges from the consideration of a jury. The number of offences which are now thus summarily triable in England is no less than three hundred and sixty-three.* I cordially echo the words of Mr. Warren, in his recent admirable abridgment and adaptation of "Blackstone's Commentaries," respecting the "inroads on the noble institution of trial by jury which are now being made incessantly." Above all, I would draw attention to his warning, that "it is matter of supreme concern to the country to beware of shaking the confidence of the humble classes of society in the administration of criminal justice, by infringing their right to an open and formal trial by their equals, and placing them at the mercy of, it may be, an interested or prejudiced superior."

With regard to civil causes, in those which are carried on in the superior courts of common law, questions of fact continue to be determined by the verdict of a jury,† and the same tribunal assesses the amount of damages where a wrong is proved or admitted. But a very large proportion of the civil legal business of the country is (and long has been) carried on in the courts of equity, before the Lord Chancellor, or the other equity judges whom the Crown appoints, and who are now more numerous and efficient than formerly was the case. Sometimes the equity judges direct a question of disputed facts to be tried by a jury; and they now, sometimes (by virtue of powers recently conferred on them), hear the witnesses of the conflicting parties examined and cross-examined in open court. But, in general, the testimony in equity

* See the list in Archbold's "Justice of the Peace," at the end of the second volume.

† By one of the late statutes for the amendment of the law, parties may, if they both please, try issues of facts before a judge without a jury. This has not hitherto been often done.

proceedings is taken by the unsatisfactory method of written depositions, or by the little better method of the witnesses being examined, *vivâ voce*, privately before an officer of the court, who writes down and transmits their evidence to the judge. It would lead me far beyond the proper bounds of this treatise if I were to enter here into an explanation of the distinction between the jurisdictions of the common law and equity tribunals, or on the attempts now made to amalgamate them. It is, however, due to our present law reformers, to bear witness to their honourable activity in sweeping away absurd technicalities, tedious processes, irrational subtleties, and other abuses of our legal system, which for ages have defiled the great constitutional maxim, that Justice and Right shall be sold, denied, or deferred to no man. In this field of reform,—

"Much has been done, but more remains to do."

Our Ecclesiastical Courts, our Admiralty Courts, our Bankruptcy and other tribunals, would require description in a more strictly legal treatise, but may be passed over here. But attention must be briefly drawn to the new County Courts, by which (with a few exceptions) all civil cases, where the amount claimed is not more than 20*l.*, *must* be tried (under penalty of the plaintiff's being obliged to pay his own costs, though successful, if he proceeds in the superior court), and where actions *may* be tried if the claim does not exceed 50*l.* Juries of five are sometimes made part of the machinery of these tribunals; but in the great majority of cases the county court judges (appointed by the Chancellor) decide in a summary manner. There can be no question that these new courts now bring justice home to the poor man in an infinity of little simple cases, in which it was formerly practically denied him. How far the extension of their authority is desirable, is a different matter. An Englishman has a right not only to ready and cheap law, but to good law; without which there cannot be justice, either ready or slow, cheap or dear. It is by increasing the activity and diminishing the cost of the best possible tribunals, that true law reform is to be effected, and not by setting up new ones of inferior quality in their stead.

We have now observed the more important parts of our legal system in which members of the great body of the people take part as jurors in the administration of justice. It is interesting to ascertain also by what classes of the people, and by what number, that privilege is exercised. Here again we find the principle of property qualification in full activity; and it is worth remarking that in this branch of constitutional power the propriety of such a limitation is tacitly admitted on all hands. The most vehement partisans of universal suffrage in parliamentary elections never require that the jury box should be open to all comers.

In early times the qualification required for jurors was the possession of freehold property,* except in the boroughs, where all burgesses were eligible. Now (with certain personal and professional exceptions) the following persons are qualified to serve on juries for the trial of all issues, civil and criminal, in Her Majesty's courts at Westminster, and at the assizes, and on grand and petty juries in the courts and sessions of the peace in the county, riding, or division where they respectively reside.

1. Every man between the age of twenty-one and sixty years residing in England, having, in his own name or in trust 10*l.* *per annum*, of clear yearly income, arising from lands and tenements, whether free-

* See p. 234, *supra*.

hold, copyhold, customary tenure, or ancient demesne, or rents issuing thereout in fee-simple, fee-tail, for his own or other person's life, or such income or rents jointly issuing, amounting together to the clear yearly value of 10*l.*

2. Every man having 20*l.* a year clear from lands or tenements held by lease for twenty-one years or upwards, or for any term determinable on any life or lives.

3. Householders assessed to the poor rate, or to the inhabited house duty, in the county of Middlesex, on a value of 30*l.*; in any other county, 20*l.*

In the municipal boroughs which have quarter sessions, all the burgesses (that is to say, all resident ratepayers) serve as jurors.

The total number of Englishmen and Welshmen who were on the jury lists in 1853, was three hundred and sixteen thousand seven hundred and forty-six for the counties, and one hundred and three thousand six hundred and three for the boroughs. The parliamentary paper from which these numbers are taken is not perfect, as some places sent no returns. On the other hand, a considerable number of the borough jurors must have also been entered in the county lists on account of their liability to serve at the assizes. Perhaps we may altogether safely estimate the total number of Englishmen and Welshmen qualified to take part as jurors in the administration of justice at four hundred thousand; a number much less than that of the total of the parliamentary electors. But it is to be borne in mind that members of the clerical, military, naval, legal, and medical professions, and persons in several other specified employments, and all persons more than sixty years of age, are exempted from being placed on the jury lists.

It may have occurred to the reader of these pages, that besides the great power now vested in the Crown by reason of the large number of magistracies and offices of every kind in the internal administration of the kingdom, which are filled by royal appointment, the great increase of our transmarine empire, of our colonies, and our Indian possessions, has placed an almost infinite mass of military and naval, and also of judicial and other civil appointments in the gift of the Crown, and thereby created an amount of influence, which an active sovereign of ambitious views and arbitrary temperament, if unwatched even for a short time by parliamentary control, might employ in a manner fatal to the national liberties. Considerations of this nature (not, however, unmingled with party motives) led a majority of the House of Commons, in the latter part of the last century, to vote, in compliance with Mr. Dunning's motion, their celebrated resolution,* that "the influence of the Crown had increased, was increasing, and ought to be diminished." Whatever foundation there may have been for such an alarm in Dunning's time, when the House of Commons was unreformed, and when the power of the press, and, consequently, of public opinion, was immature, compared with their present development, no reflecting man would join in any such protest against the predominance of royal authority now. The constant dependence of the Crown upon Parliament vests this ample amount of patronage in reality in the hands of responsible ministers, who are always subject to parliamentary inquiry and animadversion as to their use or abuse of it, and who can only retain their position as ministers by a parliamentary majority. That parliamentary majority cannot be retained by them long in the House of Commons, if the current of popular opinion sets strongly and steadily against them. The temper of the nation may not be

* 6th April, 1780.

reflected in the House of Commons so rapidly or so vividly as some may desire; but though a temporary popular caprice may be slighted, a deep-felt and wide-spread popular opinion must rule at a general election; and few members, who know this well, will expose themselves to certain rejection, by waiting for the inevitable recurrence of a general election under the Septennial Act before they adapt their votes to their constituents' desires.

It might at first sight seem that the Upper House of Parliament was inaccessible to the agency of public opinion, or only accessible to it by the extreme and perilous mode of the popular minister of the day causing the royal prerogative of creating peers to be put suddenly and largely in force. But our House of Lords has, with dignified wisdom, at all recent great political crises, rendered such dangerous measures unnecessary. The House of Lords, at present, though theoretically co-equal with the House of Commons, is notoriously and avowedly the weakest of the two, and gives way when any serious and deliberate difference of opinion takes place. All that it now does, and all that it claims to do, is, to check hasty legislation, and to give an opportunity for an appeal to the people by a dissolution of parliament. If parties are equally, or nearly equally balanced in the country, the House of Lords can peremptorily determine the fate of any measure. They are not a mere second chamber to register the edicts of the Commons; and according to the nature of each case, they may well and wisely either at once forego or repeat their refusal to acquiesce in the measures sent up to them. But on great national questions, the Lords themselves own that they are bound ultimately to give way to the clear and deliberate expression of the national feeling. The debates in the House of Peers on the recent free-trade measures have been of great constitutional interest in this point of view. The champions, in the Upper House, of the landed aristocracy, though they asserted with truth that they had a majority of the peers who in their hearts were in favour of the Corn Laws, never held out the idea or the hope that the House of Lords could permanently stop the free-trade movement, supposing the nation to be steadily resolved on forwarding it. All that they claimed was, an opportunity of taking the sense of the people on the subject by rejecting the proposal once, and compelling the ministers to try a general election of the House of Commons. Lord Derby's words on this subject are so explicit, that I will quote a short passage from the speech of that eminent Conservative statesman in opposition to the second reading of the Corn Importation Bill, May 25th, 1846 :—

"My Lords, if I know anything of the constitutional value of this House, it is to interpose a salutary obstacle to rash and inconsiderate legislation; it is to protect the people from the consequences of their own imprudence. It never has been the course of this House to resist a continued and deliberately-expressed public opinion. Your Lordships always have bowed, and always will bow, to the expression of such an opinion; but it is yours to check hasty legislation leading to irreparable evils."*

Public opinion is in truth now the great lever of political action in England, but with many valuable checks and regulations. We are free, not only from royal but from democratic absolutism. The will of the majority is justly powerful; but it must develope its power in accordance with law, and in obedience to law, even when it is proceeding to work a change in the law. Our liberty is Institutional Liberty, and not the licence of an impassioned multitude, that brooks

* Hansard, vol. lxxxvi. p. 1175.

no restraint of form or precedent; that strikes, but hears not; that cannot, or will not, reason beforehand, though it often repents when too late. Thus, too, our Constitution secures to a statesman time and means for distinguishing between the real voice of a nation, and the noise of the factious few who sometimes assume a nation's name. It enables him, also, to discern mere transitory caprices, however widespread on the surface, from the deep enduring sentiments of the people; "to see one *layer* of public opinion through another, and act accordingly."†

It is this predominant yet wisely-tempered influence of public opinion in England, that gives an intellectual and a moral value to English liberty, which, though we may mention it last, we assuredly rank not as least among the blessings of our Constitution. Our country is the peculiar domicile of mental authority. Among us, though a man be without either seat in our legislature or vote in its selection, he may largely influence public opinion, and as a speaker, or as a writer, acquire a degree of moral and political power, that may be felt far beyond his own island, and long after his own lifetime. Freedom of discussion, and the freedom of the press, are constantly claimed as peculiar glories of our Constitution; and a treatise such as the present would be palpably deficient were it to end without some notice of the laws on these subjects. Attempts to overawe the legislature by riotous mobs, under the pretence of coming as petitioners, caused a statute against tumultuous petitions to be passed in Charles II.'s time, which has been already referred to.* And when, under the guise of meeting together to discuss public matters, attempts have been made to assemble immense masses of people (sometimes armed with offen-

* Lieber. † P. 269, *supra.*

sive weapons, and sometimes with partial military organization), and by violent language to excite them to acts of treason and breaches of the peace,—whenever this, or anything similar, has been done or attempted, the common law has justly held all implicated in such proceedings to be liable to punishment for the obvious peril that they cause to society, and for the iniquitous intimidation which such proceedings, if unchecked, must exercise on the freedom of opinion in others. But the right of men to meet peaceably and discuss public matters openly and fearlessly, is "as undoubted as it is invaluable."* It is for a jury to determine, if necessary, whether this right has been fairly exercised, "making full allowance for the zeal of speakers, though they may sometimes exceed the just bounds of moderation,"† or whether in the opinion of rational and firm men, it has been abused so as to endanger the public peace, and make the commission of crime and outrage a natural and probable consequence.

The freedom of the press in this country cannot be said to have commenced before the reign of William III. It was then that the last licensing Act expired. And even after the withdrawal of that restriction, and when men were able to print and publish their thoughts without obtaining the "imprimatur" of a Government official, the law of libel pressed heavily on writers, and still more on newspaper proprietors. The growing importance of the press, as an organ both for expressing and for exciting public opinion, was felt and used by all parties; but men in power, who were most exposed to the wounds of newspaper warfare, often sought eagerly to crush their

* See the excellent chapter on the subject in Mr. Wise's little book on "Riots and unlawful assemblies."

† See Chief Justice Tindal's address to the grand jury at the Stafford special commission in 1842, cited in Mr. Wise's book.

assailants by putting in force the criminal law against libels. The judges felt naturally little predilection for a press that generally seemed presumptuous to men in authority, and which often was most licentious and calumnious. They established the doctrine, that to possess the people with an ill opinion of the Government was a libel; and they further established, that in a criminal proceeding for libel, the truth of the matters stated was no defence. Jurors were naturally, under such circumstances, unwilling to convict; and a controversy grew up as to the province of a jury in a trial for libel. The courts sought to establish the rule, that the province of the jury was simply to determine whether the defendant published the libel, and whether the libel had the meaning assigned to it in the indictment. But it was contended by many that the jury were also at liberty to consider whether that meaning was criminal or innocent, and whether the thing which was said to be a libel was a libel or not. This controversy was determined in favour of the more extended power of the jury by Mr. Fox's Act, in the 32nd year of George III. A great protection was thereby given to writers and publishers, against arbitrary and harsh prosecutions; and the benefit of it to the public has been amply proved by the increased respectability and high intellectual merit of the English press. But still the monstrous restriction remained, by which a man who was indicted for a libel was forbidden to show that what he had published was true, even though no unfair malice had made him publish a cruel truth, as sometimes might be the case. The maxim of "the greater the truth the greater the libel" continued long to be the stigma of the English law. This has been finally removed in the present reign by an Act which was framed and introduced by Lord Campbell, now Chief Justice of England. By that statute (6 & 7

Vict. c. 96), on the trial of any indictment or information for a defamatory libel, the accused party, having notified by his plea the defence that he is about to set up, may defend himself by showing the truth of the matters charged, and also that it was for the public benefit that the said matters charged should be published. If he can satisfy a jury of these points, he is to be acquitted; if not, he is justly punishable. It would be impossible to provide better for the objects which are stated in the commencement of the Act,—"For more effectually securing the liberty of the press, and for better preventing abuses in exercising the said liberty." Lord Campbell's Act, though last in date, deserves to be classed as not least in merit among the constitutional treasures of the statute-book.

We have now traced the English Constitution from its origin; and we have watched the first development of its principles at a time when the newly-formed English nation consisted of not more than two million of human beings; one-half at least of whom were in an abject state of serfdom, while the other half, the freemen of the land, the "liberi homines" of Magna Carta, were divided into proud and powerful barons, each girt with his band of armed retainers and personal dependants; into smaller landowners, equal in birth but inferior in possession to the great peers; into a class of still smaller owners of land, our free yeomanry, and into citizens and burgesses, who were beginning to revive the old Roman system of municipal self-government, and to reawaken the spirit of commercial energy and enterprise. First framed in those troubled times, and for that scanty and ill-assorted population, our Constitution has expanded with the expanse of civilization, numbers, and power; and while it has preserved all its integral parts and all its primary attributes, it has become the Government of and for us, the eighteen millions of this mighty English nation, whose language, laws, arts, arms, and institutions are overspreading every region of the world. On the blessings of that Government, on the security and order which it guarantees, and on the independent energy and freedom which it sanctions and inspires, it is surely needless to dwell further in addressing the men of 1848, who have witnessd the misery and degradation which anarchical violence and despotic coercion have caused in other lands. Our Constitution must from time to time require remedial changes; and at present the anomalies of the distribution of the suffrage, and the shameful corruption with which its exercise is too often accompanied, are pressing on our statesmen's anxious attention. He, who has studied our Constitution the most deeply, will venerate it the most; and, while he vigorously extirpates abuses, and steadily works out its vital law of growth and development, he will religiously guard its primary institutions from the experiments of the conceited theorist and the assaults of the disloyal destroyer.

# INDEX.

www.ingramcontent.com/pod-product-compliance
Lightning Source LLC
LaVergne TN
LVHW010137110826
845151LV00002B/372

* 9 7 8 1 4 2 5 5 4 0 0 3 6 *